The American Anomaly

The American Anomaly systematically analyzes the U.S. political system by way of comparison with other countries, especially other industrialized democracies. It is organized into four sections, respectively covering the constitutional order, governmental institutions, political participation, and public policy. Extended case studies in each chapter draw on all the major regions of the world.

Thoroughly revised throughout, the third edition includes:

- Updates throughout to reflect recent developments, including battles for control of Congress and the White House in 2010 and 2012, the challenges and successes of the Obama presidency, and political developments including the rise of the Tea Party and Occupy Wall Street.
- The addition of a ready-reference glossary defining key terms at the end of the book.
- Updates to examples from other countries, such as changes to the European Union in light of the Eurozone crisis, the Arab Spring, and the growth of China's global role.
- A substantive update to the domestic policy and foreign policy chapters.
- An update on online/web-based activism, with particular regard to the expanding role of social media.
- New tables and charts throughout.
- A companion website offering overview slides, links, and other supporting features.

Raymond A. Smith, Ph.D., is an adjunct assistant professor of political science at Columbia University and New York University and a Senior Fellow with the Progressive Policy Institute. He is author of *Importing Democracy: Ideas from around the World to Reform and Revitalize U.S. Politics and Government*.

The American Anomaly

U.S. Politics and Government in Comparative Perspective

Third Edition

Raymond A. Smith

NEW YORK AND LONDON

Third edition published 2014
by Routledge
711 Third Avenue, New York, NY 10017

Simultaneously published in the UK
by Routledge
2 Park Square, Milton Park, Abingdon, Oxon OX14 4RN

Routledge is an imprint of the Taylor & Francis Group, an informa business

© 2014 Taylor & Francis

The right of Raymond A. Smith to be identified as author of this work has been asserted by him/her in accordance with sections 77 and 78 of the Copyright, Designs and Patents Act 1988.

All rights reserved. No part of this book may be reprinted or reproduced or utilised in any form or by any electronic, mechanical, or other means, now known or hereafter invented, including photocopying and recording, or in any information storage or retrieval system, without permission in writing from the publishers.

Trademark notice: Product or corporate names may be trademarks or registered trademarks, and are used only for identification and explanation without intent to infringe.

First edition published by Routledge 2007
Second edition published by Routledge 2010

Library of Congress Cataloging in Publication Data

Smith, Raymond A., 1967–
The American anomaly : U.S. politics and government in comparative perspective / Raymond A. Smith. — Third edition.
    pages cm
Includes bibliographical references.
  1. United States—Politics and government—2001–2009.
2. Comparative government. I. Title.
JK275.S56 2013
320.473—dc23   2013002628

ISBN: 978-0-415-81432-4 (hbk)
ISBN: 978-0-415-81433-1 (pbk)
ISBN: 978-0-203-06748-2 (ebk)

Typeset in Galliard
by ApexCoVantage, LLC

Contents

Figures and Tables	ix
Preface to the Third Edition	xi
Acknowledgments	xvii
Chart 1 Comparison of 23 Established Democracies	xviii
Chart 2 An Overview of U.S. Politics and the Comparative View	xxvi

PART I
The Constitutional Order   1

1 The American Nation, State, and Regime   3
   Case Study: The Nation, State, and Regime in Poland   6

2 The U.S. Constitution   17
   Case Study: The South African Constitution of 1996   18

3 Federalism   28
   Case Study: The European Union   28
   Case Study: The Unitary State in Japan   32
   Case Study: German Federalism   34

4 Separation of Powers   40
   Case Study: The Westminster Parliamentary Model   41
   A Hypothetical Case Study: Parliamentary Checks and Balances   49

PART II
The Institutions of Government — 59

5 The Executive Branch: The Presidency and the Bureaucracy — 61
   Case Study: Variations in Executive Power in Southeast Asia 61

6 The Legislative Branch: The Two Houses of Congress — 77
   Case Study: Legislative Variation in the Former British Dominions 78

7 The Judicial Branch: The Supreme Court
   and the Federal Courts — 91
   Case Study: The Judiciary in France 91

PART III
Political Participation — 103

8 Conventional and Unconventional Participation:
   Activism, Social Movements, and Interest Groups — 105
   *Case Study: The Zapatistas and Indigenous Political
   Participation in Mexico 106*

9 Voting and Elections — 119
   Case Study: Voting and Elections in Israel 119

10 Political Parties — 138
   *A Hypothetical Case Study: Electoral Systems
   and the Number of Parties 139*

11 Public Opinion and Political Values — 152
   Case Study: The World Values Survey 153

PART IV
Public Policy and Policymaking — 163

12 Domestic Policy: Socioeconomic Regulation,
   Civil Liberties, and Civil Rights — 165
   Case Study: Political Rights and Social Protections in Denmark 165

13 Foreign Policy: The United States in the World — 181
   Case Study: The Foreign Policy of China 182

   Conclusion: The American Anomaly on Balance — 198

For Further Study: A Brief Bibliographic Essay
　　on "American Exceptionalism" 205
Glossary Terms 209
Index 219

Figures and Tables

Figures

3.1	Models of Intrastate Organization	38
4.1	Schematic of the Separation-of-Powers and Parliamentary Systems	44
4.2	Separation-of-Powers vs. Parliamentary Systems: Major Differences	46
4.3	Separation-of-Powers vs. Parliamentary Systems: Strengths and Weaknesses	55
8.1	The Political Participation Spectrum	106
10.1	Breakdown of a Hypothetical Four-Party Election	140
11.1	The Inglehart Values Map	154

Tables

1.1	Regional Breakdown of 60 Major Democracies	5
2.1	Principal Requirements for Enactment of Constitutional Amendments in 60 Major Democracies	24
3.1	Federal vs. Unitary States in 60 Major Democracies	30
5.1	Parliamentary, Semipresidential, and Presidential Systems in 60 Major Democracies	66
6.1	Structure of National Legislatures in 60 Major Democracies	80
7.1	Civil and Common-Law Systems in 60 Major Democracies	96
9.1	Voter Turnout in 60 Major Democracies	127
9.2	Voting Systems for Election of National Legislatures in 60 Major Democracies	131
10.1	Party Systems in 60 Major Democracies	142
12.1	Incarceration Rates per 100,000 People for 60 Major Democracies	175
13.1	Military Spending for 59 Democracies	192

Preface to the Third Edition

This book comes directly out of discussion and interaction with my students over the past twelve years. During that time, I have had the opportunity to teach introductory American politics courses in a wide variety of settings, including in small, almost seminar-style courses in an adult BA program, in a medium-size lecture format at a public college, and in large lecture-hall settings at a major university. Regardless of the school or the format of the class, I consistently found that students are eager for information about the politics and governments of other countries, particularly for the insights about the United States that can be provided by the comparative approach.

Thus was born the idea for *The American Anomaly: U.S. Politics and Government in Comparative Perspective*. This brief volume does not aim to review all aspects of the U.S. political system—that is the task of a conventional introductory American politics textbook. Nor does it seek to systematically cover all of the major variations found in the government and politics of the countries of the world—that is the job of a comparative politics textbook. Rather, this volume has a different goal: to shed new light on key institutions, participatory processes, policy domains, and other key dimensions of the U.S. political system by examining how these are organized and practiced differently in other countries of the world. The hope is that by examining the full range of democratic political processes and governmental institutions cross-nationally, students might be able to achieve greater insight into the impact of such differences for the nature and quality of democratic representation and governance in the United States.

Studying how different countries choose to organize their politics is not only a valuable academic endeavor; it is also a valuable civic undertaking, suggesting how a long-established democracy in the United States can learn from the experience of other political systems, while also identifying features of the U.S. system that might be helpful in other countries. Over the course of this book, a number of striking patterns about the anomalous character of U.S. politics will emerge, including these:

- Among the twenty-three countries that have been independent and steadily democratic since 1950, only one other (Costa Rica) employs a strict separation-of-powers political system with a powerful president, institutionally insulated from the legislature, who serves as both head of state and head of government.
- Among these twenty-three countries, most have a lower house of parliament with far more power than the upper house, unlike the United States, in which both houses have equal lawmaking authority. Also, in only a handful of others (notably Britain, Canada, and India) are the members of the lower house of the legislature elected through a simple-majority electoral system.
- Of the nearly two dozen countries in the Western hemisphere with a separation-of-powers system, every one except the United States has experienced a collapse of democracy into single-party rule, civil war, or dictatorship since World War II.
- While judiciaries around the world are growing in significance, few have the sweeping power of the U.S. federal courts to make authoritative rulings about constitutional interpretation.
- Many countries have multiparty systems in which five, six, or even a dozen or more parties routinely play a meaningful role in politics; the stable, long-term two-party system found in the United States is a true rarity.
- At first glance, U.S. public opinion appears to be in the middle of the pack among nations of the world, but on closer inspection it becomes clear that American attitudes are more liberal than those in almost all developing countries but more conservative than those in almost all developed countries.

Despite these numerous anomalies, I have found that many American students reflexively assume that the U.S. political system must be the best system in the world and that other countries are eager to emulate it. Some intuitively felt that democracy itself required that politics and government be organized as it is in the United States. A few thought that it was somehow unpatriotic or antidemocratic to critically assess the strengths and weaknesses of politics in the United States by comparing it with other countries. And a smaller but consistent number were highly critical of the United States, arguing that other countries would be better off avoiding the institutions and processes of the American political system.

This volume holds that every political system maximizes some values at the expense of others. For example, oppressive dictatorships can provide a great deal of stability, but few people would choose to live in such a system because of the freedom, equality, responsiveness, flexibility, and other values that would be compromised. Even within the family of democracies, different approaches to political institutions and processes can emphasize some values over others. To highlight these comparisons, extended case studies are presented in each chapter that draw upon all of the major regions of the world, including Western Europe, Eastern Europe, the Middle East, Sub-Saharan Africa, Southeast Asia, East Asia, Latin America, North America, and Oceania. While individual examples are drawn from dozens of political systems, a special emphasis is put on the twenty-three countries that have been independent and steadily democratic since 1950, a group consisting largely of Western European parliamentary democracies. (The political systems of these twenty-three countries are systematically compared in Chart 1 following this preface.) Given their strong historical and cultural linkages to the United States, a particular focus is placed on the English-speaking nations of the British Commonwealth, with every chapter specifically structured to include some discussion of politics or government in both Canada and Great Britain. In this third edition, many of the chapters include tables that provide additional context by situating the United States as one of sixty "major democracies." These countries represented the fully independent states in the world that in 2010 were rated by the nongovernmental organization Freedom House as being "free" (as opposed to "partly free" or "not free") in terms of the political and civil rights afforded to citizens. (Note that the exact list of which countries are categorized as "free" may vary slightly from year to year.) Only countries with populations over one million were included; most of those excluded were small Caribbean or Pacific nations whose political systems are modeled on those of former colonial occupiers and therefore follow patterns similar to those discussed in the context of Britain, France, Portugal, and the Netherlands.

A Note to Instructors

The American Anomaly is designed primarily to be used as a supplemental textbook in introductory American politics courses for those professors who wish to employ a comparative perspective that goes beyond the brief, boxed features about other countries that are so common in textbooks. To this end, it is intentionally organized to parallel the usual chapter headings found in the core introductory American politics textbooks, and it is assumed that students have or at least have access to such textbooks. However, the book can also be used profitably in other courses, most notably introductory comparative politics classes. Frequently, the textbooks for such comparative politics classes provide single-chapter coverage of the politics and governments of various countries, but often the United States is—perplexingly—*not* included in such texts. (For an overview of the comparative content of *The American Anomaly*, see Chart 2 after this preface.)

The American Anomaly may be of particular value to the increasing number of students who were raised or educated outside the United States and who may find this volume helpful in translating their understanding of politics from their own country to the American context. It can also be a useful introduction for American students who are beginning to study the politics of other countries, particularly those with parliamentary governments. The volume is organized into four sections on the constitutional order, governmental institutions, political participation, and public policy, comprising thirteen chapters that parallel the organization of many American politics courses. Extensive case studies in each chapter draw on all the major regions of the world, with examples from dozens of political systems. It is an ideal supplemental text to help college students to truly understand American politics and government in comparative perspective. This revised third edition includes updates to reflect domestic developments from the first Obama term, the emergence of the Tea Party and Occupy Wall Street, Republican victories in 2010, and the presidential election of 2012, along with global events such as the Eurozone crisis and the Arab Spring. The third edition also incorporates many new charts and graphs, and a ready-reference glossary.

To keep this volume relatively brief and readily accessible to a wide range of students, many topics have not been included. For instance, the study of how modern mass media frame political issues or how public opinion surveys achieve random samples is important, but these topics are not discussed in this volume because the comparative approach would not particularly shed much light on them. Likewise, topics that might be extremely important in the study of some other countries, such as details of how parliamentary coalitions are formed in Western Europe or how the military plays a political role in Central Africa, do not have much relevance to the study of U.S. politics and therefore are also excluded from this volume.

Similarly, *The American Anomaly* is informed by the long and rich tradition of studies on the cultural and historical roots of American exceptionalism. However, it does not directly engage that literature, partly in order to offer a fresh perspective and partly to provide an institutionally oriented approach that will make this volume a good fit for use alongside most introductory American politics textbooks. Because this book will, ideally, be just the starting point of the comparative study of the U.S. political system for many students, a brief bibliographic essay on American exceptionalism is provided at the end of the book. The third edition includes two chapters on domestic policy (including socioeconomic policy, civil liberties, and civil rights) and on foreign policy. However, discussion of public policy is also woven throughout the book. At various points, readers will find consideration of how anomalous features of the American political system have affected public policy in areas as diverse as freedom of expression, freedom of religion, the right to bear arms, due process guarantees, social welfare spending, taxation policies, education, disaster relief, racial integration, war powers, foreign policy, and immigration.

As the instructor wishes, individual chapters of this book may be assigned when various topics are discussed throughout the semester. Given the brevity of this volume, it can also be assigned as a whole at the outset of the semester, or each of the four parts of the book may be assigned together at appropriate points in the course. The parts may be read in any order, although it is recommended that Part I be read first, particularly chapter 4, which introduces the parliamentary system of government. It is also beneficial for chapters 9 and 10, respectively on voting and elections and on political parties, to be read sequentially. Each chapter includes suggestions for further reading, one exercise for Web-based exploration, and a chapter question, which can be used as the basis for a written assignment and/or a classroom discussion.

Acknowledgments

I would like to thank the students at Columbia University and New York University who provided research and editorial assistance over the course of the three editions of this book: (first edition: Victoria Kwan, Kwame Spearman, Howard Kline, and Alison Cordova; second edition: Ashley Lherisson, Carolina Rivas, and Gia Wakil; third edition: Michael Luke, Peter Capp, and Jeffrey Golladay). I am also grateful for the help and encouragement offered by friends and colleagues, including Brandon Aultman, Christian Paula, Kim Johnson, Shareen Hertel, Laura Nathanson, Martin Good, Susan Roberts, and Victoria and Bernard Candon. In addition, I would like to acknowledge the support of the chairs or heads of the political science departments at Columbia University, Barnard College, New York University, and Hunter College, in which I have taught, particularly Robert Shapiro, Kenneth Sherrill, Richard Pious, Kimberley Marten, Shinasi Rama, Bassam Abed, and Veena Thadani. Most of all, I would like to thank the many students, now numbering more than a thousand, who have studied American politics and government with me over the past decade. I have learned an enormous amount from their ideas and questions, their insights, and their enthusiasm, and I dedicate this book to them.

Chart 1   Comparison of 23 Established Democracies

Country	Year of Current Constitution	Unitary or Federal?	Separation of Powers?	Head of State
United States	1789	Federal, with 50 states and 6 territories	Yes	President elected by the Electoral College, which is allocated according to popular vote
Australia	1901	Federal, with 6 states and 2 territories	Some; upper house and High Court can check the executive	Ceremonial governor general, appointed by prime minister, represents British monarch
Austria	1920; restored in 1945 after World War II	Federal, with 9 states	No	Popularly elected ceremonial president
Belgium	1831	Federal, with 3 regions and 3 language communities	No	Hereditary ceremonial monarch
Canada	1867; Charter of Rights and Freedoms added in 1982	Federal, with 10 provinces and 3 territories	No	Ceremonial governor general, appointed by prime minister, represents British monarch
Costa Rica	1949	Unitary	Yes	Popularly elected president
Denmark	1953	Unitary, but with home rule for 2 overseas territories	No	Hereditary ceremonial monarch

Charts xix

Head of Government	Structure of Legislature	Judicial Review?	Electoral System	Party System
President elected by the Electoral College, which is allocated according to popular vote	Symmetric bicameralism; both houses popularly elected	Supreme Court and other federal courts have judicial review	Single-member plurality	Two-party
Prime minister elected by lower house of parliament	Symmetric bicameralism; both houses popularly elected	High Court has judicial review	Single-member transferable vote for lower house; proportional representation for upper house	Two-party plus
Chancellor elected by lower house of parliament	Asymmetric bicameralism; both houses popularly elected	Constitutional Court has limited judicial review	Proportional representation	Multiparty
Prime minister elected by lower house of parliament	Asymmetric bicameralism; both houses popularly elected (some seats in upper house are appointed)	High Council for Justice has limited judicial review	Proportional representation	Multiparty
Prime minister elected by lower house of parliament	Asymmetric bicameralism; lower house popularly elected, upper house appointed	Supreme Court has judicial review but can be overridden	Single-member plurality	Two-party plus
Popularly elected president	Unicameralism; popularly elected	Supreme Court of Justice has significant judicial review	Proportional representation for legislature; single-member plurality with runoff for president	Two-party plus
Prime minister elected by parliament	Unicameralism; popularly elected	Supreme Court does not have judicial review	Multimember proportional representation	Multiparty

(Continued)

Chart 1 (Continued)

Country	Year of Current Constitution	Unitary or Federal?	Separation of Powers?	Head of State
Finland	1919	Unitary	Some; president and parliament can check each other	Popularly elected president with significant powers
France	1958	Unitary	Only when president and parliamentary majority are of different parties	Popularly elected president with significant powers
Germany	1949	Federal, with 16 Länder	Some; upper house can block laws on issues related to the Länder	Ceremonial president elected by parliament and Länder legislatures
Great Britain	No single written constitutional document	Unitary, with devolved powers to Northern Ireland, Scotland, and Wales	No	Hereditary ceremonial monarch
Iceland	1944	Unitary	No	Popularly elected largely ceremonial president
India	1950	Federal, with 28 states and 7 union territories	No	Ceremonial president elected by parliament and state legislators

Head of Government	Structure of Legislature	Judicial Review?	Electoral System	Party System
Prime minister elected by parliament	Unicameralism; popularly elected	Supreme Court does not have judicial review	Multimember proportional representation; single-member plurality with runoff for president	Multiparty
Prime minister appointed by president, confirmed by lower house of parliament	Asymmetric bicameralism; lower house popularly elected, upper house indirectly elected by local elected officials	Court of Cassation does not have judicial review; there is a Constitutional Court within the executive	Multimember proportional representation for lower house of parliament; single-member plurality with runoff for president	Multiparty
Prime minister (chancellor) elected by lower house of parliament	Asymmetric bicameralism; popularly elected lower house, upper house appointed by the Länder	Constitutional Court has judicial review	Mixed single-member plurality and proportional representation	Multiparty
Prime minister elected by lower house of parliament	Asymmetric bicameralism; popularly elected lower house, mostly appointed upper house	Supreme Court does not have judicial review	Single-member plurality	Two-party Plus
Prime minister elected by parliament	Unicameralism; popularly elected	Supreme Court has some judicial review	Multimember proportional representation	Multiparty
Prime minister elected by lower house of parliament	Asymmetric bicameralism; lower house popularly elected, upper house chosen from states	Supreme Court with some judicial review	Single-member plurality for lower house; proportional representation for upper house	Multiparty

(Continued)

Chart 1 (Continued)

Country	Year of Current Constitution	Unitary or Federal?	Separation of Powers?	Head of State
Ireland	1937	Unitary	No	Popularly elected ceremonial president
Israel	No single written constitutional document	Unitary	No	Ceremonial president elected by parliament
Italy	1948	Unitary	Usually not, although Senate can sometimes check lower house and executive	Ceremonial president elected by parliament and regional delegates
Japan	1947	Unitary	No	Hereditary ceremonial monarch
Luxembourg	1868	Unitary	No	Hereditary ceremonial monarch
Netherlands	1814	Unitary, but with home-rule in overseas territories	No	Hereditary ceremonial monarch
New Zealand	No single written constitutional document	Unitary	No	Ceremonial governor general, appointed by prime minister, represents British monarch

Head of Government	Structure of Legislature	Judicial Review?	Electoral System	Party System
Prime minister elected by lower house of parliament	Asymmetric bicameralism; lower house popularly elected, upper house drawn from various sectors of society	Supreme Court has some judicial review	Multimember proportional representation	Two-party Plus
Prime minister elected by both houses of parliament	Unicameralism; popularly elected	Supreme Court has some judicial review	Proportional representation	Multiparty
Prime minister elected by lower house of parliament	Symmetric bicameralism; members of both houses popularly elected	Constitutional court has some judicial review	Proportional representation	Multiparty
Prime minister elected by lower house of parliament	Asymmetric bicameralism; both houses popularly elected	Supreme Court has some judicial review	Mixed single-member plurality and proportional representation	Multiparty
Prime minister elected by parliament	Unicameralism; popularly elected	Supreme Court does not have judicial review	Proportional representation	Multiparty
Prime minister elected by lower house of parliament	Asymmetric bicameralism; lower house popularly elected, upper house chosen by provinces	Supreme Court does not have judicial review	Proportional representation	Multiparty
Prime minister elected by parliament	Unicameralism, popularly elected	Supreme Court does not have judicial review	Mixed single-member plurality and proportional representation	Two-party Plus

(Continued)

Chart 1 (Continued)

Country	Year of Current Constitution	Unitary or Federal?	Separation of Powers?	Head of State
Norway	1814	Unitary	No	Hereditary ceremonial monarch
Sweden	1974	Unitary	No	Hereditary ceremonial monarch
Switzerland	1874	Federal, with 26 cantons	Yes	Ceremonial president, rotating each year among Federal Council members

This comparison chart is based on the list of twenty-three democracies compiled by political scientists Arend Lijphart, Robert Dahl, and others. It reflects the countries that have been independent since 1950 and have experienced uninterrupted democracy since that time. As counties with a span of several decades of democratic self-government, these countries represent many of the most relevant points of comparison for the United States. Note that India is sometimes excluded from the list because of a state of emergency that was declared there between 1975 and 1977, although this was accomplished through existing constitutional mechanisms. Other countries that have had some democratic practices since 1950 are excluded for such reasons as long stretches of single-party rule (e.g., Mexico), undemocratic intervention by the military (e.g., Turkey), or achievement of independence after 1950 (e.g., Jamaica).

Head of Government	Structure of Legislature	Judicial Review?	Electoral System	Party System
Prime minister elected by parliament	Unicameralism; popularly elected	Supreme Court has limited judicial review	Multimember proportional representation	Multiparty
Prime minister elected by parliament	Unicameralism; popularly elected	Supreme Court has limited judicial review	Multimember proportional representation	Multiparty
Seven-member Federal Council elected for fixed term by lower house of parliament	Symmetric bicameralism, both houses popularly elected	Supreme Court does not have judicial review	Proportional representation in lower house, single-member plurality in upper house	Multiparty

Chart 2 An Overview of U.S. Politics and the Comparative View

Feature	Key Characteristics of U.S. Politics and Government	The Comparative View
The American Nation, State, and Regime (Chapter 1)	The United States is a relatively new nation and state but has a strong sense of national identity. The regime is defined by the Constitution, which is nearly as old as the state itself.	Many countries are rooted in ethnic identities that greatly predate their modern states; others are more modern creations like the United States. Most states have experienced several changes in regime.
The U.S. Constitution (Chapter 2)	The U.S. Constitution is the oldest and longest continuously functioning such document, although quite brief and even vague.	Most constitutions are much longer and more detailed, are significantly changed or replaced more often, and enumerate social as well as political rights.
Federalism (Chapter 3)	The United States first introduced the idea of federalism, and both national and state governments have distinctive constitutional status and play active roles.	Most large and/or diverse countries practice federalism, but about 7/8ths of countries overall are "unitary" states with nearly all political power in the national capital.
Separation of Powers (Chapter 4)	The United States has a robust system of separation of powers with effective checks and balances among the executive, legislative, and judicial branches, each of which is largely autonomous of the others.	Parliamentary systems have no separation between legislative and executive authority. Many other countries with separation of powers, as in Latin America and Africa, tend to be strongly dominated by the executive.
The Executive Branch (Chapter 5)	The U.S. president is both the country's ceremonial head of state and hands-on head of government. Due to separation of powers, the president does not answer to Congress and can exercise significant powers unilaterally. The U.S. bureaucracy is comparatively small and dispersed between the national, state, and city levels.	Parliamentary systems have purely ceremonial heads of state, while prime ministers act as head of government as long as they control a parliamentary majority. Nondemocratic countries also tend to have very strong executives. Many developed countries have large, centralized bureaucracies that form a national elite.

(Continued)

Chart 2 (Continued)

Feature	Key Characteristics of U.S. Politics and Government	The Comparative View
The Legislative Branch (Chapter 6)	The upper and lower houses of the U.S. Congress, the Senate and the House of Representatives, have equal authority. Congress has a great deal of power, but it is widely dispersed due to relatively weak parties, independent-minded members, and strong committees.	Most parliamentary systems have very strong lower houses but much weaker upper houses that mostly review and revise rather than initiate laws. Parliaments tend to be heavily dominated by the ministers they elect. In nondemocratic countries, legislatures usually play a consultative rather than governing role.
The Judicial Branch (Chapter 7)	The courts in the United States are an independent, co-equal branch with the power of judicial review to strike down laws and executive acts as unconstitutional. Judges play an active role in the governing process.	Most court systems are more limited in their scope, dealing more with the case before them than with issuing broad legal rulings. Some countries have constitutional courts with judicial review, although few in practice can easily override executive or legislative acts.
Conventional and Unconventional Participation (Chapter 8)	Since the Civil War, the United States has only rarely experienced political violence. Political protest has been more important, especially since the 1950s, although it is only rarely violent. Interest groups flourish, although they are not usually organized along lines of class.	Many countries experience great political violence, with challengers seeking to overtake the government or form a breakaway state. Political protest, both violent and nonviolent, is also common.
Voting and Elections (Chapter 9)	The United States uses a "single-member plurality" system in which each elected office has its own election with a single winner, whoever gets the most votes.	Most countries use some form of proportional representation (PR), in which each election produces several winners from multiple parties on the basis of the percentage of the vote won.

(Contiuned)

Chart 2 (Continued)

Feature	Key Characteristics of U.S. Politics and Government	The Comparative View
Political Parties (Chapter 10)	The United States has a stable, long-term two-party system, with the two parties agreeing on many fundamental political, economic, and social questions. The two major parties are decentralized and cannot readily control their members.	Largely because of PR, most countries have multiple political parties that win votes and elect officials to office. These parties often have more means to control their members and are more powerful than most interest groups, with the possible exception of organized labor.
Political Opinion and Public Values (Chapter 11)	The United States has a long history of valuing self-reliance and personal independence, resulting in a comparatively low regard for big government. Americans are also more religious and patriotic than citizens in other developed countries.	Citizens of most developed countries hold more liberal views on issues relating to religion and morality, are generally less nationalistic, and are more in favor of activist government. Views in some developing counties are closer to the United States in these areas.
Domestic Policy (Chapter 12)	The United States has a strong tradition of civil liberties, particularly freedom of expression and religion and due process guarantees under the law. In more recent decades, there has also been greater attention paid to civil rights and the development of a social welfare system.	Most democracies also protect individual civil liberties, though attitudes vary widely toward group-based rights (i.e., civil rights). In comparison with the United States, nearly all wealthy democracies play a much greater regulatory role in the economy and provide much more of a social safety net.
Foreign Policy (Chapter 13)	After a century of relative isolationism, the United States emerged as a global power in the 20th century. Although the actual mechanics of foreign policymaking are similar to that in most other countries, the unique role of the United States in the world provides it with a distinctive foreign policy.	The *realist* perspective on international relations focuses on the role of power in world politics, which can help to explain the prominence of U.S. foreign policy in the global setting relative to other countries. The *idealist* perspective directs attention to the values of any given state, helping to explain why the United States has so prominently promoted democracy and capitalism in the world.

Part I

The Constitutional Order

Chapter 1

The American Nation, State, and Regime

Comparison is the basis of much of what we know about the world. Astronomers compare Earth with other planets to explain why the size of our globe and its distance from the Sun allow life to flourish. Biologists study the physiology of other species for clues about how the human organism functions and how diseases can be combated. Economists often contrast the performance of one economy with reference to others, determining why some countries experience growth and prosperity while others encounter stagnation and poverty.

Political scientists also make use of comparisons; indeed, one entire subfield of the discipline is known as comparative politics. The great political scientist and sociologist Seymour Martin Lipset went so far as to say that someone "who knows one country, knows no country." This was true, he argued, because, through the close examination of the politics and government of many countries, it is possible to understand the strengths and weaknesses of different systems and their ability or inability to offer stability, good governance, flexibility, deliberation, representation, and many other political values to their citizenry. These strengths and weaknesses are reflected in the historical development of many different dimensions of a political system, including its constitutional provisions, the configurations of its government institutions, the rules of its electoral system, the political culture of its citizenry, and its patterns of public policymaking. All of these are among the topics that make up the theme of *The American Anomaly*.

In the pages ahead, it will become clear that U.S. politics and government are quite unusual and atypical, indeed even anomalous. This is not to say that there are one or two models in the world from which the United States deviates. Indeed, no country has a political system that is fully representative of the countries of the world, and many have some features even more anomalous than those found in the United States (and it is Switzerland, not the United States, that would win the prize for most anomalous democratic system in the world). Still, a comparative perspective can illuminate the full range of the ways in which the human race chooses to govern itself, as well as the gains, losses, and trade-offs that result from the different political institutions and processes that have developed in the United States.

To initiate this discussion, it is useful to start with three of the broadest concepts used in comparative politics to describe and categorize the political systems of different countries: *nation, state,* and *regime.*

The *nation* can be thought of as a form of collective identity among a group of people, generally rooted in a particular geographic location and based on a set of shared cultural attributes such as religion, language, customs, and historical experience. Some nations, such as Japan and Ethiopia, have deep, even ancient roots; others, such as Australia and Costa Rica, are comparatively recent creations. Likewise, many nations possess very robust and distinctive identities and a clear sense of their place in the world. China would fit into this category, having long called itself the "Middle Kingdom" because it viewed the Chinese nation as forming the very center of the world. By contrast, some other nations have a sense of nationhood that is more fragile or indistinct, such as Ukraine, which has long been overshadowed by its much larger neighbor Russia, with which it has innumerable historical and cultural links. The terms *ethnicity* and *ethnic group* are sometimes used more or less interchangeably with *nationality* or *nation.* (Note that in everyday use, the term *nation* is sometimes used synonymously with the word *country,* but the usage of the term here is a more technical one.)

The second concept is the *state,* the term used to describe any of approximately 190 sovereign, independent countries in the world. Perhaps the simplest indicator of whether a political entity is regarded as a sovereign state within the international system is whether it has membership in the United Nations, which, despite its name, is an organization composed of states (for a listing see www.un.org/en/members/index.shtml). By definition, sovereign states have no higher political authority above them and possess such characteristics as a specified land area, a permanent population, a monopoly on the legitimate use of violence within its borders, and the ability to enter into diplomatic relations with other states; this international system of states is often traced back to a pair of European treaties signed in 1648 called the Peace of Westphalia. (Thus, the American states of the Union such as Vermont or Arizona share sovereignty within the United States, but they are *not* states in the international sense.) When one particular national or ethnic group forms the large majority of a state, as is often but not always the case, it is termed a *nation-state.* Some nations, such as the Kurds of the Middle East and the Roma (Gypsies) of Europe, do not have their own state; some nations, most notably the Arab nation, are divided among multiple states. Further, some states, such as Malaysia and Afghanistan, are composed of multiple distinct ethnic groups. Table 1.1 provides an overview of the sixty fully independent states of the world with populations of more than one million that were rated in 2010 as both electoral democracies and as "free" societies in terms of political and civil rights by the nongovernmental organization

Table 1.1 Regional Breakdown of 60 Major Democracies

Africa	Asia	The Americas	Europe	Other
Benin	India	Argentina	Austria	Australia[1]
Botswana	Indonesia	Brazil	Belgium	Israel[2]
Ghana	Japan	Canada	Bulgaria	Mauritius[3]
Mali	Mongolia	Chile	Croatia	New Zealand[1]
Namibia	South Korea	Costa Rica	Cyprus	
South Africa		Dominican Republic	Czech Republic	
		El Salvador	Denmark	
		Guyana	Estonia	
		Jamaica	Finland	
		Mexico	France	
		Panama	Germany	
		Peru	Greece	
		Trinidad & Tobago	Hungary	
		United States	Ireland	
		Uruguay	Italy	
			Latvia	
			Lithuania	
			Netherlands	
			Norway	
			Poland	
			Portugal	
			Romania	
			Serbia	
			Slovakia	
			Slovenia	
			Spain	
			Sweden	
			Switzerland	
			Ukraine	
			United Kingdom	

This list represents the 60 countries that meet the following three criteria: (1) they are internationally recognized as sovereign and independent, and are members of the United Nations; (2) they were scored by Freedom House in 2010 (www.freedomhouse.org) as "free" in terms of political participation, personal freedoms, and other rights; and (3) they have populations of more than one million, so as to avoid atypical "microstates." Note that the exact list of "free" countries may vary slightly from year to year.

1. Oceania.
2. Middle East.
3. Indian Ocean island.

Freedom House (www.freedomhouse.org). The same sixty major democracies will serve as the basis for additional tables in most of the chapters that follow.

The third concept is that of the *regime,* or the particular configuration of governing principles and institutions that prevails within any particular state. This term became widely familiar in the United States with regard to the 2003 invasion of Iraq, which had as its stated goal regime change in that country. Notably, when the regime led by the dictator Saddam Hussein and his Baathist Party was toppled by the U.S.-led invasion, Iraq's status as a sovereign *state* remained unchanged, although it was temporarily placed under U.S. occupation until the final withdrawal of American troops, in 2011. Most regimes are legitimized by a written constitution that spells out how power is organized and allocated within the country. But even the most detailed constitutions rarely capture all the dimensions of how power is actually exercised, and many regimes distort or even disregard their constitutions when it is convenient to do so.

The incumbents of any particular regime—that is to say, those currently in public office or otherwise exercising power—are often referred to as the "government." Thus, for instance, the ten-year term of Prime Minister Tony Blair of Great Britain is often called the "Blair government." In the United States, the term *government* refers to the entire multipart structure established under the Constitution; to specify the term of any one president, Americans are more likely to speak of presidential administrations, such as the Reagan administration. Generally, the nation, the state, and usually also the regime predate the individuals in power at any particular moment and also will outlast them.

Case Study: The Nation, State, and Regime in Poland

These three concepts overlap and intersect in a variety of ways, but in most cases each concept can be distinguished from the others. A useful example of these concepts is offered by the case of Poland. For at least a millennium, there has existed a distinctive Polish *nation*: a people who lived in a particular region of East-Central Europe and shared a number of cultural characteristics, such as use of a distinctive Slavic language written with Roman letters and a fervent brand of Roman Catholicism. For many years, the Polish nation, under its king, was part of a multiethnic *state*. This state disappeared in the 1790s when Poland was partitioned by the Prussian, Hapsburg, and Russian Empires and effectively vanished from political maps for a century and a half. During this time, the Polish nation, however, endured, and it was able to reassert its political sovereignty when Poland was reestablished after World War I as a *nation-state.*

At that time, the Poles attempted to create a new democratic *regime* based on a written constitution led by the government of President Jan Pilsudski.

But that regime proved unstable, and soon Poland was sequentially invaded and occupied by the German Nazi army and the Soviet Red Army. After World War II, the Soviet Union imposed a new regime that drew its authority from Communist doctrine and, more important, the threat of Soviet invasion. This new regime did not alter the basic identity of the Polish nation or state, however, but simply represented one more phase in a historical succession of regimes. In the 1980s, the last government of the Communist regime, led by General Wojciech Jaruszelski, took extreme measures to repress the burgeoning Solidarity trade union movement. The fall of the Berlin Wall and the collapse of Communism in Eastern Europe in 1989, however, led to the creation of today's restored democratic regime, with its first government led by Solidarity leader Lech Walesa.

The American Nation

The interrelationships among the American nation, state, regime, and government are not quite as clear as they are in the case of Poland. Unlike Poland and many other nations of Europe and Asia, the United States has a comparatively short history upon which to draw its sense of nationhood. Indeed, the United States has been termed the "first new nation" because it achieved independence from its mother country before any other major colony did so and because its national identity was largely self-invented.

This new American nation, of necessity, had to draw upon different markers of identity than older nations such as Finland or Korea with long histories, distinct languages, and well-established national identities. First off, the more than 99 percent of U.S. citizens who are not Native Americans clearly cannot make a claim that their ancestors have inhabited the land since prehistoric times. This is true of most countries in the Western Hemisphere, although some, such as Guatemala and Bolivia, have forged national identities with a strong component from their much larger population of indigenous peoples.

Cultural attributes also do not provide a clear path to a distinctively American national identity. Although the English language does help to unify the country, English is obviously not unique to the United States, and some Americans speak English poorly or not at all. Americans also do not share a single religious tradition; rather, religious diversity and nonconformity are American hallmarks. Much of American art, architecture, and high culture—whether the neoclassical dome and monumental sculptures of the U.S. Capitol or the gothic spires and stained-glass windows of the National Cathedral—likewise have their roots elsewhere. And the great ethnic and racial mixture that makes up the American population renders moot any notion of shared ancestry, except perhaps in the broadest sense of a common humanity.

Thus, the usual cultural, religious, and linguistic markers that might help to distinguish, say, the Polish nation from its neighbors are mostly not in place in the United States. Nonetheless, the United States does have a robust civic identity of its own, often forged in the crucible of conflict and violence. Major historical events, especially the Revolution and the Civil War, have provided the country with a pantheon of national heroes such as George Washington, Thomas Jefferson, and Abraham Lincoln. Other developments, such as the struggle against slavery and segregation, the westward expansion, the experience of immigration, recovery from the Great Depression, and victory in World War II and the Cold War, have contributed to a national sense of purpose and progress, led again by towering figures such as Franklin Delano Roosevelt, Martin Luther King Jr., and, increasingly in popular opinion, Ronald Reagan. Through all of these phases, a panoply of images, symbols, and ideas has formed the basis for a common national identity, including founding documents such as the Declaration of Independence and the Constitution; the American flag and the national anthem and the pledge of allegiance that honor it; and iconic buildings and monuments such as the Statue of Liberty, Mount Rushmore, and the Vietnam War Memorial. Thus, although Americans lack the ancient roots of many nations in Europe, Asia, or the Middle East, they nonetheless have a very clear sense of who they are as a people—a distinctive sense of nationhood.

Much of this national identity has always been based upon a specific set of principles and ideas, sometimes collectively called the "American Creed." In a feat that was at the time unique in world history, the founding generation in the United States drew upon political philosophy and their own practical experience in colonial and state government to first lay out and then to implement sweeping principles by which the United States would be governed. These principles revolve around protection of individual liberty and freedom from tyranny: as a goal established in the Declaration of Independence, as the motivating force behind the design of the Constitution, as the recurrent concern animating the Federalist Papers.

The subsequent history of the United States served to reinforce the centrality of individual liberty and freedom from tyranny, especially when compared with the perceived corruption of the Old World. The first settlers had had to cultivate a philosophy of total self-reliance in the absence of preexisting governmental or social structures. This ethos was reinforced throughout the westward expansion of the early to mid-nineteenth century, which was viewed as the manifest destiny of the American nation. Then again, throughout the late nineteenth and early twentieth centuries, the United States received millions of self-motivated immigrants who arrived in the United States to make their own way in the world. These new arrivals were accepted as full-fledged new Americans as long as they pledged fealty to the Constitution and the principles it embodied. In such an environment of capitalism, democracy, and egalitarianism, the United States viewed itself as a model for the world, "the last best hope of mankind." That the United States was a society that egregiously abused the rights of African Americans and Native Americans and that marginalized women and other groups is today usually considered a tragic shortcoming rather than an outright contradiction of the principles of liberty. And, since 1865, the arc of U.S. history has been toward greater participation and individual freedom of the entire citizenry, slowly as that arc may bend at times.

The Development of Nationhood in Comparative Perspective

Among the other new nations of the Western Hemisphere, some have a strong sense of nationhood, while others do not. Like the United States, Mexico has a unique and distinctive culture and national identity and a clear sense of its place in history and in the world. Drawing upon the historical memory of such traumatic experiences as the conquest—yet endurance—of the indigenous population, the struggle for independence from Spain, the loss of its northernmost territories to the United States, and the revolution against the established elites in the early twentieth century, Mexico has forged a strong civic identity that draws upon both native and European roots. With one-quarter of the world's Spanish-speaking population, Mexico also plays a leading cultural role among Latin American nations without submerging its identity into this broader community.

Canada, on the other hand, offers one of the clearest examples of a country where a history of evolutionary rather than revolutionary change has helped to make the question of national identity a perennial preoccupation. Spared the experience of bloody revolution, civil war, or even major internal strife, English-speaking Canadians have had to rely on the incremental development of an independent identity from Great Britain, whose queen even today remains the Canadian head of state. Although their territory is vast, Canadians are so hemmed in by inhospitable climate and terrain that more than 80 percent of the population lives in a thin strip of land within two hundred miles of the U.S. border, further diluting the development of a distinctive national identity. As one Canadian prime minister famously remarked, "Canada has too much geography and not enough history." Today, Canadians (outside Quebec) are wracked by questions about who they are as a people and about how they are distinct from the British and, especially, from Americans.

In Australia and New Zealand, comparable evolutionary historical processes have led to similar questions. Neither country ever experienced a revolution or a civil war, and both also retain the British queen as their head of state. With only small indigenous minority populations, both countries have traditionally viewed themselves as outposts of the British Empire, maintaining the English language and European culture; some have remarked that New Zealanders particularly are "more British than the British." Over the past fifty years, however, the end of the British Empire, an influx of non-European immigrants, and the economic rise of Asian countries have forced these two nations to confront whether they are still essentially transplanted European societies or distinctive Oceanic countries with strong linkages to neighboring cultures.

It should be noted that a revolutionary tradition is not essential to the development of a strong sense of nationhood among new nations. The French-speaking, largely Roman Catholic Quebecois of Canada have no revolutionary tradition per se—indeed, Quebec absorbed many highly counterrevolutionary influences when conservative nobility and clergymen fled there after the French Revolution. Still, Quebec enjoys a robust sense of its own nationhood sharpened by centuries of domination by English-speaking Protestants. One of the distinctive features of modern Canadian politics is the perennial question of whether Quebec should become an independent state—through, of course, peaceful means.

Conversely, Argentina has a revolutionary tradition and powerful patriotic symbolism, such as its much-revered sky-blue and white flag, but has often been paralyzed in part by confusion over its fundamental identity. Located on the South American continent but with a tiny indigenous population, is it a Latin country like Peru or Brazil, or is it fundamentally a nation of Italian, German, Spanish, and other European immigrants? With an educated populace, a developed infrastructure, and bountiful natural resources but recurrent political and economic instability, is it part of the developed world or the developing world? Some have argued that Argentina's twentieth-century experience of rule by charismatic figures, such as President Juan Peron and his wife, Evita, and also by a string of military dictators, was caused in part by a national desire for clear direction and decisive leadership in the face of its confused identity.

The American State and Regime

An unusual characteristic of the United States is that its state and its regime are very closely linked, indeed almost synonymous. In most countries, the state has existed for longer than any particular regime, and many states have seen a number of different regimes over time. Americans, however, have lived under the same regime now since 1789, the year that the U.S. Constitution took effect just eight years after the thirteen American colonies achieved full independence from Great Britain. Although the U.S. Constitution has been formally amended more than two dozen times and also significantly reinterpreted during crises such as the Civil War, the Great Depression, and the civil rights movement, the essential elements of the constitutional framework have endured for more than two centuries. (The U.S. Constitution is discussed in much more detail in the following chapter.)

To a degree that is quite anomalous, then, the United States as a state is largely defined by its Constitution. For instance, the presidential oath of office includes a promise to "preserve, protect, and defend" the Constitution, and naturalizing citizens must swear to take up arms, if needed, to "defend the Constitution." This fusion of the state and the regime can best be seen in the single term *The Republic* as used in the Pledge of Allegiance. When schoolchildren, new citizens, attendees at sporting events, and others pledge allegiance "to the flag of the United States of America, and to the Republic for which it stands," they are affirming their support simultaneously both for the United States as a sovereign state and for the regime that was established by the Constitution in 1789.

In contrast, some countries have had so many different regimes that they have adopted a numbering system. France, for instance, currently counts itself as in its Fifth Republic since its monarchy was overthrown by the revolution of 1789, a year in which France as a state and as a nation was already centuries old. Yet this enumeration does not even include other nonrepublican regimes that have ruled France, such as under the Emperor Napoleon and under a military government during World War II. Perhaps the most notorious example of a numbering system of regimes would be the Nazi's use of "Third Reich" to denote the third German empire. By that reckoning, the current Federal Republic of Germany could be counted as that country's fourth regime (or its fifth if the interwar Weimar Republic is counted).

Further, as the example of Germany demonstrates, any one state may have been under the control of multiple, different types of regimes. One key element in defining a type of regime is what it draws upon as the source of its authority and legitimacy—what gives it the right to govern its people. The First and Second Reichs in Germany are examples of *traditional* regimes in that the wellspring of their authority was a hereditary monarchy and aristocracy. In such traditional regimes, rulers have the right to rule because they have always had that right (or have at least had it for a long period of time). Today, many of the monarchies of the Middle East, such as those in Jordan, Morocco, and Saudi Arabia, retain powerful kings who exert a right to rule because they inherited it from their fathers and sometimes also because of their descent from the Prophet Mohammed or their role as protectors of holy sites. Notably, during the period of the Arab Spring, beginning in 2010, these monarchies have remained far more stable than the republics led by dictatorial presidents.

The Nazi Third Reich in Germany offers a quintessential example of a *totalitarian* regime. As the name suggests, these regimes seek (even if they cannot always actually achieve) total control over all aspects of the lives of their people, whose principal role is to work for and support the goals of the state. In seeking to regulate all aspects of their citizens' lives, totalitarian regimes try to destroy or at least to completely subordinate any institutions that might intervene between individuals and the power of the state, such as political parties, trade unions, churches, and even the family. To seek such absolute control, totalitarian regimes often root their claims of authority in all-encompassing ideologies, such as the sweeping Nazi vision of Aryan racial supremacy.

Other major examples of totalitarian regimes have drawn not on racial identity but on class struggle as their unifying ideology in the form of Communism. The Soviet Union under Stalin and the People's Republic of China under Mao were strongly totalitarian regimes, and North Korea under the Kim dynasty is as totalitarian as any country in history. Some other non-Communist regimes may also fall into the totalitarian category by virtue of their claims to rule based on religion, most recently Islam; the former Taliban regime in Afghanistan and postrevolutionary Iran come to mind.

Milder but somewhat similar to totalitarian regimes are *authoritarian* regimes that usually lack a totalizing ideology but instead base their right to rule on more pragmatic claims to authority. These regimes usually not attempt to regulate and direct all aspects of the personal and professional lives of their citizenry but expect them to defer to the regime on political questions. Such regimes may draw on many different sources of authority. Some might claim to have brought order or prosperity to the society, as in the case of contemporary China under Deng Xiaoping and his successors and Russia under President Vladimir Putin. Authoritarian regimes also often draw upon simple brute force wrapped in patriotic language, as has been the case in countless military-backed regimes in Latin America, Asia, and Africa. Such regimes can prove strikingly brittle when challenged, as seen when the thirty-year reign of President Hosni Mubarak of Egypt was toppled after just eighteen days of street demonstrations.

With regard to the United States, totalitarianism is an alien concept, although a case could be made that under slavery, African Americans were subjected to a form of near-totalitarian control under a totalizing ideology of white supremacy. As for authoritarianism, the U.S. government has occasionally exerted an extraordinary degree of authority during times of crisis, civil strife, or foreign war. During the U.S. Civil War, for instance, Abraham Lincoln suspended some civil liberties, and after the attack on Pearl Harbor Franklin D. Roosevelt ordered the internment of Japanese Americans and largely took command of the economy in order to focus it on military production. But such exercises of authoritarianism have occurred only in exceptional and very limited periods within the U.S. experience. Indeed, one of the most enduring features of U.S. politics has been a recurrent fear of excessive concentration of power, stretching from the preoccupation of the founders with separating, checking, and balancing power to the resistance in the 2000s from the courts, Congress, and public opinion to President George W. Bush's attempts to expand the scope of executive authority in the context of what he termed the "war on terror."

More representative of the U.S. experience are *democratic* regimes, which draw their authority from the people. The mandate of the people generally is provided in the form of free, fair, and competitive elections, but also in other types of citizen input such as public opinion, social movements, and interest-group activity. While democratic regimes may share a common source of authority, often called "popular sovereignty" or the "consent of the governed," there are many different forms that democratic political systems can take. Indeed, a major theme of this volume is that the U.S. model of government and politics is no more or no less inherently democratic than many other systems. (For one prominent organization's analysis of which states are democratic, visit www.freedomhouse.org.)

Unusual Characteristics of the United States

While much of the politics and government of the United States can be explained in terms of its historical experience and institutional structures, other factors also play significant roles. To a degree not always appreciated by American citizens, the United States is a highly atypical country: far larger, more populous, richer, and ultimately more powerful than almost all of the 190 other independent countries of the world. Its various attributes taken together arguably make the United States the most anomalous country in the world.

To begin, consider geography. At some 3.8 million square miles, the United States covers one-sixteenth of the world's surface and is the third largest country in the world, following only Russia and Canada and just ahead of China, Brazil, and Australia. The United States is, in fact, about fourteen times larger than the average country of the world, with most of the states (except for Alaska) being easily habitable territory. The United States is also enormously diverse geographically, encompassing large swaths of deserts in the southwest, several major mountain ranges, fertile farmlands, huge open prairies, and thousands of miles of coastline, features that offer abundant natural resources. This bounty has enabled the U.S. population to expand seemingly without limit, not hemmed in by vast outback desert as in Australia, by expanses of arctic tundra as in Canada and Russia, or by dense jungle as in Brazil. It has also provided enormous economic benefits in the form of a huge common market with the resources to be nearly self-sustaining, barring such problematic imports as oil.

Alongside such scale and scope, the United States possesses an unusual degree of geographical isolation, having only two directly contiguous countries, with several small island nations also nearby. For at least a century and a half, none of these countries has posed a significant direct threat to U.S. interests (although Cuba certainly tried). In the age of intercontinental ballistic missiles and terrorism, this geographic isolation is no longer as significant as it has been at some points in history, but the legacy of isolation remains significant today and was crucial in the shaping of American political history. Compare this with, for instance, Poland, which today has a land or sea border with twelve different countries, several of them historical antagonists.

If the United States is vastly large, it is also highly populated. As with geography, it places third in the world, more populous than all but China and India and well ahead of Indonesia, Russia, and Brazil. With more than three hundred million people, the United States has about ten times the average population of countries of the world. The population density of the United States is relatively low and widely scattered across its territory, much more so than in such population giants as China and India (which each has about four times the U.S. population). The average population density of the world is 43 people per square kilometer, but the figure in the United States is only 30 people—compared with France at 110, Britain at 247, and South Korea at 492.

Combining geography and population, then, provides the United States with a highly unusual profile among countries: the United States is both exceptionally large and populous, yet also highly diverse and decentralized. But the unique characteristics do not end there: it is also the only country that is large, highly populated, *and* wealthy. This is a combination that is wholly anomalous in the world; other geographically large countries are either populous but low or middle income (China, India, Russia, Brazil) or wealthy but relatively unpopulated (Canada, Australia). The United States has thus been able to construct an economy based on both a large population, offering a huge internal market of both laborers and consumers, and a diverse and well-endowed continental land mass. Further, the United States has largely been spared the devastation of war, whether originating from outside or within the United States. Even such major incidents as the bombing of Pearl Harbor in 1941 and the terrorist attacks of September 11, 2001, inflicted damage that was localized and minor compared with the destruction of full-scale armed conflict. And despite domestic crises such as the Great Depression and the upheavals of the 1960s, the United States has not seen truly crippling internal strife since the American Civil War ended in 1865.

These three major endowments—large population, extensive territory, and geographic isolation—have contributed to producing the most extensive economy in the world today and, indeed, in history. In a global economy of approximately $70 trillion per year, the United States accounted in 2011 for about one-fifth or $15.1 trillion. While the European Union collectively accounted for somewhat more, the United States far outstrips all other individual countries, with its nearest competitor being China at $7.2 trillion. The U.S. economy is so large that it is larger than the economies of the next four countries following China—Japan, Germany, France, and Britain—combined. And this figure is not simply a reflection of the fact that the United States has a large population: per capita gross domestic product (GDP) is $48,328, which, although not the highest in the world, is still higher than the average of $35,185 in the European Union. (The world as a whole ranges in per capita annual GDP from $115,809 in Luxembourg to $217 in the Democratic Republic of the Congo.) Wealth in the United States is dispersed in highly unequal pattern, more so than in other rich countries. In one ranking of 124 countries in terms of income inequality, the United States placed ninetieth, well behind every other developed country in the world and in closest company with Uruguay and Cameroon. Poverty is also heavily concentrated in certain populations, such as ethnic and racial minorities, and in certain regions, such as Appalachia, inner cities, and the rural Great Plains.

Also, the overall size of the U.S. economy is useful in projecting what have been termed hard power and soft power throughout the world. Hard power refers to military strength, in which the United States has been totally unmatched since at least the collapse of the Soviet Union in 1991. The United States has more than seven hundred military bases in other countries, located on every continent except Antarctica, and in 2011 the United States spent about $711 billion on the military—more than the rest of the NATO alliance, plus China, Russia, and Japan combined. Military strength, combined with economic muscle, provides the United States with enormous nonmilitary soft power, such as diplomatic leverage that allows it to very heavily influence—and sometimes to dominate—both other countries and multilateral institutions such as the United Nations, the International Monetary Fund, and the World Bank. Another form of soft power is the influence of American popular culture. Originating within the United States' large internal market for entertainment, U.S. films, music, television, fashion, fads, and other forms of popular culture have a huge impact on audiences and consumers throughout the world. Through the projection of both hard and soft power, the United States has become very familiar to citizens of other nations. All of these factors mean that, of necessity, most of the rest of the world pays far more attention to the United States than the United States pays to them.

Conclusion: Why It All Matters

Educated citizens outside the United States often live in proximity to and interact with countries, cultures, and languages other than their own, broadening their awareness of how different and diverse countries can be. Living in a comparatively isolated, often inward-focused nation, many Americans are aware neither of the range of variation found among the countries of the world nor of how anomalous the United States is when viewed comparatively. The focus of this book is specifically on the diverse forms of politics and government that can be found throughout the world. Learning about this diversity is a valuable goal in itself but is also an important way to understand American politics and government in comparative perspective.

Further Reading

Dahl, Robert. *On Democracy.* New Haven, CT: Yale University Press, 2001.
Fischer, David Hackett. *Fairness and Freedom: A History of Two Open Societies: New Zealand and the United States.* Oxford: Oxford University Press, 2012.

Huntington, Samuel P. *Who Are We? The Challenges to America's National Identity.* New York: Simon and Schuster, 2005.
Kingdon, John. *America the Unusual.* New York: Bedford/St. Martin's, 1999.
Lipset, Martin. *The First New Nation: The United States in Historical and Comparative Perspective.* New York: Transaction, 2003.
Wood, Gordon S. *The Idea of America: Reflections on the Birth of the United States.* New York: Penguin: 2011.

Web-Based Exploration Exercise

Visit the *CIA World Factbook* (https://www.cia.gov/library/publications/the-world-factbook/index.html) and use the drop-down menu to access statistics about the United States. Select any four significant facts about the United States, choosing one fact each from the sections on Geography, People, Government, and Economy. Then select any three other countries, and compare them with the United States in terms of the same facts. Ideally, the three countries you choose should be diverse in terms of government type, geographic region, or other characteristics. What do you think might account for these differences? What impact do you think these differences might have on the politics, government, and public policy of those countries?

Question for Debate and Discussion

This chapter lays out the basic case that the United States is so anomalous, so different from other countries, that a comparative perspective can illuminate features of American politics and government that might otherwise be overlooked or taken for granted. What is the practical value of such comparisons? Why and to what extent do you think the U.S. political system should seek to change itself to more closely resemble other political systems? To what degree do you think significant changes are even possible?

Chapter 2

The U.S. Constitution

When it was devised and enacted, between 1787 and 1789, the U.S. Constitution was a true anomaly. Until that point, political systems throughout the world had generally just evolved over time, reacting to changing circumstances with little prior thought or planning. Indeed, the founding era of the United States was the first time in history that a group of national leaders, in this case delegates from the thirteen American states, took on the explicit challenge of codifying a new political structure to govern their country and writing it down in a single document. The framers fused abstract concepts such as the "consent of the governed" and "limited government" with pragmatic considerations about how to garner popular support in enough states to ensure ratification. To an extent unanticipated by the framers, the Constitution has endured with only fairly small textual changes for more than 220 years, making it the longest continuously functioning written constitution in the world.

Today, the concept of deliberate constitution writing seems unremarkable. Indeed, the world has seen several successive waves of similar deliberations, such as after the collapse of empires during World War I, during the period of global decolonization after World War II, following the end of the Cold War in the 1990s, and most recently in the Arab world. Many of the constitutional structures created after these epochal events took forms quite different from the U.S. system, but the very idea of writing a constitutional document itself draws strongly upon the American precedent.

While the U.S. Constitution may be a global prototype, it also contains numerous elements that are relatively unusual. Unlike more recent constitutions, it is exceptionally brief, sometimes to the point of vagueness, consisting of just some 4,400 words in the original text. This brevity adds a great deal of ambiguity into the meaning of the document, the text of which is quite difficult to change. This helps to explain why the Bill of Rights (Amendments 1–10) and some other amendments provide many explicit protections of political rights, but they are virtually silent on the social and economic rights found in many later constitutions. The arduous amendment process also helps to explain why a number of anachronistic provisions, born of pragmatic compromises in the 1780s, still remain in force today.

Case Study: The South African Constitution of 1996

One of the starkest contrasts with the U.S. Constitution is the constitution of the Republic of South Africa enacted in 1996. While this document may be no more representative of constitutions as a whole than is the U.S. Constitution, it presents an extreme case against which the American document can be considered. This 1996 constitution replaced an interim document created in 1993 as part of the peaceful evolution toward majority control after decades under the brutal system of apartheid, in which power was reserved to the white minority. In some ways the South African constitutional process paralleled the development of the country's multicolored, complexly patterned, new national flag, which was often criticized as jumbled and inelegant but which reflected the valid and compelling interests of multiple elements within the society. Indeed, one of the express purposes of the new South African constitution is to "heal the divisions of the past and establish a society based on democratic values, social justice and fundamental human rights."

One notable characteristic is the document's length and attention to details. The original text of the U.S. Constitution contains just a short preamble and seven fairly brief articles that can be printed in as little as five pages, with a few more pages for the twenty-seven amendments. But the South African constitution runs to 140 pages and includes fourteen chapters consisting of 243 sections, plus an additional seven lengthy schedules. As might be expected, the document establishes the branches of government, such as the presidency, the parliament, and the supreme court. It also establishes many of the basic political rights seen in the U.S. Constitution, including freedom of religion, belief, opinion, expression, assembly, association, property, and political participation, as well as guarantees of legal due process and prohibitions on slavery.

The most striking aspect of the South African constitution, however, is its broad-ranging social guarantees, which have led legal scholars to regard it as the most progressive in the world. For instance, it acknowledges ten official languages and encourages the promotion of three other African languages, eight languages spoken among immigrant communities, three languages used in religious services, and even sign language for the hearing impaired. By contrast, the U.S. Constitution never mentions language, and the United States has no "official" language, notwithstanding the historical predominance of English.

Likewise, where the Fourteenth Amendment to the U.S. Constitution briefly and rather vaguely provides for "equal protection of the law," the South African constitution specifies nondiscrimination on the basis of "race, gender, sex, pregnancy, marital status, ethnic or social origin, color, sexual orientation, age, disability, religion, conscience, belief, culture, language and birth." Explicit protections are offered for "the right to bodily and psychological integrity," including reproductive rights and access to abortion.

Rights are also guaranteed in areas as diverse as the formation of unions and the right to a safe environment, health care, food, water, social security, education, and even access to information held by the state.

Although the legacy of apartheid, the persistence of poverty, political corruption, a raging AIDS epidemic, and many other factors limit the ability of South Africa to enforce many of these provisions, their very existence makes that country's constitution a starkly different document from its American counterpart, and one with real-world consequences. For instance, in 2005 the Supreme Court of South Africa ruled that the constitution's specific ban on discrimination based on sexual orientation required the legalization of same-sex marriage. After some discussion, parliament the next year extended full marriage equality to all of its citizens, making South Africa the first jurisdiction outside North America and Western Europe to do so.

The U.S. Constitution: Brevity and Vagueness

Although the U.S. Constitution is both brief and, at times, quite vague, it is far more meaningful than those of some countries that have elaborate, formal documents that are not worth the paper on which they are printed. The 1972 constitution of North Korea, for instance, lavishes rights to freedom of speech, the press, assembly, association, demonstration, and religion and rests its legitimacy upon the "workers, peasants, soldiers, and working intellectuals," all of whom are in fact subject to the whims of the brutal dictatorship of the Kim dynasty. Still other countries may have constitutions that their governments are too weak to actually enforce in all or part of the national territory; notable cases in this category would be "failed states" such as Somalia and Afghanistan, where regional warlords wield most power outside the capital city.

Conversely, several flourishing democracies have no written constitution or, more precisely, no single authoritative document. The constitutions of these countries actually do incorporate many important written documents, such as acts of parliament or international treaties, alongside conventions and precedents that have become so well established that they are considered binding. This is particularly the case in countries of the British parliamentary tradition, especially the United Kingdom and New Zealand. Strikingly, in some of these systems, the single most important political figure—the prime minister—is rarely if ever mentioned in constitutional documents. Indeed, the shifting power relationships among the monarch, the prime minister, the cabinet of ministers, the speaker of the House of Commons, and the rank-and-file members of parliament have never been explicitly codified, but it is nonetheless quite clearly established in each of those countries. The other prominent example of a democracy with an unwritten constitution is Israel, where nine basic laws establish the outline of the political system, augmented at times by Jewish laws and customs. Despite ongoing discussion, disagreements among various religious, ethnic, and political factions in Israel have precluded consensus on a single authoritative constitutional document.

Within the realm of written constitutions, the text of the U.S. Constitution is quite lacking in detail, as noted in the comparison with the South Africa constitution (which is actually not the most extreme: the 1950 constitution of India contains 395 articles divided into twenty-two parts with twelve schedules and three appendices). The U.S. Constitution has sometimes been called a "citizen's charter" in that it is intended more to set a process in motion than to carefully identify and provide for all contingencies. In part, this is because the very act of writing up a national constitution was a novel concept in the 1780s (although it did draw very heavily on earlier experience with enacting state-level constitutions as well as the Articles of Confederation, which ineffectually governed the United States between 1781 and 1789). The framers were not always sure what they wanted in the new constitution and had few relevant precedents upon which to draw in creating such features as a democratic bicameral legislature, an elected executive, and a national judiciary.

As a result, a number of crucial features of the American political system are nowhere to be found in the text of the Constitution. The sprawling structure of committees and subcommittees of Congress that are so indispensable to its work are only vaguely implied in the fleeting provision of Article I that "each House may determine the rules of its proceedings." The crucial division of each chamber into two party caucuses, which determine the leadership of both chambers and the chairs of all committees, is also entirely unmentioned. In fact, political parties are completely absent from the Constitution even though they are absolutely central to the organization of Congress, as well as to elections and many other features of American political life.

Similarly, Article II clearly gives the president the power to appoint "heads of the executive departments" (subject to Senate confirmation). But nowhere does it explicitly provide the power to direct them once in office, reassign them, or fire them; these powers became established only through actual practice and later court rulings. Article III, creating the Supreme Court, is the vaguest of all. In fact, the court's single greatest power, the ability to review and overturn acts by Congress and the president, is never explicitly stated. Although implied in early constitutional discussion, such as *Federalist 78*, judicial review was not fully articulated and established until the 1803 legal case of *Marbury v. Madison.*

The Process of Constitutional Change

The brevity and vagueness of the U.S. Constitution has meant that throughout history, it has been exceptionally subject to interpretation by citizens, by the president, by Congress, and, most of all, by the federal courts. On the one hand, this has provided the flexibility needed for a single document to endure for more than two hundred years, during which time the country expanded from the shores of the Atlantic Ocean across the North American continent and changed from a preindustrial, agricultural society to a postindustrial, information-age economy.

On the other hand, the vagueness of the Constitution has allowed competing political forces to make seemingly legitimate constitutional claims, leading to sharp conflict. Early in the Republic, both proponents and opponents of slavery could argue that the Constitution was on their side, precisely because it was largely silent on the issue. During the Civil War, both the Union and the Confederacy could claim that their view of states' rights (as well as slavery) was the one promulgated by the Constitution. During both the Progressive Era and the Great Depression, the Constitution was invoked both by those who opposed government regulation of the economy, because such powers are not specifically enumerated in the text, and by those who sought a vigorous role for a government in meeting the changing needs of an industrializing, urbanizing country. More recently, the civil liberties and civil rights guarantees of various constitutional amendments went from a fairly limited interpretation as late as the 1940s to one ensuring far broader protections by the 1970s. Today, a major fault line in debates over the Constitution is whether it is best understood as a steadily evolving, living document that adapts to the times or whether it is a static legal instrument that must be interpreted solely in the light of the original intent of the framers.

Such a process of adaptation and accommodation is also commonly found in countries with unwritten constitutions, where all that is needed to enact sweeping constitutional change is an act of parliament. For example, New Zealand eliminated its provinces in 1875 and abolished the upper house of its parliament in 1950, all by a simple majority vote of parliament. Similarly, in the late 1990s, the British government enacted far-reaching constitutional changes, again all with a simple majority vote of the House of Commons. Among the major innovations were removing most hereditary nobility from their seats in the House of Lords; establishing regional legislatures in Scotland, Wales, and Northern Ireland; and expanding local self-governance in the great metropolis of London.

In countries with written constitutions, however, new interpretations are much more likely to be integrated directly into the text of the constitution through some more or less complicated process. In some cases, countries simply scrap their old constitutions and approve entirely new ones. When the parliamentary government created by the French constitution of 1946 proved weak and unstable, an entirely new constitution with a much stronger executive was enacted just twelve years later. This was possible because, unlike the understanding in the United States, the French regime and the French state are not closely associated, with the long history of the state encompassing many successive monarchical, revolutionary, imperial, democratic, and other regimes. Other countries have experienced many more changes of constitution, sometimes within the space of a few years; in the twentieth century, Ecuador had six different constitutions, Haiti had seven, Nigeria had eight, and Ghana had nine. Such frequent changes in constitutions are usually reflective of a volatile political situation with frequent shifts in power, in which new constitutions may become little more than justifications for those who seize power by military or other illegal means.

It is technically possible in the American system to promulgate amendments or even an entirely new constitution via a Constitutional Convention called by three-quarters of the states, but the ever-growing weight of history creates a huge disincentive for such a step. A Constitutional Convention could well be a chaotic process, if only because there are so many more divergent voices in American politics today than at the time of the founding. Thus, any new constitution would probably more closely resemble the detailed law code of the South African document than the lean quality of the existing U.S. Constitution. (Many U.S. state constitutions, which are much more easily amended or replaced than the federal Constitution, are long, convoluted documents.) It is also widely and almost certainly correctly assumed that any new constitution, shorn of the weight of history, could never command the respect and deference that the Constitution of 1789 enjoys.

Of course, part of the reason that there has never been a need for a new Constitutional Convention is that the framers established another, quite brilliant solution to the question of formal textual change. Article V provides for amendments on any constitutional issue (with the exception of equal representation for each state in the U.S. Senate). However, Article V deliberately makes an amendment quite difficult: two-thirds of the members of each house of Congress must approve an amendment, followed by ratification by three-quarters of the states, generally through a vote in the state legislatures. Such a high threshold, or supermajority requirement, guarantees that only those amendments that enjoy enormous consensus in the country will actually be enacted. Although the Constitution was not framed in terms of political parties, the two-thirds requirements in Congress mean that in practice amendments require significant bipartisan support to make it out of Congress, as well as broad support across a wide variety of states.

The requirement of supermajority support in the national legislature for constitutional amendment is a common feature of written constitutional systems, with the necessary percentage usually varying from three-fifths to two-thirds. It is also common that when a country has a bicameral legislature, both houses must approve the bill. In Brazil, amendments take effect if just 60 percent of both houses vote to ratify on two separate occasions, meaning that a relatively small legislative majority can make enormous changes after each election. (However, certain provisions are shielded from changes, and amendments cannot be introduced during times of declared emergencies.) In some countries, particularly those with a single legislative chamber, such as the Nordic states, an additional restraint is added by requiring two consecutive convenings of the legislature to approve the amendment, meaning that any given legislative majority must have earned reelection by the people at least once. Many countries, like the United States, require a second step of ratification after action by the national legislature. One common form in federal states is to require support by a majority vote in some proportion of the provinces, such as half in the case of Mexico and two-thirds in Ethiopia. Another method is to submit the amendment to a direct vote of the people via a referendum. Australia goes further still by requiring a double majority of half the population and majorities in at least four of its six states. Table 2.1 provides an overview of amendment processes in sixty major democracies.

The U.S. requirements for amendment are not the most arduous in the world; Argentina, for instance, must convene a constitutional convention to enact an amendment. But the U.S. system of amendment remains unusually difficult and would be ill suited for countries with highly detailed constitutions that require frequent fine-tuning and adaptation. The threshold of three-quarters of the states (thirty-eight of the fifty) is high in itself, but the usual route of ratification requires a majority vote in *both* houses of the legislature in the forty-nine states that practice bicameralism (Nebraska is the sole exception). Thus, opponents of an amendment need only defeat it or even keep it from coming to a vote in just one chamber in thirteen states (out of a total of ninety-nine chambers in fifty states) to prevent the amendment from taking effect. This helps to explain why more than ten thousand amendments have been proposed to Congress throughout American history but only twenty-seven have actually been ratified; just seventeen of these have been since 1791 and only four over the past half century.

Anachronistic Elements of the U.S. Constitution

In part because of the difficulty of the amending process, historical features of the U.S. Constitution have remained in place that, at best, are of questionable value and, at worst, may be viewed as antidemocratic. The most obvious in this regard is that each state of the Union is guaranteed equal representation in the U.S. Senate regardless of its population, one of the pragmatic compromises that made possible the ratification of the Constitution. This feature of the Senate is discussed in more detail in chapter 6, but it is hard to make a democratic argument that the roughly 580,000 people of Wyoming should have the same number of U.S. Senators as the more than thirty-seven million citizens of California. Another oddity in the U.S. Constitution, reviewed at greater length in chapter 9, is the Electoral College. This method for selecting a president is cumbersome and peculiar, and, as the American people learned in 2000, it is possible for the candidate who received the most popular support to not become president. Yet neither of these anomalies has ever been effectively addressed, in part because these provisions empower smaller (i.e., less populous) states, whose support would be needed to pass a constitutional amendment. Given the extremely high supermajority requirements

Table 2.1 Principal Requirements for Enactment of Constitutional Amendments in 60 Major Dttemocracies

Additional approval requirements (listed from most to least difficult to enact)	Amendment requires simple majority (50%) in Legislature	Amendment requires supermajority (>50%) in legislature
Approval also required by federal units (usually by state or provincial legislatures)	Canada	Mexico **United States**[1]
Approval also required by popular referendum	Australia Denmark France Ireland Switzerland Uruguay	Austria Benin Japan Mali Romania
Approval by a second session of the legislature also required (often after another election has been held)	Panama	Argentina Belgium Brazil Bulgaria Costa Rica El Salvador Estonia Finland Ghana Greece Netherlands Peru South Korea
No further approval required	Czech Republic Guyana Hungary Israel[2] Jamaica New Zealand[2] Trinidad & Tobago United Kingdom[2]	Botswana Chile Croatia Cyprus Dominican Republic Germany India Indonesia Italy Latvia Lithuania Mauritius Mongolia Namibia Norway Poland Portugal Serbia Slovakia Slovenia

(Continued)

Table 2.1 (Continued)

Additional approval requirements (listed from most to least difficult to enact)	Amendment requires simple majority (50%) in Legislature	Amendment requires supermajority (>50%) in legislature
		South Africa
		Spain
		Sweden
		Ukraine

1. A Constitutional Convention can also be called to propose amendments by petition of two-thirds of the states.
2. No single Constitutional document but a body of conventions.

for amendment, representatives of about 3 percent of the U.S. population, if they all worked together, could block a constitutional change favored by the representatives of the other 97 percent of the country.

The other major area of the U.S. Constitution that remains anomalous, even anachronistic, is the near-total absence of any mention of social and economic protections. The example of the South African constitution may be extreme in its articulation of numerous detailed rights, but most constitutions contain at least some provisions about the health and well-being of the citizenry. The 1991 constitution of the formerly Communist country of Bulgaria, for instance, includes a version of the political guarantees found in the U.S. Bill of Rights, such as freedom from illegal search and detention, the right to a fair hearing at trial, and freedom of religion, expression, and association. But the document also goes much further, including clauses that declare mothers "shall be guaranteed prenatal and postnatal leave, free obstetric care, alleviated working conditions, and other social assistance" and that workers "shall be entitled to healthy and nonhazardous working conditions to guaranteed minimum pay and remuneration for the actual work performed, and to rest and leave." Other constitutional guarantees include social security and welfare aid, the protection of the physically and mentally handicapped, affordable medical insurance, education, and a clean environment.

By contrast, it is impossible to point to the text of the U.S. Constitution as justification for social and economic protections, beyond perhaps the fleeting mention of promoting the "general welfare" in the Preamble and in Article I. This is a reflection in part of the great age of the U.S. Constitution. It was created at a time when improving citizens' quality of life was not seen as a major goal of government, and it was designed by wealthy elites who needed no such assistance. The absence of explicit social and economic protections is also rooted in a longer-term skepticism of big government in American political culture, a theme discussed in chapters 11 and 12.

Today, of course, national, state, and local governments, as well as court rulings and bureaucratic decisions, have in fact enacted many of the types of social and economic protections described in other constitutions, such as minimum-wage laws and environmental regulations. In fact, the United States actually delivers many of these protections more effectively, in practice, than countries that, due to poverty, corruption, neglect, or other factors, do not live up to their loftily worded constitutions. Yet it remains the case that attempts by the government to improve the social and economic conditions of its citizenry remain among the most contested and controversial issues in American politics. Indeed, one of the major points of conflicts between liberals and conservatives throughout the twentieth century was over whether to expand or contract the New Deal, Franklin Delano Roosevelt's Depression-era plan for government intervention into the economy and the promotion of a safety net of government-run social programs.

This debate continues down to the current day, although in somewhat more muted form. In most democratic countries, an expansive role for the government in offering social welfare programs is well established and largely uncontroversial. But in the United States, a large swath of the American public, and in particular the American political class, remains opposed to such a role. Had the U.S. Constitution been textually altered to guarantee certain protections, the country would likely have moved further beyond these debates and more closely resemble other countries. But in the absence of such an authoritative statement, the issue of welfare policies remains a potent political topic, and the proper role of government in the health-care system is an issue of perennial disagreement.

Conclusion: Why It All Matters

More than 215 years after its enactment, the U.S. Constitution remains partly a global prototype and partly an anachronistic anomaly. Constitutions are important in all countries, in that they set the basic parameters for the political process, safeguard key rights, and establish the institutions of government. Because of its great longevity and the enormous reverence with which it is treated, the U.S. Constitution is even more central to American political life, even political identity, than almost any other such document in the world. Yet its exceptional age and its brevity mean that the U.S. Constitution is also full of idiosyncrasies and silences. Understanding its form, content, and even its quirks is an essential first step in understanding the country itself.

Further Reading

Dahl, Robert A. *How Democratic Is the American Constitution?* New Haven, CT: Yale University Press, 2002.

Goldsworthy, Jeffrey Denys. *Interpreting Constitutions: A Comparative Study.* New York: Oxford University Press, 2006.

Levinson, Sanford. *Our Undemocratic Constitution: Where the Constitution Goes Wrong (and How We the People Can Correct It)*. Oxford: Oxford University Press, 2006.

Maddex, Robert L. *Constitutions of the World*. Washington, DC: Congressional Quarterly Press, 2007.

Sartori, Giovanni. *Comparative Constitutional Engineering: An Inquiry into Structures, Incentives and Outcomes*. New York: New York University Press, 1997.

Web-Based Exploration Exercise

Find and read through the constitutions of any two countries of the world other than the United States; ideally, you should choose one democratic country and one nondemocratic country. Then compare the constitutions with the U.S. Constitution. Identify and report back on two significant similarities and two significant differences that you found among the three documents. A comprehensive portal to constitutions of the world, many but not all in English, can be found at http://confinder.richmond.edu/.

Question for Debate and Discussion

The U.S. Constitution includes a provision by which it could be replaced: the Constitutional Convention. Because this has never occurred in U.S. history, it is unclear what exactly would transpire at such a convention and what its limitations might be, if any. Critics note that the first Constitutional Convention completely eliminated the existing system, the Articles of Confederation. Others argue that in today's far more established governmental structure, Congress would be able to set effective parameters for the process. What advantages might there be to starting with a clean slate in the United States? Could these outweigh the dangers and disadvantages? What sweeping changes might be desirable? Could these changes be more effectively enacted through the more common procedure of the amendment process?

Chapter 3

Federalism

Virtually all countries have two levels of government in common. *National-level* government generally deals with foreign affairs, defense, managing currency, and the regulation of commerce, although often much more. *Local-level* government tends to focus on more mundane and smaller-scale issues, managing day-to-day concerns in areas such as police departments, sanitation, and land-use zoning. Where countries differ significantly is the organizational structure they create for the national and the local governments, at the level most commonly termed provinces, but also known by such terms as departments, states, cantons, or prefectures.

Three principal models exist to describe the interrelationship between governments at the national and provincial levels. *Confederations* or *confederal states* are those in which there exists an identifiable national-level government but in which most or all final decision-making remains vested at the provincial level. By contrast, in *unitary states,* governing authority is clearly concentrated at the national level, with all or most important decisions made in the capital city and then merely delegated for enactment and administration at the provincial level. The third model, that of the *federation* or *federal state,* strikes a middle path between confederal and unitary approaches, with decision-making authority carefully divided between and shared by the national and provincial levels. The United States is an example of a robust federal system, in which the fifty states of the union (the provincial level of government in the United States) have distinct areas of authority within which the national government may not freely encroach or interfere. Figure 3.1 presents the major forms of intrastate organization. Table 3.1 provides an overview of the federal and unitary states among sixty major democracies.

Case Study: The European Union

Although it is not a state per se, the European Union (EU) most closely reflects some of the key characteristics of a confederation in the contemporary world, with sovereign power retained by member countries that voluntarily cede significant decision-making authority to the EU capital in Brussels. Over the past half century, the EU has mostly been a remarkable success story, the wealthiest political entity in the world, with a population of nearly a half billion across twenty-seven member states. But it began in the grim years after World War II as a way primarily to prevent a repeat of the horrors of the two world wars by linking coal and steel production among six former antagonists on the continent: France, Germany, Italy, the Netherlands, Belgium, and Luxembourg. In this way, it was hoped that no one country would be able to militarize against its neighbors, but the additional economic benefits that resulted from the pooling of heavy industry soon also became apparent. Over the next several decades, new member states were added and cooperative efforts were successively extended to cover a huge range of economic issues, including the flow of labor and capital, "harmonized" policies for consumer goods and manufacturing, common environmental standards, and eventually even issues of social and human rights.

Despite their high degree of economic coordination, the EU national governments retain far greater latitude than the provinces of any country could maintain. In particular, the states of the EU have retained near-total control over their foreign and military policies. For example, slightly more than half of the EU member states sent troops to Iraq in 2003, while the rest—including major players France and Germany—did not, making a coordinated EU position impossible. Indeed, on the international scene, EU countries mostly steer their own courses, especially Britain and France, which have independent nuclear arsenals, veto-bearing seats on the UN Security Council, and special links to their former overseas colonies. In this way, the EU actually has reversed the usual pattern of the confederal model, in which power over diplomatic and military issues is the major form of delegation to the central government while domestic policy remains under the control of the member states.

Along the way, the EU has developed an elaborate institutional infrastructure, most notably including a Council composed of heads of government, a Commission to oversee the operations of the Union, a Court of Justice with strong enforcement powers, and an increasingly important Parliament directly elected by the people of the member states. Governance of the EU is thus often said to have a dual character, partly federal in nature—with central institutions having binding authority and powers of enforcement—and partly intergovernmental in nature, with some dimensions more closely resembling the diplomatic than the legislative process.

The near doubling of the number of member states since 2005 to include a number of much less prosperous Eastern European countries has further complicated governance, leading to a period of "enlargement" of the Union at the expense of "deepening" of intra-Union relations. In the mid-2000s, a proposed constitution, which would have moved the institutions of the EU closer to the confederal model, was rejected by member states, although the subsequent Treaty of Lisbon in 2007 achieved many of the same aims in a simplified manner.

Table 3.1 Federal vs. Unitary States in 60 Major Democracies

Unitary		Federal
Benin	Lithuania	Argentina
Botswana	Mali	Australia
Bulgaria	Mauritius	Austria
Costa Rica	Mongolia	Belgium[1]
Croatia	Namibia	Brazil
Cyprus	Netherlands	Canada[1]
Czech Rep.	New Zealand	Chile
Denmark	Norway	Germany
Dominican Rep.	Panama	India
El Salvador	Peru[2]	Mexico
Estonia	Poland	South Africa
Finland	Portugal	Switzerland[1]
France	Romania	**United States**
Ghana	Serbia	
Greece	Slovakia	
Guyana	Slovenia	
Hungary	South Korea	
Indonesia	Spain[2]	
Ireland	Sweden	
Israel	Trinidad & Tobago	
Italy[2]	Ukraine	
Jamaica	United Kingdom[2]	
Japan	Uruguay	
Latvia		

1. Decentralized federal systems that include some confederal characteristics.
2. Unitary states with considerable power devolved to the provincial level, approximating some characteristics of federal systems.

Since then, however, the intrinsic weaknesses of the confederal model have come to haunt the Europe Union, or at least those members of the so-called Eurozone, which share a common currency. The inability of the EU as a whole to restrain the spending of its more profligate members, such as Greece, Italy, and Portugal, has led to deep recessions and full-blown political crises in those countries. The wealthier northern nations, especially Germany, have attempted to impose harsh austerity measures, but the national electorates of the southern tier have resisted. At this stage, it remains unclear whether the EU will continue to reflect a "united Europe of states," whether it will gravitate toward becoming the "United States of Europe," or—most intriguingly—move toward some new confederal model never before seen in the world.

The Confederal Model: Many Weaknesses, Few Strengths

Although far from a confederal system today, the first, short-lived regime in the United States was not that of the Constitution but the often overlooked Articles of Confederation. In 1781, in the immediate aftermath of the American Revolution, the thirteen states recognized their need to coordinate among themselves but still jealously guarded their newfound freedom and independence. They thus enacted the Articles of Confederation, which created an extremely weak national government with no president or other national executive leadership, no power to tax or to regulate interstate commerce, and no power to act on major issues without the unanimous consent of the states. This led to an eight-year period of ruinous instability, with the national government unable to carry out even basic functions, the states engaging in economic conflict that threatened to turn into actual warfare, and each state wielding an effective veto over the national government. It was in specific response to the weaknesses of the Articles of Confederation that the Constitution was enacted in 1789 "in order to form a more perfect union" and to serve as the "supreme law of the land," creating strong, national-level government and turning the United States into a federation.

The idea of confederation would not disappear in American history, resurfacing during the U.S. Civil War under the banner of states' rights. Although the Confederate States of America never had the opportunity to govern outside wartime, there is little reason to believe that its decentralized structure would have proven effective. Some historians have, in fact, argued that the power that each Confederate governor had over the deployment of the troops from their state hindered the development of a coherent national defense strategy and contributed to the military defeat of the South. Overall, the American experience with confederation has not been anomalous but rather a prototypical example of the need for reasonably strong, national-level government.

Reviewing the world today, it is difficult to find an example of a true confederation. Switzerland was a confederation for more than five hundred years and today remains the functioning state with perhaps the greatest devolution of power to its provinces (called "cantons"); still it is regarded as a federation because its national government does retain some key areas of distinct authority. The term used for the founding of Canada was "confederation," but it is nonetheless now better described as a fairly decentralized federation, with a great deal of authority exercised both in Ottawa and in the ten provincial capitals. Ongoing decentralization of power in Belgium from the central government to the linguistic regions has pushed it ever closer, but not yet fully, to the confederal model.

In practice, the closest example of a confederal state to be found in the world today is probably the fragile country of Bosnia and Hercegovina, which emerged after the disintegration of the multiethnic country Yugoslavia following a brutal war between 1992 and 1995. Under international pressure, the three major ethnoreligious groups—Muslims, Serbs, and Croats—agreed to a complex new political architecture that the peace accords termed a federation but that was, in theory and especially in day-to-day reality, really a confederation. Thus, postwar Bosnia and Hercegovina has an extremely decentralized, three-part system, reflected in the existence of a three-member collective presidency at the national level and in the establishment of political, fiscal, and administrative autonomy within each group. The central government was tasked with conducting most aspects of foreign and trade policy, managing currency and finances, and coordinating some aspects of relations among the three groups. But the three entities managed almost all other aspects of governance, had the sole authority to tax, could exercise a veto over most national legislation, and even maintained their own armies under only nominal national control. In practice, the confederal system in Bosnia obscured lines of responsibility, made governmental accountability all but impossible, discouraged interregional cooperation, and promoted corruption and economic stagnation—all while doing little to create a viable state.

Case Study: The Unitary State in Japan

One of the major political tasks facing the United States and its allies at the end of World War II was to construct new modes of governance in the defeated states of Germany and Japan that would help to prevent future aggression on their part. Both political systems had become deeply dysfunctional in the prewar period, Japan under the influence of an expansionist military, Germany under the control of the Nazi Party. Part of the solution was a long-term military occupation, but part of it was to create new constitutional norms that promoted democracy and decentralized power. With regard to federalism, however, the two states ended up with radically different systems, Japan emerging as a classic unitary state, Germany a robust federal republic.

In 1945, Germany was a nation located in the middle of a continent and had been unified into a single state for less than a century. But Japan was an isolated island nation claiming more than 2,500 years of unbroken continuity from the first emperor and the founding of the early Japanese state. The U.S.-imposed constitution of 1946 focused its attention on the elimination of the political role of the emperor, reducing him to a powerless "symbol of the state," but it could not overcome the legacy of centralized rule. Democratization was achieved by strictly limiting the role of the military and promoting a parliamentary democracy, with virtually all decision-making authority remaining vested in politicians and bureaucrats located in Tokyo.

Today, Japan has forty-seven prefectures (or provinces), and, although each has its own elected government, their roles are largely administrative. Tokyo defines political structures and laws that are binding on the prefectures (and also on the country's many municipalities below the prefecture level). Municipal and prefecture governments may be delegated the task of figuring out how best to apply a centrally made decision, such as in the construction of schools or the organization of hospital systems. But rulings handed down by the national government always take precedence over prefectures, and there are numerous topics with which the prefectures cannot become involved. Further, they rely on subsidies from the central government rather than having their own power to levy taxes. In short, prefectures are used by the central government when convenient, disregarded when not.

Unitary States: Centralized Decision Making

The most common form of government in the world by far is that of the unitary state in which final decision-making authority rests squarely at the national level. To be sure, provincial governments may exist in unitary states, but they are created by the central governments for their own convenience and may be directed and overridden more or less at will. Before the American Revolution, the thirteen colonies were subject to the unitary authority of the British king, who appointed and directed the work of powerful colonial governors. Such strong central government was the norm not only in the American colonies but also among many monarchies in which centralized power had been concentrated in the hands of a single sovereign. Indeed, one of the major breakthroughs of American constitutional theory was the idea that sovereignty could be divisible, *shared* at both the national and state governments. This was possible because the ultimate source of the authority of both national and state government was the people themselves, hence the new concept of popular sovereignty.

Today, the unitary model of government remains the most common form of government in the world, used by nearly seven-eighths of the world's national governments. Among nondemocratic states, it is in practice the norm for all final decision-making authority to reside with the executive branch of the national government. Thus, centralized decision making and almost exclusively top-down lines of authority can be found in most nondemocratic countries, such as China, in which the Beijing-based Communist government can and routinely does direct the affairs of the entire country, and Saudi Arabia, where the royal family dictates public policy. Even some marginally democratic countries that are formally federations, such as Nigeria and Pakistan, may in practice operate as unitary states, at least during frequent periods of military or other dictatorship.

Although the unitary model is closely associated with nondemocratic systems, many democracies are also unitary states. The unitary model is particularly well suited to small countries in which it is relatively easy for the entire country to be administered from the capital city. But there are also a number of larger states that are unitary states. In addition to the example of Japan, another prominent unitary state is France, where various *départments* are established almost entirely for the convenience of the national government, to which they are wholly subordinate. So entrenched is the sense of France as a single, indivisible whole that even some overseas departments, such as Réunion Island in the South Pacific and French Guiana in South America, are formally considered to be as integral a part of France as Normandy or the Loire Valley. The idea of giving quasi-autonomy to the island of Corsica in order to quell separatist fervor there was rejected as compromising the unitary character of the state. However, not all unitary states are as rigid as France (and even France does have active local governments). Great Britain is a unitary state but since 1997 has undertaken significant devolution of power to Scotland, Wales, and Northern Ireland.

In the United States, the unitary model is an alien idea at the national level. The fifty state governments exercise many powers in their own right, without such powers having been granted by or devolved from Washington. Notably, however, the *internal* political organization of U.S. states follows a unitary model. Whereas the states of the Union preceded the national government and are in some regards equal to it, thousands of city and county governments established *within* states are wholly creations of those state governments. In practice, cities may exercise a great deal of home rule and, because of their large populations, may be quite influential in the politics of their states and even the country. Still, even entities as sprawling and complex as Los Angeles or Chicago are mere expressions of the will of the states of California or Illinois, which retain final authority over their cities. Constitutionally there is little to keep a determined state government from managing almost all aspects of governance throughout the state. In 2005, for example, the State of New Jersey took direct control over the failing school system and police department of the City of Camden. (One major exception to the unitary aspects of state government is the territories held by Native American tribes, which have direct relations with the U.S. government and largely bypass state authority.)

Case Study: German Federalism

Even a casual tourist to Germany can discern that the unified country is a relatively recent political construct, with multiple historical power centers ranging from Berlin to Munich to Hamburg to Frankfurt to Cologne. Unlike long-established unitary states such as France and Great Britain, which are utterly dominated by Paris and London, respectively, the diversity of major cities in Germany reflects the reality that the country was unified only in 1871. In seeking to dismantle the highly centralized Nazi regime after World

War II and to deter renewed military aggression, the Allied Powers tapped into this history by creating a new Federal Republic of Germany, commonly called West Germany during the Cold War era to distinguish it from Communist-controlled East Germany.

The Allies' imposition of federalism, along with other measures, worked extraordinarily well: postwar West Germany became a model democratic, even pacifist, country with powerful provinces called *Länder*. So strong was the force of these constitutional arrangements that after the collapse of Communism, East Germany simply abolished itself as a country and reorganized into separate *Länder*, each of which was then individually unified into the Federal Republic of Germany.

Today, the sixteen *Länder* continue to enjoy an exceptional degree of influence, all part of the enduring plan to prevent a return to tyranny in Germany. Indeed, the central government has relatively few powers entirely to itself, mostly relating to military, border, and diplomatic issues. Some powers are reserved to the *Länder*, such as those pertaining to police, public order, and education, but most areas of legislation are subject to the concurrent jurisdiction of both. Similarly, the power to tax and allocate revenues is exercised by both the federal and Länder governments.

The German system even goes so far as to give the leaders of the *Länder* the ability to directly influence federal lawmaking. Members of the upper house of parliament, the Bundesrat, are essentially ambassadors from the governments of the *Länder*, not elected by the people but appointed by the governors of the *Länder* and subject to their direction. The upper house has a veto over any issues falling under concurrent jurisdiction and can even block any legislation relating to federal jurisdiction unless overridden by 60 percent of the lower house. This direct influence of the *Länder* on national politics is exceptional, so in this regard German federalism represents an unusually strong system of checks on national authorities.

The Federal Model: Unity in Diversity

Only about twenty-five countries, just over one-eighth the world's total, have federal political systems. But because federal systems are particularly well suited to diverse, populous countries, these twenty-five countries represent some 40 percent of the world's population, most notably India, Brazil, Germany, Mexico, Nigeria, Russia, and the United States. Federalism is also well suited to sparsely populated states with large territories to govern, such as the huge but underpopulated landmasses of Canada, Australia, and Argentina. Even in relatively small countries, federalism can be helpful when the population is deeply divided along ethnic, religious, linguistic, or other lines, as in Belgium and Switzerland. (The other officially established federations in the world are Austria, Bosnia, Comoros, Ethiopia, Iraq, Malaysia, Micronesia, Pakistan, St. Kitts and Nevis, Sudan, the United Arab

Emirates, Venezuela, and, arguably, Spain; all others are formally unitary states.)

The advantages of federalism are manifold. Simply put, the larger and more diverse the territory and population of a country, the harder it is to find "one-size-fits-all" solutions. This challenge is all the greater in democratic systems, in which government must demonstrate high degrees of responsiveness to the wishes of the people. The relatively few populous countries that do not employ a federal system are either undemocratic, such as China, or largely homogenous in population, such as Japan. A noteworthy exception is the large, populous, and diverse country of Indonesia, which has long rejected federalism—a decision that has contributed to armed insurrections and civil strife ranging from one end of the country at Aceh to the other at East Timor, which won independence in 2002.

The relevant political science concept here is that of *subsidiarity,* or the idea that as many decisions as possible should be made as close as possible to the people. Hence, the state government in Bismarck, North Dakota, is seen as better able to decide on the distribution of public-health resources within its geographically large but thinly populated state than a model designed in Washington, which might be weighted toward states with larger and denser populations. The same basic logic of subsidiarity also helps lead the state of North Dakota to provide its largest cities, such as Fargo and Grand Forks, with local latitude to run their own health departments geared toward those more urban settings.

This distribution of authority can help to tailor programs and maximize the effectiveness of services. It also relieves the burden from national government of managing huge array of varied concerns, allowing it to focus on its own major responsibilities, such as foreign policy and national defense. In addition, a federal system allows for flexibility and innovation, from which the entire system may benefit. This led U.S. Supreme Court Justice Louis Brandeis to call the states "laboratories of democracy" in which different approaches to governance and public policy can be tried out and evaluated for their effectiveness. True federalism, however, involves more than merely operational latitude in implementing priorities set at the national level. In this regard, federal systems fall along a spectrum, with some provincial-level leaders clearly able to refuse or resist orders from the national leadership while others can only protest or perhaps delay such orders. The governors of U.S. states or the premiers of Canadian provinces would fall at the stronger end of that spectrum, their counterparts in Mexico and India at the weaker end.

Despite the generally democracy-promoting aspects of federalism, there are also some troublesome features. One major concern arises when areas of responsibility become too intertwined. The educational system in the United States, for example, has sometimes been criticized as being directed at too many levels, with different agencies that operate in competing or even conflicting ways at the national, state, county, and local levels. American students lag behind their counterparts in many other countries, and rates of functional illiteracy are strikingly high among some segments of the population. Similarly, health programs are awkwardly funded and administered by multiple levels of government. The United States spends far more than other countries on health care yet has produced troubling results in areas such as preventive medicine and maternal health care. Shortcomings in education and health care are not necessarily *caused* by federalism but may be exacerbated and prolonged by the decentralization and lack of coordination that federalism can bring.

In times of crisis, tangled lines of authority can also lead to problems, such as when the national government, the Louisiana state government, and the New Orleans city government failed to properly coordinate their efforts during the 2005 Hurricane Katrina crisis. Partly as a result of this failure, no entity—not city emergency services, not the state National Guard, not the Federal Emergency Management Agency—was able to effectively evacuate the city or come to the aid of the survivors. On the other hand, the response in New York City to the September 11, 2001, terrorist attacks highlighted some of the flexibility and adaptability of a federal system, with national, state, and local governments each responding in a coordinated fashion within the respective spheres of their expertise and responsibility. Within an hour of the attacks, the city police and fire forces took command of "Ground Zero," the state mobilized health-care resources and disaster relief, and the U.S. Air Force secured the city's airspace.

Beyond problems of coordination, there are also serious dangers in federalism that has gone too far or in which the balance of power between the national and provincial government is unclear or unstable. Indeed, the great constitutional failure in the American experience, the catastrophic American Civil War, was directly rooted in differing interpretations of states' rights. Although resolved by bloodshed in the 1860s, many of the same issues resurfaced in the 1950s and 1960s during the civil rights movement, when the national government finally moved to protect its African American citizens from state-level segregation policies. (It should be noted that while American regional identities, particularly those of the South, may have a significant de facto influence on politics, such regions have no distinctive constitutional status. This is a typical feature of federal systems worldwide, in which there usually are not regional governments established between the national and provincial level.)

The form of federalism in different countries is also greatly shaped by the reasons that the federal model was adopted in use in the first place. Some countries at the time of their founding were created out of preexisting entities, as was the case in the United States and Canada. In such cases, federalism can be the price of national unification; states or provinces may be unwilling

Confederation (Confederal state):
The members remain to cooperate and cede some authority, but the central government is very weak

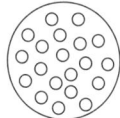
Federation (Federal state):
The members retain important roles, but a strong central government is supreme

Unitary state:
Nearly all power is concentrated in the national capital

Figure 3.1 Models of Intrastate Organization

to accede to a strong national union unless they are guaranteed a significant continuing role. In other democracies, federalist principles can be introduced into previously unitary states to dampen separatist impulses among ethnic minorities. Spain, for instance, has increasingly reinterpreted its constitution to allow greater and greater regional autonomy in the far north, hoping that this will deter separationist impulses among ethnically and linguistically distinctive Basques and Catalans. Given Spain's recent economic crisis, however, it looks more likely than ever that Spanish federalism may lead to an independent Catalan state.

Conclusion: Why It All Matters

The United States was the first federal country, and it has had an enormous influence on the subsequent development of federalism throughout the world. Despite some failings, federalism has, on the whole, served the geographically vast and demographically diverse country well, as it has many other countries with large populations and sprawling territories. By allowing for effective decision making at the level best suited to a particular task, federalism multiplies opportunities for democratic self-governance by introducing multiple layers of government. But federalism today remains a system employed by only a minority of countries in the world, with many flourishing democracies functioning under a unitary system, making it emphatically clear that federalism is an option rather than a requisite condition for democracy. Confederation, on the other hand, is a largely failed model that the United States was wise to put behind it with the passage of the Constitution of 1789.

Further Reading

Griffiths, Ann Lynn, and Karl Nerenberg. *Handbook of Federal Countries.* Montreal: McGill-Queen's University Press, 2005.

Hueglin, Thomas O., and Alan Fenna *Comparative Federalism: A Systematic Inquiry.* Peterborough, Ontario: Broadview, 2006.

Kincaid, John, and G. Alan Tarr. *Constitutional Origins, Structure, and Change in Federal Countries.* Montreal: McGill-Queen's University Press, 2005.

Watts, Ronald. *Comparing Federal Systems in the 1990s.* Kingston, Ontario: Institute of Intergovernmental Relations, Queen's University, 1996.

Web-Based Exploration Exercise

Visit the website for the government of any state in the United States. (The website of any state can be reached at www.state.XX.us by substituting the state's two-letter postal code in place of the X X; for instance, Maryland can be reached at www.state.MD.us.) Then visit the website for one of the provinces or states of another country; a useful listing can be found at http://www.forumfed.org/en/federalism/by_country/index.php. Identify and explain any two similarities and two differences between the governmental structure and activities of a U.S. state and those of the other province or state you explored.

Question for Debate and Discussion

As a federal country, the United States has a complex and multilayered system of government. What advantages would you see to reorganizing political power in the United States to be more along the lines of a unitary state? What might be lost if the United States were to do so? Can you see any arguments for moving toward a more confederal model?

Chapter 4

Separation of Powers

A distinctive institutional feature of the U.S. government is its strict separation of powers into clearly divided executive, legislative, and judicial branches. This separation of powers is in many ways the cornerstone of the U.S. Constitutional edifice, and, according to the founders, democracy is virtually impossible without such a separation of powers. As James Madison wrote in *Federalist 47*, "the accumulation of powers, legislative, executive, and judiciary . . . may justly be pronounced the very definition of tyranny."

The separation of powers established in the U.S. Constitution has several different dimensions. First are the institutional separation of the president from Congress and of both these political branches from the Supreme Court and the rest of the federal court system. Because no single person can simultaneously hold a position in more than one branch, senators or representatives who wish to become cabinet secretaries must leave Congress to do so, and members of Congress must resign before becoming president or vice president (although the vice president does ceremonially preside over the Senate). Federal judges, likewise, cannot hold legislative or executive positions, and no one can hold state and federal office simultaneously.

Separation of powers is further reinforced by the president, senators, and representatives having different terms of office (four, six, and two years, respectively) and different constituencies (the entire country, states, and congressional districts, respectively.) Federal judges, meanwhile, have lifetime tenure, and their only "constituency" is the U.S. Constitution itself, as an enduring expression of the will of the people. Finally, the goal of preventing tyranny is further advanced by the system of checks and balances, most notably the presidential veto, the congressional impeachment authority, the senate's power to advise and consent to presidential appointments, and the Supreme Court's power of judicial review of executive and legislative acts.

Given this emphasis that "ambition must be made to counteract ambition," in Madison's words, many Americans are surprised to learn that the strict separation of powers is a rarity among established democracies. In fact, the United States is the *only* advanced industrialized democracy to have a full *separation-of-powers* or *presidential* system in which a powerful president must contend with a powerful, separately elected Congress and an independent judiciary with final say on constitutional issues. Further, there seems to be little desire for newly emerging nations to adopt an American-style strict separation-of-powers system. Even in Iraq, where the United States had a major role in establishing the new governmental structure after the overthrow of Saddam Hussein, a separation-of-powers system was rejected. Indeed, among the established democracies, the separation of powers may be regarded as perhaps the most anomalous of all American institutional features.

The system encouraged in Iraq and employed in most democratic, industrialized nations is the *parliamentary system*. Many Americans are aware that most other democratic countries call their national legislatures not a congress but a parliament and that the chief leader is not a president but a prime minister. But there may also be a tendency to think that these are simply differences in terminology rather than substance and that the two systems function in largely the same way. In fact, however, the two types of governmental arrangements are not simply different but in some ways are outright opposites. The single most crucial difference is that in a parliamentary system, executive authority *arises out of* control of the legislature. Whereas one cannot hold a seat in Congress and be president at the same time in the U.S. system, one generally must be both a member of and the uncontested leader of the majority in the lower house of the legislature in order to be prime minister. This fusion of legislative and executive authority means that the goal of a parliamentary system is the *concentration* of power, while the U.S. separation-of-powers system is specifically designed to achieve the diametrically opposite result of a *dispersal* of power. Whereas a measure of inefficiency is deliberately built into the U.S. system as a way of countering tyranny, streamlined efficiency is the key attribute of most parliamentary systems.

Case Study: The Westminster Parliamentary Model

Although they all bear certain key characteristics, parliamentary systems vary widely in their specifics. But the prototype for all such systems is that found in Great Britain, which is regarded as the "Mother of Parliaments" and as the source of the "Westminster model," a name derived from the area of London in which the government is located. The British parliamentary system is considered particularly important because it was the earliest such system to develop and the longest to be in continuous operation, and most other parliaments are to some extent based on the British precedent. In many countries of the former British Empire, such as India, Jamaica, Canada, Australia, and New Zealand, the Westminster model was explicitly imported, although always with some local modifications. Parliaments found in many other countries, such as in continental Western Europe, contain stronger homegrown elements but are nonetheless to one degree or another similar to the Westminster model.

Unlike most other modern systems, the British parliament evolved over the course of many centuries, shifting, adapting, and accruing various idiosyncrasies along the way and never being codified into a single written constitution. Today, sovereign power—or the right to govern—is said to emanate from "The Crown in Parliament." The Crown, or the monarchy, remains a hereditary office invested in one person from the time of accession to natural death; the current queen, Elizabeth II, has held that title since the death of her father, in 1952. The parliament is composed of two separate chambers, the House of Lords and the House of Commons, working in conjunction with the monarch.

Traditionally, most of the members of the House of Lords were noblemen (along with a few women) who inherited titles such as duke, earl, and baron upon the death of their fathers or other close relatives and then held office for the rest of their lives. However, beginning in 1958, there also began the practice of granting "life peerages" to accomplished individuals in British society, entitling them (although not their descendants) to the title of lord or lady and to a seat in the House of Lords until their deaths. Others with seats in the House of Lords have included the bishops of the Church of England (called the "Lords Spiritual") and the "Law Lords," who meet separately to hear legal cases as the final and highest court of appeal in the judicial branch in Great Britain, though the Law Lords have been phased out since 2009.

Early in British history, most political power was wielded by the monarch, who claimed a right to rule based on divine mandate as well as military power. The growing power of land-based British nobles forced a power-sharing arrangement, as enshrined in the Magna Carta of 1215, leading eventually to the founding of a House of Lords in London to serve as a voice for the interests of the nobility. While British monarchs remained politically potent, they began to choose a principal officer, called a "prime" minister, from the House of Lords to manage the day-to-day affairs of government. As power began to shift from the countryside to the cities, another, initially less powerful chamber called the House of "Commons" was added to parliament to note that it reflected the interests of people who were neither royalty nor nobility but rather parts of communities. Indeed, it is still referred to as the "lower" house of parliament, a term used in many other countries to describe the house that is in some electoral sense closest to the people. Throughout the nineteenth century, more and more of the authority that was once wielded by the monarchy in concert with the nobility was slowly transferred to the Commons, in particular to the prime minister that it elects and to the cabinet of ministers that is appointed by the prime minister. By the mid-1800s, the British political journalist Walter Bagehot famously described the monarch and the House of Lords as the "dignified" rather than the "efficient" parts of government, representing tradition and authority rather than practical governance.

Today, the House of Commons has the final say on all legislative matters and yields all executive authority. The British monarch performs only ceremonial functions, acting as the country's formal head of state by embodying the historical continuity and national unity of the country while staying entirely out of politics and above partisanship. The executive power once wielded by monarchs is now vested in a cabinet of government ministers led by a prime minister, all drawn from among the members of Parliament. The basis for their exercise of executive authority resides not in selection by the monarch but from support of a majority in the House of Commons. Meanwhile, the House of Lords has been reduced to an essentially consultative role and remains a body very much in transition, with most of the hereditary lords removed from office and other changes under consideration.

The Fusion of Power in Parliamentary Government

As described in the case study, it is possible to talk about distinctive forms of executive, legislative, and judicial power in the British parliamentary system. What is *not* possible is to neatly disentangle them into separate institutions and spheres of influence. In parliamentary systems, executive, legislative, and (to a considerably lesser extent) judicial powers overlap and intersect in a variety of ways that are quite distinct from the U.S. system, with significant results for the functioning of those governments. Figure 4.1 provides an overview of the key differences between the presidential system (based on the U.S. model) and the parliamentary system (based on the British or Westminster model). What follows is an overview of the ways in which power is concentrated rather than separated in parliamentary systems, based largely on the Westminster model.

Under the separation-of-powers system, the U.S. president serves as both the symbolic head of state and the hands-on head of government. As seen in the case study of Great Britain, however, parliamentary systems employ a dual executive system in which the loftier ceremonial duties of office are separated from the partisan and political work of making policy and running a government. In parliamentary systems, the role of ceremonial head of state is played by either hereditary monarchs, such as the king of Spain, or figurehead presidents, such as the president of Germany, who lend their dignity to proceedings of state, such as the opening of parliament and the accreditation of foreign ambassadors but who wield little or no actual executive authority. These heads of state, then, generally play no role in the separation-of-powers scheme precisely because they do not wield any real power. (A few countries, notably France and Russia, have so-called semipresidential systems in which the head of state does exercise real power. The head of state role is discussed in more detail in chapter 5).

To find the institution where power is actually exercised in a parliament, it is necessary to look to the lower house of the legislature and in particular to its leader, the prime minister (an office sometimes also called premier or chancellor). In democratic systems, these lower houses are invariably elected

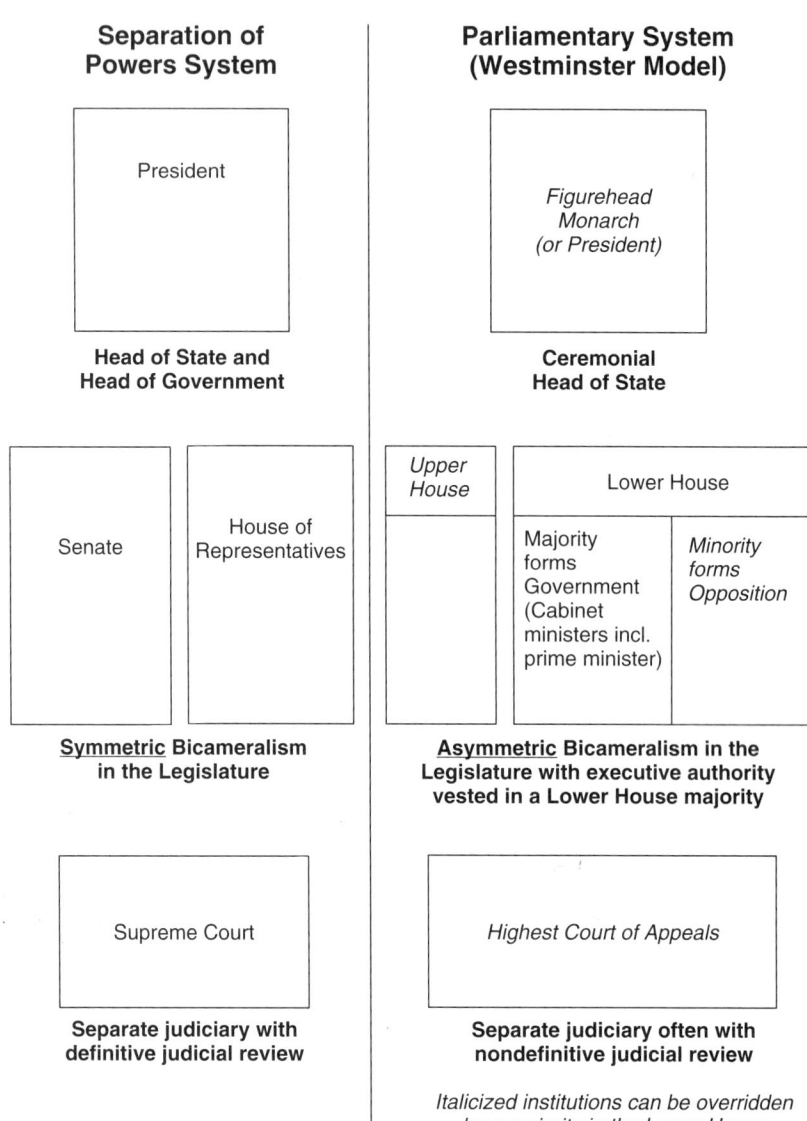

Figure 4.1 Schematic of the Separation-of-Powers and Parliamentary Systems

directly by the people and thus draw their claim to rule from the consent of the governed. Control of a majority of seats in the parliament, then, is equated with the support of a majority of the population—the ultimate form of democratic legitimacy. At the start of each new parliament, a prime minister is selected on the basis of his or her ability to garner the support of more than half the members of the chamber. Because they must have worked their way to the top of a major political party, prime ministers are usually well-known, long-established politicians on the national stage, perhaps even household names in their countries. (The American experience of electing such relative "Washington outsiders" as Barack Obama or Bill Clinton to the top office is quite unusual in parliamentary systems.)

In countries with only two main political parties, the prime minister is generally the leader of the party that holds an outright majority of seats. In countries with multiple political parties, the picture can be somewhat more complicated if no single party holds an outright majority. In this case, negotiations may be necessary to form a coalition of parties that collectively control a majority of seats; ordinarily, the leader of the party with the largest number of seats becomes the prime minister. Sometimes, the choice of a coalition partner is clear, and one or more small parties join the larger party, usually in exchange for control of a key ministry or area of policy. Thus, for instance, a small, rural-based party might join a coalition in exchange for control of the agriculture ministry and an outsized influence on farm policy. As might be expected, the more numerous and diverse the coalition partners, the harder it becomes for a prime minister to assemble a stable coalition. Thus, coalitions tend to expand only to the point needed to ensure the support of more than half the members of the lower house. (The politics of parliamentary coalitions contain many more complexities, which are beyond the scope of this discussion.)

Whatever the specific circumstances, the prime minister next appoints a cabinet of ministers to compose the new government. Ministers of the cabinet are subject to appointment, reassignment, and termination by the prime minister but share the same source of authority as the prime minister, namely the support of a majority in the lower house of parliament, which can remove them at will. Thus, cabinet government is in many ways a collective undertaking, with real group deliberation and decision making and shared responsibility for governance, although the prime minister is the single most important player.

The newly formed government exercises executive powers for as long as it maintains a parliamentary majority or until the maximum time elapses before the law requires that a new election be called (a period usually of three, four, or five years). At any time during the life of a parliament, many systems allow the prime minister to call for a new election. This often comes at a time when only a year or so is left before elections must be called. The prime minister in many countries can call a "snap election" at such time that she or he perceives some political advantage, such as when his or her party is particularly popular or when political opponents are in disarray. This can be a risky gambit, however, as in 2005, when Chancellor Gerhard Schroeder, the prime minister of Germany, called a snap election, only to see his party lose its majority. On the other hand, a few months later Prime Minister Junichiro Koizumi of Japan was successful in calling a snap election to win a fresh electoral mandate for economic privatization initiatives that had been meeting opposition in parliament.

Thus, parliamentary terms of office can vary widely and unpredictably, and national elections can be scheduled with just a few weeks' notice. This is a marked contrast to the American system, where both executive and legislative terms of office are highly fixed and inflexible—presidential and congressional elections in the United States have been held on a rigid schedule, remarkably without interruption, since 1789. Members of parliament are also all elected on the same day and serve for the same amount of time, another important distinction from the deliberately staggered election dates and terms of office for U.S. representatives, senators, and the president.

One of the first tasks of a new prime minister is to appoint other ministers to run portfolios including foreign affairs, defense, finance, justice, and the environment. Like the prime minister, these ministers generally must be members of parliament, and together they compose a cabinet that shares collective responsibility for the actions of the government. Formally, the prime minister is regarded as just another member of parliament and as a "first among equals" within the cabinet. Not being directly elected by the people, the prime minister, unlike an American president, claims no independent personal mandate to govern and is accountable to parliament as a whole (although *not* to the cabinet). In practice, however, voters in parliamentary systems often know—and have their choice of party influenced by—which person will be prime minister when they cast their votes, which can give a prime minister a greater individual standing. Further, while a parliament can remove a prime minister from office, this is usually much easier said than done, as is discussed further later in this chapter. Indeed, as long as they enjoy a solid parliamentary majority, prime ministers often wield extensive powers that are largely unchecked by other political actors and institutions. Figure 4.2 summarizes the major differences between the separation-of-powers and parliamentary systems.

Separation of Powers	Parliamentary
Executive and legislature elected separately: members cannot overlap	Executive power arises out of majority control of the legislature
Executive and legislature act independently, with checks and balances, thus **dispersing power**	Executive is allied with the legislature, thus **concentrating power**
It is very slow and difficult for the legislature to remove the executive	Legislature can remove the executive at any time
All elections are held on a rigid schedule for fixed terms of office	Elections can be held at any time

Figure 4.2 Separation-of-Powers vs. Parliamentary Systems: Major Differences

Prime Ministerial Power

Prime ministers are formidably powerful precisely because they not only lead the executive but also exert control over their majority in the lower house, ensuring that they usually can pass any legislation they choose. It may not be easy to maneuver oneself to become the prime minister, but once in office the prime minister has an array of institutional prerogatives. In addition to appointing ministers, he or she can dismiss them or reassign them, making members of the cabinet unable or unwilling to challenge the prime minister, at least not in public once a decision has been taken. Cabinet ministers are required to support the official position of government on all matters, on threat of dismissal and even expulsion from the party. While cabinet ministers often do have a good deal of autonomy within their departments and can certainly bring pressure to bear on the decisions of government, they cannot hope to prevail in direct conflict with a prime minister. About the most that a cabinet member can do is resign on principle, perhaps briefly embarrassing the prime minister. This happened, for instance, to Prime Minister Tony Blair of Great Britain in 2003 when two high-level cabinet officials resigned to protest his decision to join in the invasion of Iraq. While a headline-grabbing move, the resignations ultimately had no effect on British participation in the war.

The prime minister also has tremendous control over the rank-and-file members of his or her party who hold seats in parliament (often called "backbenchers" because of where they are seated in the chamber). Ideally, the relationship between backbenchers and their leaders should be one of cooperation and mutual support, with leaders carefully soliciting and heeding the wishes of their backbenchers. And while this is often the case, in times of conflict or dissention prime ministers have formidable means by which to exert party discipline to ensure that backbenchers vote as their party leaders wish them to. In the United States, members of the Senate and House of Representatives can and do vote against their party leaders in Congress, often with few lasting consequences to themselves or to the leaders.

But in parliaments, party leaders have the means to destroy the careers of backbenchers of their own party who challenge or oppose them. Party leaders are highly influential in the selection of their party nominees for office because most parliamentary systems do not have primary campaigns in which nominees are selected by the voters. Thus, party leaders can often deny renomination in the next election to members of parliament who do not vote as the party wishes. Party leaders also control who will be promoted out of the back benches to a junior ministerial position, then to a full ministerial position with a minor portfolio, and then to a top ministerial position. In an extreme example, in 2011, a Greek legislator who opposed his party's emergency economic measures was immediately and publicly expelled from the party itself. Thus, it can be seen that displeasing the party leadership in parliamentary systems can be the equivalent of career suicide; U.S. politicians face far fewer such constraints.

As might be expected, prime ministers whose majority is based on a coalition are often in a weaker position and must work more actively to allay the concerns of their coalition partners—particularly any party whose defection from the coalition would cause the loss of a parliamentary majority. In this case, prime ministers must negotiate with the heads of other parties, who in turn are expected to keep their own backbenchers in line. As will be seen, coalition partners and even the prime minister's own party do have the final say over the fate of a prime minister, so prime ministers have multiple incentives to keep their coalition partners and their own party backbenchers relatively contented and cooperative. But during ordinary times, they also have a much broader array of threats and inducements to ensure the support of their legislative majority than do congressional leaders and certainly more than do U.S. presidents, who have no direct power over members of Congress.

Finally, prime ministers are also able to largely ignore the members of parliament who are not from their party or coalition of parties. Such individuals are even less powerful than backbenchers in the majority, who at least have the ear of those in power. Their major role is to form the "Opposition," which has the right to challenge, question, and berate the government from the floor of parliament, use the media to air their grievances, and propose alternative programs to the public. The leader of the largest party outside government may even take the official title "Leader of the Opposition" and appoint a shadow cabinet paralleling the existing cabinet to serve as a government-in-waiting prepared to assume control of government on short notice. But for as long as they are outside the government, the opposition enjoys no executive and quite little legislative power.

Other Checks and Balances?

Thus far, we have seen that prime ministers are mostly unchecked in their executive authority by either the formal head of state (who plays a symbolic role) or by the members of their own cabinet (who are subject to prime ministerial control). Likewise, we have seen that prime ministers are rarely limited in their legislative power by either the backbenchers of their own parties or the opposition in the lower house. Are there, then, other potential checks and balances on prime ministers that serve to rein them in?

One possibility would be the upper house of parliament in those very frequent cases where such an upper house exists. Depending upon the particular system, the upper house may at times be able to frustrate the goals of the prime minister. However, the case of the British House of Lords is not atypical in that formal or informal procedures often constrict the types of issues that the upper house can influence, particularly when they are revenue-related bills. Likewise, there are often formal and informal means by which lower houses can override the upper houses in the case of conflict. (The role of upper houses varies greatly and is discussed in more detail in chapter 6.) Broadly speaking, some upper houses can sometimes act as a check on prime ministers, but only in the legislative arena; they generally play little or no role in executive decisions.

Another possibility for checks and balances would be the judicial branch, and here again systems vary widely. There are some countries in which national supreme courts have the final say on issues relating to constitutional questions and may have the ability to check the prime minister in some cases. By their very natures, however, many unelected judiciaries tend to avoid so-called political questions that they deem better left to the elected branches of government. Some Westminster model systems go even further by enshrining the concept of parliamentary supremacy in which the nation's highest court may issue a ruling, but that ruling can be reversed by a simple act of parliament. (The role of the judiciary is considered further in chapter 7.)

Could federalism serve as a check on a prime minister? As seen in chapter 3, federal systems usually designate specifically particular areas of authority for the national and the state or provincial governments. Within those areas designated as solely under national control, states or provinces have few tools to challenge a prime minister. Within the areas of concurrent jurisdiction, states and provinces might be able to curb or limit the authority of a prime minister, although various constitutional supremacy doctrines and the superior resources of the national government may still provide the prime minister with the upper hand. Thus, the prime minister of a federal state might have less comprehensive powers than one in a unitary state, at least on certain domestic issues.

One final possibility to consider is whether some supranational entities can check the actions of a prime minister. Even two decades ago, the answer would have been "no" because national sovereignty generally trumped all other considerations. Today, the answer is a qualified yes, in that once a country has willingly entered into an international treaty or multinational organization, it may well be bound by rulings from outside sources. This is particularly the case with strong organizations, such as the European Union and the World Trade Organization, that have the power to enforce their rulings. That said, member states within these organizations usually have recourse to a variety of strategies to appeal and delay such rulings and, at the extreme, always have the right to withdraw. In addition, many areas of crucial national concern are exempted from international agreements.

A Hypothetical Case Study: Parliamentary Checks and Balances

Suppose that a prime minister wished to double his or her country's existing gasoline tax in order to build new highways. Could the prime minister's bill be challenged—or halted—and, if so, how, when, and by whom? (Because specifics vary from country to country, the following is a generalized case study based on practices in the Westminster model.)

- The head of state would likely be limited simply to officially approving the bill once it had been passed by the parliament.
- The cabinet would have the opportunity to discuss and debate the bill in closed session, perhaps offering modifications and counterarguments. But the prime minister would generally still be able to introduce the bill, and, after that, all cabinet members would be required to support it or else lose their positions.
- Parliamentary backbenchers of the prime minister's party or allied parties in the lower house probably stand nothing to gain and much to lose in terms of their career prospects by openly opposing the bill. They may privately air grievances, but they are unlikely to publicly challenge it.
- The opposition parties in the lower house may loathe the bill and may say so loudly and publicly. They may even gain an electoral advantage on the issue when the next election is held. But, until then, they are powerless to stop the prime minister.
- The upper house of parliament may have the opportunity to delay the bill, to suggest amendments to it, or to hold public hearings criticizing the bill. But if it comes to an outright confrontation between the two houses, the upper house is unlikely to prevail.
- The states or provinces in a federal system may (or may not) have some say over how the funds are allocated in the highways that pass through their territories. But as to the actual passage of the bill, they are unlikely to have much influence because the action is being taken by the national government on its own authority.
- The court system may be asked to adjudicate various elements of the bill at some later point, but unless and until that happens, it will have little say. And, in some countries, parliaments are free to override court decisions if they wish.
- International agreements are likely to be silent regarding internal revenue and infrastructure. In any case, international agreements can be very hard to enforce over the will of an elected national government.
- The electorate, of course, will have the final say in the next election, and public opinion may sway a prime minister. But during the life of a parliament, the voters have no direct control, and many prime ministers defy short-term public opinion in hopes of bringing voters around to their position before the next election.

In sum, then, a prime minister may be challenged and constrained by multiple political actors, but a determined prime minister is unlikely to be stopped. Unlike an American president who must contend with the U.S.

House, the U.S. Senate, and a federal court system with judicial review, prime ministers are able to act far more unilaterally.

Prime Ministerial Accountability to Parliament

At this stage, it may seem that prime ministers have unfettered power. Unencumbered by the elaborate web of checks and balances that limits U.S. presidents, prime ministers usually get their way. Still, there is one Achilles' heel from which prime ministers suffer that presidents do not and that may serve as the ultimate brake on their actions. As we have seen, presidents are institutionally sealed off from Congress, which limits their ability to control Congress—but also means that they are not required to be accountable to Congress. Indeed, drawing on their own vast array of constitutional and statutory powers, presidents have wide latitude to operate largely independent of Congress. This is especially true in the conduct of military operations and the making of foreign policy, in which Congress has a very limited say.

Prime ministers, however, are embedded in parliament and are accountable to that institution, which is never more clearly manifest than when ministers are required to appear on the floor of parliament to be publicly questioned by rank-and-file members. Perhaps the best-known example of this is the raucous "Prime Minister's Question Time" during which the British prime minister appears in the House of Commons chamber for half an hour every Wednesday. During this televised spectacle, the prime minister is grilled, mocked, cajoled, and otherwise berated by members of the opposition, while being cheered and jeered from the back benches as well. Armed only with a briefing book, prime ministers must spontaneously speak on a wide variety of issues, sometimes making statements that make news headlines. Question Time is a vivid manifestation of the reality that prime ministers hold their positions *only* because they continue to be supported by a majority of the lower house—and that they can be deposed by parliament. The same is true of all cabinet ministers, who must also answer questions and can be forced to resign if enough members of parliament are displeased with their work. (To view this remarkable spectacle, visit http://www.c-span.org/Series/Prime-Ministers-Questions/).

To be sure, no prime minister or other minister has anything like the job security enjoyed by the U.S. president, who is guaranteed a fixed term of four years barring death, disability, resignation, or impeachment and removal from office. Besides losing an election, a prime minister can be removed in either of two principal ways. The first way is if enough members of parliament from the prime minister's party (or party coalition) decide that the prime minister is leading them in the wrong direction on policy or has become a liability for the next election. Because the prime minister's sole personal claim to power is the support of a majority in parliament, once that claim is lost, the prime minister can no longer remain in office.

Most prime ministers are acutely aware of their standing within their party and use their considerable powers to threaten those who would challenge their leadership and to reward their supporters. But it was a challenge from within her own party that toppled even as formidable a figure as the British prime minister Margaret Thatcher, who for eleven years concentrated enormous power to herself—so much so that other members of her party long felt that their views were not being heeded. With growing evidence that she was becoming an electoral liability in forthcoming elections, a rare but successful "backbench revolt" was fomented against Thatcher, led by a rival whom she had earlier vanquished. Under the imminent threat of replacement as prime minister, the Iron Lady stepped aside in favor of her preferred successor, John Major. Sometimes, a more carefully orchestrated hand-off can also occur between elections, as in 2003 when Prime Minister Jean Chretien of Canada more or less willingly handed over the prime minister's office to his Liberal Party colleague Paul Martin. Similarly, in June 2007, Prime Minister Tony Blair of Britain stepped down under pressure in favor of his longtime rival Gordon Brown with hopes of reviving the electoral standing of the Labour Party. (Less dramatically, a prime minister can also be quickly replaced without an election if he or she dies in office, resigns for health or other nonpolitical reasons, or becomes disabled.)

Replacement of the prime minister as party leader, while at times dramatic, is actually the *less* volatile way to bring about a change in leadership. The other mechanism—called a "vote of no confidence"—topples not just the prime minister but also the entire cabinet of ministers (that is to say, "the government") and triggers a new election. A vote of no confidence can be brought up as a special motion, but it can also take place if the government loses a crucially important vote, such as on its budget. Since executive power in a parliamentary system is drawn solely from the support or confidence of a majority in the lower house of parliament, the loss of such a vote is taken as prima facie evidence that majority support has been lost. When this happens, the government is said to have "fallen," which is not nearly as dire an event as it sounds to American ears. An election will then be held to get a new mandate from the people. Paul Martin's prime ministership in Canada, for example, proved quite short-lived, and his government was toppled by a vote of no confidence in late 2004.

Votes of no confidence are unusual when one party holds a majority and thus has the less radical option of simply replacing the prime minister rather than run the risk of calling a new election that the party might lose. However, votes of no confidence are much more likely in coalition governments, where the defection of any single party can lead to a loss of a parliamentary majority. The more parties that are in a coalition, the greater is this danger because as a government makes real-world decisions, it can become harder and harder to please all groups. Further, the smaller the party, the narrower its electoral base and the more likely it is to have a few deeply entrenched interests that are nonnegotiable to it. Thus, if a party coalition that relies on a small rural-based party must also bring in a city-based party to survive, the two may have irreconcilable goals. If the government must decide between preserving countryside and expanding urban zones, for instance, the small party on the losing side may no longer see any advantage to remaining in the coalition and trigger a vote of no confidence. For example, the two governments led by Prime Minister Romano Prodi of Italy fell to votes of no confidence in 1998 and then again in 2008, both times because of the defection of one small but decisive part of his majority coalition.

The ability of a parliament to topple a prime minister and his or her government at any time can go a long way toward reining in prime ministers and promoting democratic participation. In the United States, Congress does have the power to impeach and remove the president from office, but this cannot constitutionally be done purely out of political disagreement; the Constitution requires that it be based on evidence of "high crimes and misdemeanors." The 1998–99 impeachment and trial of Bill Clinton represented a troubling break with the tradition of reserving the congressional removal power for serious abuse of power, both because Clinton's offenses were comparatively minor and because they had no relationship to his role as president. But even in this highly partisan proceeding, the Senate did not come close to reaching the two-third majority required to remove Clinton. The impeachment and conviction powers of the Congress involve an arduous process that is a far cry from the clean efficiency of a parliamentary vote of no confidence.

The ability to topple governments at any time certainly can also have some negative consequences in terms of stability. Perhaps the most notorious example of this is Italy, as noted in the earlier example. In Italy, the extreme fragmentation of the party system has meant that coalition governments of six, eight, or more parties are the norm. In the sixty-year period between the formation of a democratic government at the end of World War II and 2006, Italy had more than sixty governments, most lasting less than a year. Indeed, it was not until the period 2001–6 that any government survived for its entire five-year term (only to be narrowly defeated when elections were called). This extreme pattern of instability fostered a sense of chaos in the politics of the nation and contributed mightily to the persistent inability of the Italian state to effectively address such problems as extreme regional inequalities, entrenched corruption, the mafia and other types of organized crime, and terrorism by both right-wing and left-wing political factions.

Another element offering greater stability in the United States is fixed-term elections. Since the first unanimous election of George Washington, a president has been elected exactly every four years, as have members of Congress every two years. Once a U.S. presidential election is held, it is impossible for there to be another until another four years have passed. Most likely, the person elected president will serve out the term, but if not it will almost surely be a senior politician from the same political party who had been chosen by the president—namely the vice president. The composition of Congress is nearly as stable, even if a few individual members might change between regularly scheduled elections. Such executive and legislative stability is in stark contrast to that found in parliamentary systems, especially those with multiparty coalition governments. Patterns of change are thus far more predictable under the U.S. system, enabling longer-range planning and fostering a sense that elected officials have a legitimate right to govern for the duration of their terms.

Despite their contribution to stability, however, fixed terms of office also add an element of rigidity to the political system, making it all but impossible to replace a president who proves to be ineffectual or a Congress that is paralyzed or deadlocked before the next regularly scheduled election. President Jimmy Carter was widely considered to be ineffective for at least the last two years of his term, yet there was no way to replace him with a leader better suited to the challenges the country was facing in the late 1970s. If he had been a prime minister, Bill Clinton would probably not have survived in office after his sex scandal with Monica Lewinsky, sparing the country more than a year of distractions. And the strongly pro-Democratic vote in the congressional elections of 2006 amounted to a vote of no confidence in President George W. Bush and his policies, yet Bush remained in office as commander in chief right up until January 20, 2009.

In all, the fusion of powers in a parliamentary system offers some significant strengths when compared with the U.S. system. Almost by definition, the sort of divided government that is often found in the United States—such as a Democratic president and a Republican-controlled Congress—cannot occur in a parliamentary system (especially when the upper house is clearly subordinate to the lower house). Even when the United States experiences unified government—when the White House and both Houses of Congress are under the control of the same party—they are still institutionally separated, and there is no guarantee of cooperation. This was seen, for instance, in 2005 and 2006 with the demise of President George W. Bush's plans to overhaul Social Security and to reform immigration policy at a time when his Republican Party controlled both the Senate and the House of Representatives. More recently, President Barack Obama and the House Republican majority clashed over raising the nation' debt ceiling and avoiding a so-called fiscal cliff of massive budget cuts, with neither side willing to concede ground to the other.

Of course, it was part of the original design of the U.S. Constitution for government to be inefficient in order for it not to become tyrannical. Such inefficiency, however, can have deleterious real-world outcomes in the realm of public policy. Health care provides one of the most vivid examples of the failure of the separation-of-powers system in the United States. More than forty million Americans are uninsured, and a crisis looms in which tens of millions of baby boomers are likely to need extensive care in their old age. Yet the two Houses of Congress and the president long remained incapable of reforming a cumbersome and inefficient health-care system that costs far more per capita than that of any other country in the world. Even the landmark Patient Protection and Affordable Care Act of 2010 (commonly called "Obamacare") passed through Congress and survived Supreme Court scrutiny by the narrowest of margins, and its ultimate impact remains unclear as of this writing.

In a parliamentary system, coordination between the legislative and executive powers is automatic because they are both wielded simultaneously by the same people from the same party (or coalition of parties)—the prime minister and the cabinet. This means that in parliamentary systems, there is much less likely to be inaction—often called "gridlock" because of conflict between different parties and/or different branches of government. Reform of the health-care system or almost anything else could be accomplished nearly at the stroke of a pen. This is not always necessarily an advantage: after several elections, Labour and Conservative governments in Britain successively nationalized and privatized the British steel industry, creating an instability that destroyed its ability to compete internationally. Still, governments of both parties were simply keeping their campaign promises, which were well known to voters before the election.

In fact, one political consequence of the parliamentary system is that voters can much more easily hold political parties accountable for their accomplishments at the next election, a concept called responsible government. In the U.S. system, the president can blame Congress, the House of

Separation of Powers	Parliamentary
Contains "checks and balances"	Prime minister is largely unchecked
Susceptible to "gridlock" especially under "divided government"	Total coordination between executive and legislature
Rarely able to carry out sudden major changes	Can readily respond to changing needs rapidly
Can lead to centrist, compromise policies	Can create sharp shifts, some highly unpopular
Can be hard for voters to assess responsibility for outcomes	Easy for voters to assess responsibility for outcomes
In theory, prevents tyranny (but in practice may promote it)	In theory, can lead to tyranny (but in practice rarely does)

Figure 4.3 Separation-of-Powers vs. Parliamentary Systems: Strengths and Weaknesses

Representatives can point to the Senate, the state and local governments can excoriate the national government, and all can claim judicial interference, making it hard for voters to know where to place credit or blame. Because of the concentration of power in parliamentary systems (especially in unitary states), the success or failure of any given government is much more readily discerned by the voters. Parliamentary governments have all the tools they need to enact their campaign promises, and the voters are unlikely to be very forgiving if they fail to do so. Figure 4.3 summarizes the major strengths and weaknesses of the separation-of-powers and parliamentary systems.

Conclusion: Why It All Matters

Although distinctive executive, legislative, and judicial roles can be found in most of the countries of the world, they are not always institutionally separated. The separation-of-powers system has, on the whole, functioned effectively in the United States, but it has proven much more problematic in other countries in Latin American and Africa. The system of separation of powers has significant implications for the workings of each of the three branches, which is the focus of Part II of this book.

Further Reading

Cheibub, José Antonio. *Presidentialism, Parliamentarism, and Democracy.* New York: Cambridge University Press, 2007.

Gunlicks, Arthur B. *Comparing Liberal Democracies: The United States, United Kingdom, France, Germany, and the European Union.* Bloomington, IN: IUniverse, 2011.

Manuel, Paul Christopher, and Anne Marie Cammisa. *Checks and Balances? How a Parliamentary System Could Change American Politics.* Boulder, CO: Westview Press, 1999.

Lijphart, Arend. *Patterns of Democracy: Government Forms and Performance in Thirty-Six Countries.* New Haven, CT: Yale University Press, 2012.

Sartori, Giovanni. *Comparative Constitutional Engineering: An Inquiry into Structures, Incentives and Outcomes.* New York: New York University Press, 1997.

Web-Based Exploration Exercise

Visit the website of any country with a parliamentary system of government. Identify and explain two similarities and two differences between the roles of these parliamentary institutions and their counterparts in the United States. A comprehensive portal to the governmental websites of countries around the world can be found at www.gksoft.com/govt/en/world.html.

Question for Debate and Discussion

While it is possible to generalize about the parliamentary system of government, its actual operation varies significantly from country to country. Some differences are institutional, such as whether the prime minister is largely shielded from votes of no confidence (as in Germany) or is appointed by the president (as in France). Other differences are political, such as when minority governments are permitted by the parliamentary opposition to rule (as is fairly common in Scandinavia) or when the extreme fragmentation of the party system makes it difficult to form stable coalitions (as in Israel). Examine the particulars of a parliamentary system with an unusual feature, and determine how and why that feature has emerged, then make a direct comparison between that country's system and the U.S. system.

Part II

The Institutions of Government

Chapter 5

The Executive Branch
The Presidency and the Bureaucracy

The one indispensable, common element across all forms of government is the existence of executive power—the ability to act, backed by the threat or use of force. In the evolution of governing structures of all types, three of the crucial factors have always been the power to muster force of arms, to collect taxes, and to enforce the will of the rulers among the people. In the modern world, another characteristic of all sovereign states is their ability to enter into and conduct relations with other states. And as society has grown more complex, most states have developed executive-branch bureaucracies for regulating and supervising various aspects of society and the economy and for providing programs and services. Legislative bodies and law courts in many authoritarian countries do not have much real political power and may even just be showpieces, but expansive executive authority can be found in all functioning states. For this reason, this chapter delves more deeply than any other in this book into nondemocratic as well as democratic regimes.

The same essential core areas of authority and responsibility can be found in the executives of nearly all states, including the United States. Indeed, it is common to speak of the American president as playing a number of distinct roles encompassing the full range of executive power based on Article II of the U.S. Constitution. In the commander-in-chief role, the president has the command authority to deploy and direct the military. As the chief diplomat, the president has the right to send and receive ambassadors and, more generally, to conduct relations with other countries. In the head-of-government role, the president has the ability to appoint and direct the federal bureaucracy. And as head of state, the president serves as the symbol of the unity of the country and continuity of national history. (This chapter considers the constitutional parameters and institutional setting of the executive branch; the actual making of domestic policy and foreign policy by the executive is considered in further detail in chapters 12 and 13.)

Case Study: Variations in Executive Power in Southeast Asia

Executive power may be universal, but the institutional configurations of executive power are many and varied. This variety can be readily seen by examining five neighboring countries of Southeast Asia, each with entirely distinctive executive arrangements: Brunei, Malaysia, Indonesia, Myanmar, and Vietnam.

The tiny, oil-rich Sultanate of Brunei represents the most traditional of all forms of executive power: autocratic control by a hereditary monarch. There are no checks or limits of any kind on the extremely wealthy sultan, who is head of state, head of government, commander in chief, religious leader, prime minister, minister of defense, and minister of finance. The sultan receives nonbinding advice from various consultative bodies, all of whose members he appoints, and then rules by royal decree.

Malaysia has a robust parliamentary system, with a clear-cut division between the head-of-government and head-of-state roles. A former British colony with a highly diverse population, Malaysia has adopted a system quite similar to the Westminster parliamentary model, with effective executive power exerted by a prime minister who is the leader of the majority in the lower house of a bicameral legislature. The prime minister serves as head of government and appoints and directs a cabinet to oversee the military, foreign affairs, and other government ministries. The prime minister is not the head of state, however; that role is played by a king, whose responsibilities are chiefly ceremonial and religious.

In nearby Indonesia, a country consisting of an archipelago of thousands of islands and home to the fourth largest population in the world, the system is much more akin to that found in the United States, especially since major constitutional reforms in 2004. Today, the country has a strict separation-of-powers system, with a president who is directly elected by the people and who appoints and directs the work of a cabinet of ministers. The Indonesian president directly carries out all four of the principal executive roles: head of state, commander in chief, chief diplomat, and head of government. Much as in the United States, the president must contend with an elected, bicameral legislature, one house of which is elected on the basis of population and the other on the basis of regional representation, with joint lawmaking powers. Having become a multiparty democracy only after the forced 1998 resignation of longtime, military-backed dictator Mohammed Suharto, Indonesia faces an uncertain future with regard to executive power.

One possible and troubling trajectory for Indonesia is the situation found in Myanmar (formerly Burma), where a group of military officers long ruled the country by force, with no constitution, no legislature, no independent judiciary, and no other checks and balances on their decrees. Through a State Peace and Development Council, the military officers appointed one among their number to serve as prime minister and also to appoint a cabinet, judges, and regional governments, all subject to the officers' will. The elected People's Assembly was prevented from meeting after 1990, and the nation's democratically elected leader, Aung San Suu Kyi, winner of the Nobel Peace Prize, was kept under house arrest. A very promising liberalizing trend began in 2010 with elections and the freeing of Suu Kyi. But for decades, Myanmar's military leaders turned their country into an international pariah—and an unusually blunt throwback to the concept of might-makes-right. What happens next in that country remains a question of great international interest.

Might also makes right in neighboring Vietnam, although the exercise of executive power is much more elaborately justified by the Communist Party, which has concentrated all authority to itself since 1975. Constitutionally, executive authority is wielded by a president who serves as head of state and a prime minister who is head of government. But, in practice, Vietnam continues to exercise the system prevalent in the former Soviet Union even some fifteen years after the demise of that country: real power resides with officials of the Communist Party. In this regard, then, the president, prime minister, and other ministers are not independent executive actors but are more akin to government bureaucrats who implement and administer programs and policies that are set by the Party.

Nondemocratic Executives

In the contemporary world, the case of Brunei is extreme in the absolute powers invested in the sultan, but several other, primarily also Muslim countries invest their kings with final authority. To one degree or another, these include Morocco, Saudi Arabia, Jordan, the United Arab Emirates, Oman, Qatar, and Kuwait. Some of these states may have written constitutions, elected legislatures, and federal structures, and their day-to-day governance may be carried out by an appointed prime minister and a professional government, but these are all clearly subject to the ultimate authority of the throne. In some other countries, executive power is monopolized by a single political faction, often one that emerged victorious from an era of revolution or civil war as did a number of Communist Parties in Asia. Such states often try to project a veneer of democratic legitimacy, but mostly rely on authoritarian means such as heavy-handed media censorship, threats to jobs and livelihoods, and police forces able to act with impunity. The case of direct rule through raw military force is relatively rare as of 2010, though in many countries the armed forces are capable of independent action and may intervene directly in the political system from time to time. Military regimes lack the legitimacy of traditional monarchies or even single-party states, however, and often resort to brute-force tactics of intimidation, torture, and murder. Militaries also rarely have the skills or inclination needed to manage an entire country, and economic and social problems tend to proliferate under their leadership, often leading to an eventual return to civilian government—a cyclical pattern that has been especially prevalent in Central and South America.

This discussion of executive power in nondemocratic countries is relevant not only because many powerful states are nondemocratic but also because, even in democratic countries, the executive is the part of government most likely to display authoritarian and antidemocratic impulses. However, such tendencies should not be overstated. First, the American president is emphatically not a monarch. Having just fought a war of independence, the founders rejected any thought of installing a hereditary king or even of a highly powerful executive with lifetime tenure of office. Crucial early precedents set by George Washington, such as declining to be called "Your Majesty" and voluntarily stepping down from office after two terms, further underscored that the president is a citizen, not a monarch. With the possible exception of the president's unilateral power to grant pardons—a holdover from monarchical practices—all presidential powers are subject to multiple checks and balances. A strong tradition of noninterference in politics by the U.S. military and its very limited role on U.S. soil have prevented it from becoming either the political servant—or the master—of American presidents.

The U.S. presidency has also never been a platform for full single-party rule. True, electoral cycles and patterns of voter allegiance have from time to time consolidated the rule of one party or another. Most recently, the presidency was held by the Democratic Party for all but eight years from 1933 to 1969 and by the Republican Party for all but twelve years from 1969 to 2010. Still, during these periods opposition parties won five out of twenty presidential elections and often also controlled Congress and many statehouses. The U.S. presidency has also never become a platform for personal rule by the president. Richard Nixon egregiously abused his office, covering up break-ins of the offices of the Democratic Party and using the IRS to audit his political enemies, and also promulgated an "Imperial Presidency" by disregarding the will of Congress and acting secretly in the prosecution of the Vietnam War. But, of course, Nixon was ultimately forced to resign the presidency under the immediate threat of impeachment and removal from office, albeit only after many months of political paralysis and nearly a constitutional crisis.

Democratic Dual Executives

Although the U.S. presidency bears little resemblance to the executive power in most nondemocratic countries, its institutional contours are also quite different from those found in most other democratic countries. Indeed, of the twenty-three countries that have been continuously democratic since 1950, only Costa Rica also concentrates all executive power in a single individual who is entirely separated from the legislature. The others, including nearly all of the countries of Europe, all have a dual executive, with one person filling the ceremonial role of *head of state* and another acting as *head of government,* deriving authority as prime ministers from control of a majority in parliament. (The executive role of prime ministers is discussed in some detail in chapter 4 and therefore is excluded from this chapter. Table 5.1 indicates the use of presidential, semipresidential, and parliamentary executives in sixty major democracies).

In systems with dual executives, the head of state role historically originated with powerful kingships, and today a number of these countries retain hereditary constitutional monarchs who play a ceremonial and symbolic role while all real power resides with prime ministers and cabinets drawn from parliament. However, monarchs also personify the grandeur of the nation and of the state and its glories in ways that no ordinary politician can hope to match: consider the stark contrast between the splendors of Buckingham Palace and the modest townhouse at 10 Downing Street that houses the prime minister.

Constitutional monarchs carry out a range of formal public functions that offer continuity and legitimacy to the government, such as officially opening sessions of parliament and proclaiming the government's agenda from the throne. They may also formally appoint the prime minister and other ministers, provide their assent to legislation and treaties, act as the ceremonial commander in chief of the armed forces, and officially receive foreign ambassadors assigned to their countries, all without exerting actual influence over the substance of the work of government. Constitutional monarchs sometimes in theory retain wide-ranging "reserve powers," such as the power to reject legislation or issue orders to the military, but they know that if they were to ever actually try to exercise them, it would most likely lead to the abolition of the monarchy.

Kings and queens can lay a special claim to represent historical continuity and the enduring values of the state, but what of those parliamentary democracies that do not have their own monarch? With only rare exceptions, those countries have chosen *not* to make their prime minister into the head of state and instead to create new structures. In a number of countries of the former British Empire, such as Canada, Australia, and New Zealand, a governor general is appointed by the prime minister from the local population to fill in for the queen as ceremonial head of state, with essentially the same responsibilities and limitations.

A more common solution is to create as figurehead a president to serve as head of state, in somewhat pale imitation of ceremonial monarchs (although, notably, they often reside in the grand palaces once occupied by royalty). Although the specifics vary widely, ceremonial presidents generally wield little or no independent authority. Most, such as the presidents of Germany and Israel, are elected by the parliament; a few, such as those in Austria and Ireland, are directly elected by the people, although this popular mandate does not particularly lead to enhanced constitutional powers. Generally, ceremonial presidents are respected and accomplished individuals in society—central bankers, prominent journalists, retired politicians, former diplomats—who are intended to be above politics.

In times of crisis, heads of state may also play an important stabilizing role, particularly when democratic practices are not well established or are under threat. In 1981, King Juan Carlos of Spain used his role as com-

Table 5.1 Parliamentary, Semipresidential, and Presidential Systems in 60 Major Democracies

Parliamentary Executive power is exercised by a prime minister	**Semipresidential** Executive power is shared between a president (head of state) and a prime minister (head of government)	**Presidential** Executive power is exercised by a president who is head of state and head of government
Australia[1]	Finland	Argentina
Austria	France	Brazil
Belgium[1]	Guyana	Chile
Benin	Mongolia	Costa Rica
Botswana	Romania	Dominican Republic
Bulgaria	Ukraine	El Salvador
Canada[1]		Ghana
Croatia		Indonesia
Cyprus		Mali
Czech Republic		Mexico
Denmark[1]		Namibia
Estonia		Panama
Germany		Peru
Greece		South Africa[2]
Hungary		South Korea
India		**United States**
Ireland		Uruguay
Israel		
Italy		
Jamaica[1]		
Japan[1]		
Latvia		
Lithuania		
Mauritius		
Netherlands[1]		
New Zealand[1]		
Norway[1]		
Poland		
Portugal		
Serbia		
Slovakia		
Slovenia		
Spain[1]		

(Continued)

Table 5.1 (Continued)

Parliamentary	Semipresidential	Presidential
executive power is exercised by a prime minister	Executive power is shared between a president (head of state) and a prime minister (head of government)	executive power is exercised by a president who is head of state and head of government
Sweden[1]		
Switzerland[3]		
Trinidad & Tobago		
United Kingdom		

1. Head of state is a constitutional monarch.
2. Head of state is a president who is elected by and can be removed by parliament.
3. The two legislative houses choose a seven-member collective executive; a ceremonial head-of-state presidency rotates among the members annually.

mander in chief of the military to make a television broadcast in which he ordered an end to an attempted military coup during which senior officers had seized control of the parliament. Heads of state, particularly monarchs, can also offer political legitimacy and continuity to governments that are disrupted by foreign invasion or civil war. The Norwegian king and the Dutch queen did this during World War II, and more recently the exiled King Mohammed Zahir Shah played this role in Afghanistan when a post-Taliban government was established there in 2002, albeit without actually reclaiming the throne.

Even in less extreme circumstances, heads of state can also play an important role as neutral political arbitrators. Indeed, the one key nonceremonial responsibility of the head of state is to ensure that there is always a head of government. This is usually not a concern because most parliamentary elections produce a clear winning party or coalition of parties. Then, the head of state simply can—indeed, must—invite the head of the winning party or coalition to form a government. If no clear legislative majority emerges after an election, the head of state may assist in negotiations to help form a new governing coalition. He or she can also help during times of political turmoil, as did the presidents of Greece and Italy while those countries struggled with the Euro currency crisis in 2010.

In the case of complete deadlock, some heads of state may play a hands-on role as a political broker and might even exercise personal discretion in choosing whom to invite to form a government. This has been the case particularly in parliaments composed of many fractious parties, such as those in Italy and Israel. Still, the choice of prime minister is always subject to a confirmatory vote by parliament. And. even if there were an absolute impasse and negotiations failed, the head of state would still never take direct power. The previous prime minister and cabinet or a temporary replacement would generally continue to exercise executive authority in a caretaker capacity with the head of state calling new elections with hopes that a revote would decisively change the balance in parliament. In Belgium, just such a caretaker arrangement was in place for more than a year in 2010–2011.

It should be noted that a number of countries with parliaments have chosen both to directly elect their presidents *and* to invest them with a significant degree of real power, an arrangement often called a semipresidential system. Since 1958, the president of France has been directly elected by the people as head of state, commander in chief, and chief diplomat. The president also directly appoints the prime minister, who must be confirmed by parliament. When there is a parliamentary majority of the same party as the president, final executive authority is, in practice, wielded by the president; at other times it becomes necessary for the president to name a prime minister from the majority party and for the two to share power under an arrangement called *cohabitation*.

Such a situation is awkward, although France has generally handled it well. More problematic was the case of the Palestinian Authority in 2007, in which a moderate president from one party and a radical prime minister from another both claimed executive authority, leading to civil strife. Likewise, in Ukraine, an intense rivalry between presidents and prime ministers has led to governmental paralysis and the rollback of post-Soviet reforms. For exactly these reasons, few established democracies employ a semipresidential system, with some countries, such as Greece, Finland, and Portugal, moving away from that model toward a more standard parliamentary system.

The American Presidency in Comparative Perspective

As seen in the examples from Southeast Asia, executive power can take many configurations. The U.S. presidency is but one of those configurations, and it combines a number of different attributes seen in the case studies, along with some specific features of its own. U.S. presidents enjoy enormous democratic legitimacy because they are elected directly by the people (albeit via the rather problematic Electoral College). They are also the only elected officials, along with their handpicked vice presidents, who represent the entire country. Further, presidents have a fixed term of office independent of any actions by other political actors. This makes U.S. presidents quite unlike prime ministers, who are not directly elected by the people, who represent just one of many districts, and who hold their office only as long as they retain the support of a parliamentary majority.

Of course, the U.S. presidency (and those presidencies that draw on the U.S. model, especially in Latin America) is also unusual in that it concentrates essentially *all* executive roles and authority in a single individual. But does it matter that the U.S. president is expected to simultaneously play a symbolic role as head of state while also being immersed in day-to-day politics as head of government? From a purely pragmatic perspective, the answer is probably no. Because heads of state in other countries generally play little or no role in practical politics, they can largely be overlooked when seeking to understand the workings of government. But the investiture of head-of-state responsibilities in the U.S. presidency serves in other, more subtle ways to alter the essential nature of the office. Even as they are criticized in the press and parodied in popular culture, U.S. presidents also enjoy a tremendous degree of deference and respect, viewed at once as ordinary politicians and yet also as figures who are in some contexts above everyday politics. The so-called bully pulpit of the president—the ability to garner attention and shape public opinion—is greater than that of most prime ministers, who are always immersed in workaday politics. Yet it can also mean that the president is held to higher personal and professional standards. In many ways, the 1999 impeachment of Bill Clinton was framed much more about his violation of the dignity of his office than any abuse of presidential power or other serious offense.

The head-of-state role of the U.S. presidency is most clearly manifested in the annual State of the Union address, when the president addresses the nation from the dais of the House of Representatives. Certainly this triumphal occasion, attended by the Congress, the Cabinet, Supreme Court, top military officers, and the foreign diplomatic corps, is a far cry from the often merciless grilling on the floor of parliament to which prime ministers are subjected every week during Question Time. In fact, it more closely resembles the "throne speech" that is read by constitutional monarchs (although written by the government of the day) at the annual opening of parliament. The ceremonial role of the presidency also rises to the fore in times of crisis, such as after the September 11 terrorist attacks, after which George W. Bush spoke at a prayer service in the National Cathedral, or when Barack Obama addressed the nation after the massacre of children by gun violence in Connecticut in 2012. No other social or political figure in the country has anywhere near comparable standing to address and lead the nation in troubled times, when public opinion tends to "rally round the flag" by providing soaring approval ratings to presidents whatever their actual actions.

The fusion of head-of-state and head-of-government roles thus clearly strengthens the position of the U.S. presidency (and other presidencies based on the American model), enabling presidents to mobilize public opinion and pressure and giving them leverage over Congress and other political actors. This fusion also has a number of problematic effects as well. For instance, the symbolic role of the president as leader of the nation has long influenced who can be elected to the office. A disengaged but visionary leader such as Ronald Reagan would rarely if ever be found in a prime ministerial office, but he was well suited to the American head-of-state role. Countries with parliamentary systems seem more ready to accept leaders who are politically adept and technically skilled but who may be less than charismatic or who do not connect with the public on an emotional level. The need to be widely perceived and accepted as a potential leader of the nation has also affected which candidates are deemed viable for the presidency and helps to explain why it took until 2008 for a woman or an African American candidate to be taken seriously as contenders for the top job.

Even more troubling is that making the president the head of state can make it difficult to separate the person from the office—and the office from the state itself. In Britain, this distinction is nicely captured by the convention of calling the members of the party that is out of power "Her Majesty's Loyal Opposition," stressing that they oppose the *government* of the day but not the *state* itself. In the United States, by contrast, Richard Nixon famously (and inaccurately) believed that anything the president does is by definition legal. In the aftermath of September 11, some White House staff members went so far as to suggest that questioning the president in times of crisis was intrinsically unpatriotic, even bordering on the treasonous. In countries with a dual executive, however, it is much easier to distinguish between the particular politician currently serving as head of government and the more enduring values of the state itself. And, of course, the fact that prime ministers are ultimately responsible to—and can be replaced by—parliaments also keeps in check their ability to aggrandize their own power and status.

Other Presidential Systems

The United States has mostly managed to navigate the dangers of fusing the head-of-state and head-of-government roles, but most other countries with presidential systems have not been so fortunate. The separation-of-powers system, with a directly elected president and a separate bicameral Congress, is by far the predominant system adopted throughout Latin America. This is in part because of the historical influence of the United States as a neighboring country but also because the other countries of the Western Hemisphere found themselves in a similar historical situation as the United States. After achieving independence from Spain or Portugal, the countries of Latin America generally saw no more compelling reason to separate the two roles than did the United States. And far more so than in the United States, many Latin countries had strong traditions of rule by *caudillos* or powerful individual leaders.

In general, the presidential system has not proven an effective means for Latin American countries to deal with the often severe poverty, gross inequalities, endemic corruption, and other challenges they face. When legislatures, courts, interest groups, and the general public are politically active, Latin American presidents have often found themselves too weak institutionally. In some cases, this has led to political paralysis and a loss of legitimacy for the government, leading to further social and political problems and, often, interventions and coups by military generals. In other cases, Latin

American presidents have made use of their control of the military and police to declare states of emergency, suspend constitutional rights, dissolve parliaments, and rule by executive decree. This pattern is typified by the Latin American president who is perhaps best known around the world, the populist Juan Peron, who ruled Argentina for ten tumultuous years after World War II. Working within a constitutional framework explicitly modeled on that of the United States, Peron and his political party nonetheless completely dominated all sectors of Argentine society, corralling public opinion, marginalizing congress, manipulating the courts, and either coopting or suppressing his political opponents. His strongman rule laid the groundwork for the three decades of direct power by the military over Argentine government, including periods of brutal dictatorship.

The vacillation between excessively weak democratic presidents and excessively strong antidemocratic presidents has contributed greatly to internal conflict, governmental corruption, and political repression throughout Latin America. Presidential systems have similarly faltered in other parts of the world. An example would be those African countries that rejected parliamentary systems after their decolonization in the 1950s and 1960s in favor of strong presidencies that have served as vehicles for personal dictatorships, one-party states, and military rule. In the 1970s and 1980s, dictators from Idi Amin of Uganda, to Jean-Bedel Bokassa of the Central African Republic, to Haile Mariam Mengistu of Ethiopia terrorized their populations with actions ranging from localized massacres to outright genocides. More recently, the shocking memory of these brutalities has helped to curb autocratic governments and promote multiparty democracy across Africa, although the future of democracy on the continent remains uncertain.

There may be times, particularly in regimes undergoing a transitional phase, when a strong presidency offers benefits. In post-Taliban Afghanistan, the new constitution created a powerful, independently elected president because power in the country was at that time fragmented among multiple competing warlords controlling various regions. One hope was that a strong president could serve as a symbolic rallying point and unifying symbol, which President Hamid Karzai appears to have achieved to some degree. But, as of this writing, he has not been able to assert effective military or political control outside the capital city, leading some to dub him the Mayor of Kabul.

The U.S. Vice President, Cabinet, and Bureaucracy

Although all executive power in the United States is vested constitutionally in one person, the U.S. president is not, of course, the only actor in the executive branch. Of these other actors, the U.S. vice president is one of the most anomalous of all the structures created by the Constitution. For most of American history, the sole tasks of the vice president were from time to time to ceremonially preside over the Senate and break the occasional tie vote—and to wait for the president to die. In recent decades, vice presidents have evolved into senior advisers to the president, assisting with policy formulation, political salesmanship, and some ceremonial duties. Vice Presidents Al Gore, Joe Biden, and, especially, Dick Cheney have exercised influence well beyond what their nonexistent constitutional authority would suggest is possible.

In general, however, vice presidents are a nonessential feature of presidential systems and, indeed, can pose a danger in less-established democracies if they conspire to seize the presidency. Mexico abolished the office in the nineteenth century after a volatile period during which a number of vice presidents supported coups that enabled them to ascend to the top job. One advantage of a vice presidential office is that it enables the party in power to stay in charge should a president die, resign, be removed from office, or be temporarily disabled, all without the need for a special election. Unfortunately, vice presidents are often chosen not for their governing skills but for their appeal in elections or, worse, because they are perceived as politically weak and thus not a potential threat to the president. Countries without vice presidents are generally able to find other satisfactory ways to fill a presidential vacancy, such as temporary replacement followed by a quick special election, while suffering no great loss to their governing structures. France, which has had a powerful presidency since 1958, has twice had to hold elections within ninety days to fill a presidential vacancy, experiencing no difficulty either time.

Beyond the vice president and perhaps some high-ranking members of the White House staff, the most high-profile figures in the executive branch are the members of the president's cabinet, which is composed mostly of the heads of fifteen of the largest departments in the federal government. Some of these are relatively small departments dealing with functional areas of the economy, such as commerce, transportation, and energy. However, some of the cabinet positions can be extremely influential, particularly those that closely relate to core functions of government, including the secretaries of state, defense, and Treasury, as well as the attorney general, who leads the Department of Justice. Many cabinet secretaries have had impressive careers of their own, as governors, senators, generals, or business leaders or in other prominent roles.

As significant as these cabinet figures may be, however, their power relationship to the president is entirely unambiguous; they are chosen by the president to advance the president's agenda and can be directed, reassigned, and dismissed, serving only "at the pleasure of the president," as the phrase goes. *All* executive authority exercised by members of the cabinet, the heads of noncabinet executive agencies, and indeed by members of the federal bureaucracy (except for a few regulatory commissions) technically is carried out on behalf of the president. While presidents may rely on the guidance and expertise of members of the cabinet and other top-level officials, they are completely free to disregard such counsel if they wish.

This idea of a "cabinet" is quite different from the way that term is used in the parliamentary tradition, in which members of a cabinet—that is to say, the ministers who direct major government bureaucracies—usually must also be sitting members of the majority in parliament. Far more than in the United States, parliamentary cabinet ministers are chosen because of their political standing and support rather than for their substantive expertise. Most ministers in parliamentary systems are long-seated members of the party who are well-established politicians in their own right, often formally or informally heading factions within parliament. This was long the case in Japan, where the Liberal Democratic Party ruled for all but ten months of the period 1955–2009. Despite this seeming monopoly control, the existence of multiple intraparty factions has meant that power in Japan is in fact dispersed across many different ministries, with prime ministers merely being first among equals. A similar situation pertains in countries such as Israel and Italy where the cooperation of multiple small parties is usually needed to assemble a majority coalition. In these cases, prime ministers must fill their cabinets with leaders of many parties and engage in ongoing negotiations to keep small parties from withdrawing from the coalition and triggering a vote of no confidence.

The parliamentary system also affects how cabinet ministers relate to the bureaucrats in their ministries. In the United States, the entire top tier of government is essentially decapitated after each presidential election, often making for complex transitions between presidential administrations. All of the officials at the several highest levels of the U.S. federal bureaucracy are political appointees, and it is standing practice that they will resign their offices upon the completion of the term of the president who appointed them. It is only several layers down from the top of each department or program in the United States that one finds long-term civil servants who are insulated from dismissal for political reasons.

Parliamentary systems, in contrast, are likely to have ministries with two heads: the elected minister and a civil servant (sometimes called a "director-general") who is the permanent chief of the bureaucracy. The job of the minister, working with a few junior ministers also drawn from parliament, is to express the political will of the government and to oversee the general direction of a particular ministry. The director-general, by contrast, is a technical specialist who will have served many different governments over decades, providing a note of continuity amid parliamentary majorities that come and go, sometimes quite abruptly. In theory, the director-general and his or her bureaucratic subordinates are nonpartisan, politically neutral servants of the state who simply respond to the elected government of the day. In most cases, they are chosen through a competitive system of exams and promoted for their technical expertise rather than for their political ties. Of course, in practice, bureaucracies do have their own political preferences and, even more so, their own established way of doing things. The minister of the day may at worst be viewed as a passing nuisance to be managed and outlasted rather than obeyed. In the United States, placement of political appointees in so many top-tier jobs in the bureaucracy diminishes its autonomy from political control. Yet another level of supervision is created by the oversight of the federal bureaucracy by standing committees of Congress, which can alter programs' funding, organization, or authority.

Another difference between the U.S. bureaucracy and those of many other countries is its size. The United States has a much smaller national bureaucracy than other wealthy countries, particularly outside the realm of defense (which is proportionately much larger in the United States than in most other democracies). Indeed, the United States has long had an ideology of small government, preferring to leave many areas to the private sector (and to adjudication in the courts) rather than to create new government programs to directly administer them. The strongly federal nature of the United States can mask the extent of bureaucracy, however, because state, county, and local governments in the United States also administer extensive government programs. (Broadly speaking, most state and local governments tend to have the same basic structure as the federal government, with a single, directly elected governor or mayor naming all the top bureaucrats as political appointees to lead a permanent civil service.)

The comparatively modest size of government bureaucracy in the United States and its scattering across fifty states, more than three thousand counties, and nearly twenty thousand municipalities, means that a powerful, unified national civil service has never emerged in the United States. By comparison, in some unitary states with large bureaucracies, such as France and Japan, the civil service plays a potent quasi-autonomous role in the political system, positions are highly coveted, and many young people aspire to government jobs. Indeed, drawn from top educational institutions and recruited through dense personal networks, civil servants in some countries constitute an elite corps that is highly influential in many sectors of society. In the United States, being a civil servant is not particularly prestigious, and many of the most ambitious people in society gravitate instead toward elected positions or influential slots in the private sector.

Conclusion: Why It All Matters

The office of president of the United States has been occupied in unbroken succession for over 220 years, making it history's oldest democratic executive still in operation. Fusing the roles of head of state, head of government, chief diplomat, and commander in chief, the American presidency is a formidably powerful and demanding role. On the domestic front, American presidents must contend with an array of other players, including Congress, the courts, and organized interest groups, any of which can frustrate a presidential agenda. In terms of foreign policy, U.S. chief executives are far more unfettered, often able to act under the own authority. The implications of this difference on the making of domestic and foreign policy are discussed in greater detail in chapters 12 and 13.

Because of the military, diplomatic, and economic might of the United States, the American president is perhaps the most prominent political office in the world. Yet it is also an atypical one in many respects: most established democracies do not have U.S.-style presidencies, and most countries that have adopted the system have found it an all-too-convenient platform for dictatorship. To be successful as a democratic institution, an office this powerful must be checked and balanced by other powerful political actors. Fortunately, the United States also has developed exactly such active and robust institutions in its Congress and Supreme Court, the subjects of the next two chapters.

Further Reading

Elgie, Robert. *Political Leadership in Liberal Democracies.* New York: St. Martin's Press, 1995.

Helms, Ludger, ed. *Comparative Political Leadership.* Basingstoke, UK: Palgrave Macmillan, 2012.

Tsurutani, Taketsugu, and Jack B. Gabbert, eds. *Chief Executives: National Political Leadership in the United States, Mexico Great Britain, Germany, and Japan.* Pullman: Washington State University Press, 1992.

Tummala, Krishna K. *Comparative Bureaucratic Systems.* New York: Lexington Books, 2003.

Web-Based Exploration Exercise

Visit the website of the White House (www.whitehouse.gov), and find examples of recent activities of the president in the four major roles of the office: head of state, chief diplomat, commander in chief of the armed forces, and head of the federal bureaucracy. Explain how each of these activities might or might not have been carried out differently if the United States had a parliamentary system.

Question for Debate and Discussion

The separation-of-powers system has been criticized for creating presidencies that are either too weak or too powerful. Hemmed in by pressure from the legislative and judicial branches, presidents in some countries are unable to effectively lead. Institutionally insulated from other political actors, presidents in some countries abuse their power and dominate other political actors. Is the U.S. presidency too weak or too strong? Should the U.S. presidency be changed to strengthen or weaken the office?

Chapter 6

The Legislative Branch
The Two Houses of Congress

In the previous chapter, we saw that executive power is always relevant in the study of governments: all functioning states have a significant role for the executive in carrying out the work of government. By contrast, the role of legislatures varies widely. At one extreme are powerless assemblies convened purely to offer legitimacy and to provide a show of support for the work of an authoritarian executive. At the other end are legislatures that are fully autonomous and that exercise considerable power within their sphere of influence. The U.S. Congress, the most powerful national legislature in the world, is the paradigmatic example of this category of legislature. In between these extremes are legislatures whose work is mostly consultative or technical, providing input and suggestions but deferring most actual decision making to the executive, whether a prime minister chosen from the legislature's own ranks or a separately elected president.

The U.S. Congress has sweeping powers to pass laws on issues ranging from taxation and expenditures, to the regulation of interstate commerce, to the declaration of war; it can also check and balance other political actors by overriding presidential vetoes, structuring the federal court system, impeaching and removing high officials, approving constitutional amendments, and, in the Senate, confirming presidential appointees and ratifying treaties. Despite the enormous power of the U.S. Congress, however, it is not unusual for students of American politics to misunderstand or discount the role of Congress relative to that of the more high-profile presidency. This is in part because Congress, like most legislatures, is a large and cumbersome institution with complex structures, arcane procedures, and multiple participants. Yet, to understand the nature and role of different types of legislatures, it is necessary to examine these very dimensions. As will be seen, the institutional configuration and legislative processes of the U.S. Congress offer just one of many possible types of democratic legislature, with significant implications for the functioning of American democracy.

Case Study: Legislative Variation in the Former British Dominions

Although the British Empire included many colonies, only a few countries were granted the special, largely self-governing status of "dominions of settlement." Three of these, New Zealand, Canada, and Australia, were in regions of the world that were only sparsely populated, so they formed new societies largely transplanted from Britain. All three of these dominions chose to adopt nearly identical configurations of executive power, maintaining the British monarch (represented by a governor general) as head of state and investing governing responsibility in a prime minister and cabinet drawn from the majority in the lower house of parliament. Strikingly, however, all three also chose rather different structures for their legislative bodies, exemplifying the three distinctive models of how a national legislature can be designed: *unicameralism, asymmetric bicameralism,* and *symmetric bicameralism.*

For several decades, New Zealand had an upper house of parliament called the Legislative Council. Because New Zealand is a unitary state with a largely homogenous population, in the 1950s it was broadly agreed that there was no compelling need for the extra layer of representation offered by the upper house, and it was abolished. Since then, New Zealand has functioned well with just a single 120-member House of Representatives, elected directly by the people, out of which the government is formed. Occasional calls for the reinstatement of an upper house have not met with interest from the population, who feel adequately represented by a *unicameral* legislature.

Since its founding in 1867, Canada has had a bicameral parliament focused on a popularly elected House of Commons, from which the government is drawn. But, unlike in New Zealand, the Canadian upper house, the Senate, has endured; today it has 105 members who are appointed by the government for a life term up to the mandatory retirement age of seventy-five. Senators are chosen according to a formula that draws them from all the different provinces, regions, and territories of the country, even those that are very sparsely populated.

In theory, the Canadian Senate has the same legislative powers as the Commons except that it cannot initiate bills related to revenue. Because it is an appointed body and lacks direct democratic validation, however, the Senate rarely seeks to block or even resist the will of the Commons, even when the two houses have majorities from different political parties. The Senate today generally does not undertake major actions but serves as a chamber of "sober second thought," offering critiques, suggestions, and amendments to bills introduced by the Commons. Free of electoral concerns, senators can offer perspectives from underrepresented groups and from the smaller provinces and can hold open hearings to examine long-term considerations, which it did in the 1990s, for instance, on the theme of euthanasia and assisted suicide. But, in the end, the will of the Commons prevails, not because of written constitutional provisions but because of established conventions and practices. This difference in power renders the Canadian parliament an example of *asymmetric bicameralism*.

Australia also maintains a bicameral parliament, but with some very significant differences. Members of the Australian Senate are elected directly by the people of the six states and two territories, with equal representation guaranteed for the six states despite wildly different populations. As a result, senators are every bit as much elected officials and politicians as their counterparts in the Australian House of Representatives, and they jealously guard their constitutional equality to the House in both theory and practice. The deference of the Canadian Senate to the lower house, thus, is not to be found in Australia. When the two chambers of parliament have majorities of different parties, as is frequently the case, the Senate is much more likely to stand its ground and effectively veto the legislation, arguing that it has as much of an electoral mandate as does the House of Representatives. The Senate also makes vigorous use of its investigatory authority to keep the government in check. The relative parity of legislative power between the two houses in Australia is an example of *symmetric bicameralism*.

Unicameralism

As a small unitary state with all political power emanating from the national government, New Zealand is nearly a textbook case of a country that can thrive with a unicameral legislature. Without provinces or states to demand direct representation in their own right and with a largely homogenous population of less than 4.5 million, New Zealand has little need for a second chamber to represent a great diversity of interests. (One unique adaptation in New Zealand is that it provides several guaranteed seats in the House of Representatives for members of the indigenous Maori peoples.) Most countries that have unicameral legislatures are similarly unitary states with a small and fairly homogenous population; all of the Nordic countries, for instance, also practice unicameralism. However, for historical or other reasons, a significant number of unitary and/or homogenous states continue to maintain bicameral legislatures. Table 6.1 provides an overview of how the national legislatures are structured in sixty major democracies.

As might be expected, unitary states with unicameral parliamentary systems are able to act with a great deal of efficiency. Indeed, it was the fear that such legislative efficiency might lead to tyranny that was part of what prompted the American founders to subdivide Congress into two parts, creating a type of check and balance within the legislative branch. However, in countries with well-established democratic traditions, other informal political practices and independent judiciaries have helped to prevent unicameralism from leading to an abuse of power.

Table 6.1 Structure of National Legislatures in 60 Major Democracies

	Unicameral	Asymmetric Bicameral	Symmetric Bicameral
Parliamentary Systems	Benin	Austria	Australia
	Botswana	Belgium	Italy[1]
	Bulgaria	Canada	Switzerland[3]
	Croatia	Czech Republic	
	Cyprus	Germany[2]	
	Denmark	India	
	Estonia	Ireland	
	Greece	Jamaica	
	Hungary	Japan	
	Israel	Netherlands	
	Latvia	Poland	
	Lithuania	Slovenia	
	Mauritius	South Africa	
	New Zealand	Spain	
	Norway	Trinidad and Tobago	
	Portugal	United Kingdom	
	Serbia		
	Slovakia		
	Sweden		
Presidential or Semipresidential Systems	Costa Rica	France[4]	Argentina
	El Salvador	Indonesia	Brazil
	Finland[4]	Romania[4]	Chile
	Ghana		Dominican Republic
	Guyana[4]		Mexico
	Mali		Namibia
	Mongolia[4]		**United States**
	Panama		Uruguay
	Peru		
	South Korea		
	Ukraine[4]		

1. The upper house has equal legislative authority and also plays a role in electing the prime minister.
2. The upper house can block the lower house on issues relating to the provinces.
3. Both houses choose a seven-member collective executive rather than a single prime minister.
4. Semipresidential system, with a separately elected president with considerable power.

Unicameralism is not an entirely unknown structure in the United States. One state, Nebraska, maintains a unicameral state legislature, to no apparent detriment to the people of that (fairly low-population, fairly homogenous) state. Since U.S. states are unitary in nature, it is unclear how much a second state legislative chamber really adds to either the quality of representation or governance in the U.S. states, particularly in the quite common event that both chambers are controlled by the same political party. Many state upper houses seem to continue due to history, tradition, inertia—and politicians who are unwilling to vote themselves out of a job. The same phenomenon appears to explain the persistence of upper houses in a number of small countries, such as a number of Caribbean island nations.

In the United States, unicameralism is also strongly the norm at the local level of government, with most municipalities having a single-chambered city or town council. Even its largest and most diverse metropolis, New York City, in 1989 abolished its de facto upper house, which was called the Board of Estimate. City and town mayors are usually directly elected by the people, although there are some municipalities that function on a quasi-parliamentary system in which the unicameral council chooses one of its own members to serve as mayor. Some U.S. municipalities even adopt a sort of head of state/head of government split, with the mayor setting broad policy and a city manager carrying out day-to-day governing.

Asymmetric Bicameralism

Among countries with parliaments, asymmetric bicameralism, as seen in the example from Canada, is the norm. This has been dubbed the "one-and-a-half" house solution: all executive and most legislative power resides in the lower house of parliament, but the legitimate interests of federal units or regions are recognized through the existence of a weak upper house. Indeed, nearly all federal countries practice bicameralism and use the upper house to represent groups and interests that might otherwise be overlooked. Even a number of larger unitary states maintain upper houses to provide representation to their provinces; in France, the relatively weak upper house is even commonly called the "rural chamber" because it offers a voice for low-population, largely agricultural areas.

Unlike the case of the appointed Senate in Canada, the members of weak upper houses are generally elected, either directly by the people or by provincial legislatures. Whichever the case, members of weak upper houses understand that their positions have less power than those of their counterparts in the lower house. Indeed, in asymmetric bicameralism, the upper house is often a revising chamber that mostly offers divergent viewpoints and makes recommendations. Its main purpose is to add an opportunity for further deliberation and refinement of laws that might otherwise be rushed through a unicameral legislature. Weak upper houses can often influence or delay legislation but rarely have a decisive impact when they clash with the lower house. Members of upper houses may sometimes also serve as government ministers, although rarely in major positions, and almost never as prime minister. In a recent innovation in Canada, however, Prime Minister Stephen Harper has endorsed a process through which the people of the various provinces would hold votes to determine who they wish to have appointed as senators from that province. Should this practice take hold, the Canadian Senate would gain a much greater measure of democratic legitimacy that could lead it to use its power more proactively. This, in turn, might help to address the long-standing tensions between the less populated provinces and the two giants of Ontario and Quebec, which account for 181 of 308 seats in the House of Commons.

The two halves of the U.S. Congress were deliberately designed to be equal in power. However, to the extent that any aspect of asymmetric bicameralism can be detected in the U.S. Congress, it is actually the *upper house* that has greater powers—a distinctive feature of the U.S. Constitution (and those constitutions based on it, especially in Latin America). The U.S. Senate is constitutionally invested with two significant types of authority lacking in the U.S. House of Representatives: the confirmation of presidential appointees to high office and the ratification of international treaties. The Senate also has the final say in the impeachment process, being the sole arbiter of whether to remove an impeached president, federal judge, or other official from office. However, none of these is a specifically *legislative* power; rather, they are part of the checks-and-balances scheme of the U.S. Constitution. While the House of Representatives does have the sole right to introduce bills relating to revenue, this does not greatly enhance the power of the House because the Senate ultimately must also approve such bills.

Symmetric Bicameralism

The norm in parliamentary systems is for the lower house to be decisively more powerful than the upper house in both legislative and executive authority. Indeed, there are no countries in the world in which the government is formed solely or even primarily out of the upper house. Thus, all parliamentary systems, in terms of executive power, are asymmetric. A few parliamentary systems do, however, provide equal (although never greater) legislative power to their upper houses.

One such example, Italy, has mostly avoided clashes between the two chambers because it uses an electoral formula that all but guarantees that both houses will have the same composition in terms of political-party affiliations. Australia has no such electoral formula, however, and when the two houses have majorities from different parties, it can seriously undermine the ability of the government to function. The Australian government formed in the lower house can continue to function independently only until it needs to have pass a crucial piece of legislation, such as the budget, which requires Senate approval as well. The Australian constitution has a special provision requiring that the most serious impasses between the two houses be resolved by the drastic step of dissolving parliament, calling a national election, and then having the newly elected members of the two houses meet and vote in joint session as a single body. Given that the lower house has twice as many members as the upper house, it is almost certain to prevail. Still, this is a clumsy and difficult procedure, and in 1975 exactly such a scenario led to the country's most serious constitutional crisis. Thus, the Australian system enjoys neither the inherent stability afforded by a separation-of-powers system nor the efficiency normally found in parliamentary systems, leading some observers to regard it as an argument against symmetric bicameralism in a parliamentary government.

By contrast, in separation-of-powers systems, symmetric bicameralism is the norm. In the United States, this separation intentionally reinforces the dispersal of power by requiring the equal consent of a majority of both houses of Congress to pass a law or enact appropriations. Thus, for example, in 2006, badly needed immigration reform was blocked because the two Republican-led chambers could not find a middle ground between a House bill focused on border enforcement and a Senate bill that would have created a guest-worker program. Further, the U.S. Senate and House of Representatives also play an equal role in the constitutional amending process; either house may introduce an amendment, and both must pass it by a two-thirds majority for it to be sent to the states for ratification. A constitutional amendment to ban the desecration of the American flag garnered two-thirds support in the House several times in the 1990s, only to be blocked repeatedly in the Senate, where it was deemed to undermine the First Amendment's guarantees of freedom of speech. Similarly, symmetric powers tend to be invested in the two chambers of other national legislatures with separation-of-powers systems, such as in Latin America.

Symmetric bicameralism does not necessarily create problems for governance in the United States, but it does raise some serious issues from the perspective of democratic theory. In institutions of representative democracy, it is usually not possible to ensure that every legislator represents exactly the same number of constituents, but great pains are taken to reapportion the House as well as state and city legislative chambers periodically to address imbalances. The enormous disparities in the populations across the fifty states, however, grossly violate this proposition because all states, regardless of population, have equal representation in the Senate. Of course, part of the original argument for guaranteeing two senators for each state was to ensure the support of the less populous states, whose influence is minimal in the House, where seats are apportioned by population.

Whenever membership in upper houses, representing provinces, states, or regions, is based on geography rather than population, the potential exists for individual legislators to represent widely differing numbers of constituents. However, when upper houses are weak, this violation of the one person–one vote standard is mitigated by the subordination of the upper house to a lower house elected on the basis of population. In strong upper houses, the problem becomes clearer. In Australia, the most populous state, New South Wales, has about fourteen times the population of the smallest state, Tasmania, but both states have twelve federal senators. In Switzerland, the largest canton, Zurich, has nearly twenty times the population of the smallest canton, Jura, but each has two seats in the Swiss upper house. In the United States, the disparity is far more pronounced: California has more than *seventy* times more people than the least populous state of Wyoming, yet both states have two votes in the Senate.

Today, the fifty-two senators from the twenty-six least populous states represent only about 20 percent of the U.S. population, yet they form a majority that can thwart the will of the representatives of the other 80 percent. In the United States, a small number of states representing just 4 percent of the population can also block a constitutional amendment, which must pass the Senate by a two-thirds majority and then be ratified by three-quarters of the states. Further, smaller states have a mathematical advantage in the Electoral College that chooses the president. This is because each state has the same number of electoral votes as it has members of Congress, in which small states are overrepresented by virtue of their disproportionate number of Senate seats.

In actual practice, the small-state senators do not particularly tend to vote as a bloc: Rhode Island and Delaware have little in common with Alaska and South Dakota. Still, the U.S. Senate represents a severe distortion of the one person–one vote standard of democracy. Ironically, the U.S. Supreme Court ruled in 1964, on the basis of the U.S. Constitution, that state and city legislatures cannot apportion their districts in ways that grossly violate the principle of one person–one vote. But that ruling did not affect the U.S. Senate because the rule of equal representation for the states is clearly required in Articles I and V.

Thus, equal representation in the U.S. Senate is a classic example of a compromise made at the time of the founding that was essential for garnering support for ratification by the smaller states. The argument for equal representation of the states was questionable even at the time of the founding, but the emergence of a strong national identity, mobility across states, stronger linkages via mass media, and many other factors make it profoundly anachronistic today. Although the Senate's equal representation is widely considered unalterable, it would theoretically be possible to move toward a system of asymmetric bicameralism by passing a constitutional amendment to weaken the powers of the Senate to make it into more of a revising chamber, perhaps by giving the House the power to override it by a two-thirds vote. Such a change remains a practical impossibility, however, precisely because any such amendment would require the support of many of the smaller states whose power would be diluted.

The Dispersal of Power in the U.S. Congress

By their very nature, separation-of-powers systems lead to the dispersal of power across three branches of government. This dispersal is further increased by bicameralism, and particularly symmetric bicameralism, in which the equal consent of both houses is required to pass legislation. But power in the U.S. Congress is *even further* dispersed because of the very limited control of the political parties over individual members and because of the powerful role played by congressional committees.

Relative to legislators in other countries, members of Congress have an exceptional degree of autonomy from their party leaders. One major reason for this is that the leadership of political parties in the United States does not simply choose its own party nominees in elections, as is the case in many other countries. Rather, the system of primary elections means that elected officials must win the support of the registered voters of their party rather than the party's leaders. While U.S. political parties can offer or withhold considerable monetary and other resources, candidates for office must ultimately prioritize the needs and wishes of their constituents rather than their parties. In parliamentary systems, the power of party leaders is further strengthened by their ability to determine which backbenchers will be promoted through the ranks of parliament to ministerial office. Thus, parliamentarians who resist their party leaders run the risk of not only losing renomination in the next election but losing any upward mobility within government. By contrast, American politicians who aspire to higher office are largely on their own and may even find electoral advantages to distinguishing themselves from their party's leadership.

Thus, members of the U.S. Congress can and do routinely vote against their own party leaders in ways that members of parliaments rarely do. The only time that there is a rigid norm requiring members of Congress to support their parties is after each election, when a vote is taken to determine which party has a majority and thus will be in control of the leadership of each chamber and of all committees. In practice, however, members of the same party in the U.S. Congress do tend to vote together in large numbers, in part because of broad ideological agreement within parties and in part because individual members may calculate that it is in their own interest for their party to succeed. It also reflects a belief that party leaders in Congress know better than to bring a bill up for a vote until they are assured of broad agreement within the party, thus keeping dissension behind closed doors rather than revealing it in open votes. However, there are times when the members of Congress defy even the most powerful leaders in the country; in late 2008, President George W. Bush, presidential candidates Barack Obama and John McCain, and the Democratic and Republican leaders in both houses of Congress strongly endorsed a bailout for the nation's banking industry, only to have it rejected by a bipartisan majority in both chambers until the bill was substantively revised. Likewise, staunch conservatives in the House repeatedly blocked Speaker John Boehner, a Republican and thus the head of their party in the House, during budget negotiations with President Obama in 2011 and 2012

This weakness of party leadership is most pronounced in the Senate, where the rules of debate mean that each individual can threaten a filibuster, which would bring work in the Senate to a halt. To a degree that is astonishing when viewed in comparative perspective, any single U.S. senator—not just party leaders or even just members of the majority—wields an enormous ability to influence and obstruct the passage of legislation by means of a filibuster threat. Further, the requirement that sixty senators vote for cloture in order to end a filibuster further extends power to the minority party. Thus, it is not unusual for a bill to have the support of more than fifty senators but still fail to be passed because a filibuster prevents the Senate from taking a vote.

By contrast, in the House, tighter procedural rules make that chamber more like a parliament. Still, the speaker and other leaders of the majority party are not able to simply ram through their own agendas and sometimes must modify their goals in order to ensure majority support. Most commonly, they must set forth policies that balance the interests of the more ideologically driven and the more pragmatically centrist members from their own party, while also perhaps trying to win some votes from the opposing party. Such an influential role for individual rank-and-file legislators is almost unheard of in the world; unlike most members of national legislatures, members of the U.S. Congress genuinely do play a fundamentally important role in the governance of the country.

Individual members of Congress also have an enhanced degree of autonomy because they are provided with their own extensive staffs and offices, in both Washington, D.C., and in their constituencies. Membership in Congress is a full-time job with commensurate pay, unlike some legislatures in which those who do not serve in government positions or in legislative leadership roles maintain outside careers and work only part time. The resources and professional time available to members of Congress enable them to provide services directly to voters, such as intervening on their behalf when they are having problems with some part of the government bureaucracy. Such constituency service has little or no bearing on the legislative duties of members of Congress, but it enables them to enhance their likelihood of reelection, thus further reinforcing their individual autonomy. This is, however, also another manifestation of the commonly cited concern that members of Congress must spend so much of their time on reelection activities that they have inadequate time and energy to actually be effective legislators.

Power is also dispersed in Congress because of the strength of the committee system. Most legislatures employ a committee structure because of the practical benefits it provides, such as division of labor and specialization of expertise, and individual bills to be assigned to standing committees for closer scrutiny and amendment. No legislative chamber can, as a whole, address all the issues that come before it with anything near the attention to detail or expert knowledge that committee structures allow. What is unusual in the U.S. Congress is the high degree of participation in the process enjoyed by committees, which allows multiple players to have direct input into the shape of legislation. Thus, only about 10 percent of bills that are proposed in the U.S. Congress ever become law, in large part because there are so many points at which a bill can be stopped during the process. Whereas committees in many legislatures play an advisory role, congressional committees can make or break a bill. It is a very common occurrence for a bill to "die in committee" either because powerful committee chairs choose not to allow it to come up for a vote or because it is defeated in a vote of committee members. While there do exist some procedures for getting around the committee structure that can be invoked by each chamber's leadership or membership as a whole, these are cumbersome and seldom used.

Not only are congressional committees important for determining which bills will or will not make it to the floor of each chamber for a vote, but they also play a major role in shaping the substance of the bill. By holding public hearings, debating bills, markups, and carefully analyzing provisions, committees play a major role in determining the scope and provisions of bills. Additional changes can be proposed by the leaders of each chamber and sometimes also through amendment offered by the members of the chamber, especially in the Senate. While members of the majority party usually have more opportunities for input, the voices of members of the minority party tend to be heeded rather more than in parliamentary systems, where they are relegated to the role of a marginalized opposition.

For a bill to become a law, in summary, it must pass through an extraordinary number of hurdles in the U.S. system. These include but are not limited to the chairs and memberships of at least one subcommittee and one committee in each house, the leadership and the memberships of both houses, a conference committee to iron out differences between the House and Senate versions, and the president. Some bills must also go through a second, comparable appropriations process to determine the level at which they will receive funding. This complicated procedure has been cited as an inertial force in U.S. politics, making it difficult to change the status quo or tackle new problems quickly or efficiently. Whereas the loyalty of members of Congress to their individual districts or states may make them better representatives in a narrow sense, this can also obstruct the development of coherent national legislative agendas.

Certainly, the legislative process in the U.S. Congress is vastly more complicated than in those parliamentary systems where the government is essentially assured that any bill it proposes will quickly and easily pass into law. This is not to say that parliamentary party leaders are free to completely disregard the wishes of their backbenchers or even that they would wish to do so. Government ministers can benefit from the constructive input of rank-and-file members of parliament and try to avoid debates in parliament or anonymous comments in the press that might cast the work of the government in a bad light. However, when push comes to shove, the executives in parliamentary systems can almost always get their way over the legislature.

The Power of Congress in Comparative Perspective

The dispersal of power within the U.S. Congress across houses, committees, and individual members should not detract attention from the fact that the U.S. Congress still exercises a great deal of power—far more than most other legislatures. Indeed, there is not even much point in examining the legislative role in nondemocratic countries because such legislatures are likely to be simply rubber stamps for laws submitted from the executive, offering a veil of legitimacy for executive actions. At most, they may serve in a nonbinding advisory capacity and perhaps sometimes offer constructive ideas and technical expertise in the crafting of the laws, but ultimately they are completely dominated by the executive.

Even in democratic countries, legislatures sometimes play only secondary roles. In parliamentary systems, legislative majorities are the ultimate source of and check on executive authority because the prime minister must maintain the confidence of a majority to continue in office. The power to bring down the executive through a vote of no confidence or by replacing a party leader is the ultimate power that is invested in parliaments but denied to Congress, as discussed in chapter 4. However, once a solid parliamentary government has been formed, most of the legislative initiative usually comes from government ministers.

The U.S. Congress, on the other hand, really is a coequal branch of government. In the United States, presidents certainly can and do propose legislation, but such proposals represent only starting points in the process. And, although presidents can veto laws (subject to a congressional override), they cannot prevent Congress from taking up any issue it wishes, nor can they force Congress to pass a law against its will. Even after a bill is authorized, Congress must also vote to appropriate funds because many laws are meaningless without access to the funding needed to implement and administer them. Presidents may take the initiative to introduce a budget but know that it will be substantially altered by Congress in exercise of its power of the purse. This authority also gives Congress formidable leverage over the federal bureaucracy, which is closely overseen by committees in both houses.

In theory, separation of powers can also help to enhance the role of national legislatures in other presidential systems, especially throughout Latin America. But most such countries still tend to be more heavily president centered. Constitutionally, many Latin American presidents have more far-reaching powers than the American president. Some, in Brazil for instance, have a line-item veto that enables them to pick and choose which parts of bills they wish to sign into law (some U.S. state governors have this power, but the president does not). More important, many Latin American presidents have—whether legally or extralegally—the ability to declare a state of emergency and to rule directly by presidential decree, backed by their control of police and military forces. In the 1970s and 1980s, nearly every country in South America experienced direct rule by a president supported by or sometimes manipulated by the military. As recently as 2009, a military coup ousted the president of Honduras and was followed by a state of emergency.

In many of these cases, presidents squared off directly against legislatures, with the latter almost invariably proving to be the losers. In one striking example, in 1992, President Alberto Fujimori of Peru used his control of the military, amid economic crisis and threats from the Shining Path guerrilla fighters, to forcibly disband both houses of the Peruvian congress. When he came under international pressure, Fujimori called new elections for a congress only one-third the size of its predecessor and used his control over the electoral process to ensure that the new congress would be filled with his supporters. The new congress then obligingly amended the Constitution to strengthen the formal powers of the president and to allow multiple terms of office. In some other cases, Latin American presidents have dominated their political systems not explicitly through the use of force but by suppressing opposition parties and factions. In perhaps the clearest example, for nearly seventy years Mexican presidents totally dominated the Congress because of the near monopoly of the ruling Revolutionary Institutional Party. The Mexican Congress was reduced largely to a consultative and technical role rather than that of a coequal branch of government.

Conclusion: Why It All Matters

Perhaps more than any other national legislature in the world, the U.S. Congress not only represents the people but also plays an active role in the governance of the country. Unlike parliaments, the U.S. Congress is not subject to direction by the executive branch; unlike the congresses in other separation-of-powers systems, it has managed to hold its own against the power wielded by presidents. Yet, if the power of Congress is enormous, it is also dispersed between two houses of equal authority, across a network of influential committees and subcommittees, between the parties, and, ultimately, among the elected members themselves. At its best, this dispersal of power can promote the building of political consensus and the passage of well-crafted centrist public policy. At its worst, Congress can serve as an instrument of delay and dysfunction, as when conservative Democrats from the South blocked civil rights bills in the 1950s and 1960s and Republicans frustrated immigration reform in the 2000s.

Certainly, the presence of 535 empowered legislators in the nation's capital provides a robust form of political representation, with each member of Congress heavily focused on his or her electoral constituency. Congress also provides multiple points of entry into the political system, which can also be a boon in influence for well-moneyed interested groups that can provide campaign contributions or offer endorsements and the mobilization of voters.

As powerful as it may be, Congress is ultimately subject to the constitutional structure of checks and balances through means such as the presidential veto and, as is discussed at greater length in the next chapter, the judicial review of the federal court system.

Further Reading

Arter, David. *Comparing and Classifying Legislatures.* London: Routledge, 2007.
Fish, M. Steven, and Matthew Kroenig. *The Handbook of National Legislatures: A Global Survey.* Cambridge: Cambridge University Press, 2009.
Loewenberg, Gerhard, Peverill Squire, and D. Roderick Kiewiet, eds. *Legislatures: Comparative Perspectives on Representative Assemblies.* Ann Arbor: University of Michigan Press, 2002.
Norton, Philip, ed. *Legislatures and Legislators.* Brookfield, VT: Ashgate, 1998.
Power, Timothy J., and Nicol C. Rae, eds. *Exporting Congress?: The Influence of U.S. Congress on World Legislatures.* Pittsburgh: University of Pittsburgh, 2006.

Web-Based Exploration Exercise

Visit the website for the U.S. House of Representatives (www.house.gov). Then use the parliamentary Web page of the Inter-Parliamentary Union (www.ipu.org/english/parlweb.htm) to visit the website of the *lower* houses of at least two other legislatures. Identify at least one similarity and one difference that you find with regard to the role of that house in the passage of a bill into a law.

Question for Debate and Discussion

One of the major hallmarks of the U.S. Congress is the way power is dispersed among both houses, multiple committees, and even the members. Could power be consolidated in Congress in order to make it more like a parliament? How could this be done? Would this be desirable? What would be the disadvantages of a concentration of power in the hands of a few leaders?

Chapter 7

The Judicial Branch
The Supreme Court and the Federal Courts

While executive and legislative branches are always indisputably political, the judicial branch of government is often viewed as quite separate and distinct from politics and is also notably less powerful than the other branches. Executives have the power of the sword, the ability to use force to achieve their goals, while many legislatures have the power of the purse, the ability to choose how funds are allocated. Denied these two sources of power and removed from day-to-day politics, judiciaries are generally a distant third force in government. In the famous words of Alexander Hamilton, the judiciary is "the least dangerous" branch in terms of its ability to dominate a political system or tyrannize the people. Still, the Supreme Court is a major player in American politics, and in political systems throughout the world courts are playing an increasingly autonomous and influential role.

Judiciaries vary greatly from country to country, even more so than do executive and legislative structures. The role they play also extends beyond the realm of politics into such areas as criminal justice, contracts, land use, family law, and many other areas that are beyond the scope of this book. To assess the political role of the judiciary in any country and to serve as a basis of comparison for the U.S. judiciary, there are three major questions to consider: Are the courts impartial and independent? Are they a separate and coequal, or a subordinate, branch of government? And do they have the power of judicial review—the ability to strike down executive and legislative acts that conflict with a nation's constitution? As might be expected, in nondemocratic countries, the answer to all of these questions is no. And the answer to all three of those questions in the United States is a definite yes. Yet, to a degree that might surprise many Americans, there are many democratic countries in which the answers to these questions are rather less clear cut.

Case Study: The Judiciary in France

To an even greater degree than in the United States, the government and politics of France are defined by its revolutionary tradition. Historically, judges in France were viewed as agents of the king, and they were thus on the losing side of the French Revolution of 1789. In an attempt to rationalize legal proceedings and ensure the authority of the state, detailed legal codes were promulgated by Napoleon in the early nineteenth century and then exported throughout the European continent both by his armies and by the force of his example. Ever since, courts in France and throughout much of continental Europe have remained subordinate to—indeed, almost extensions of—the executive and legislative branches.

Today in France, law courts are viewed as administrative organs of the state, playing a supporting role rather than acting as an independent force. Judges are civil servants, some directly employed by the Ministry of Justice, and are expected more to assist the executive in enforcing the law than to uphold or protect the rights of individuals or the society at large. In cases of criminal prosecution, for instance, the principal task of judges is to help to determine the guilt or innocence of the accused rather than act, as in the United States, as impartial referees in an adversarial confrontation between a prosecutor and a defendant. French courts also have no right to strike down actions taken by the executive branch of government. This power is reserved to a semiautonomous body set up *within* the executive branch called the Council of State, assisted by a system of subordinate administrative courts that hear complaints against the bureaucracy.

Limits on the French judiciary do not stop there. The development of highly detailed legal statutes beginning with the Napoleonic Code means that courts in France are required to rule on particular cases as narrowly as possible. While the rulings of judges are binding in the specific case before them, they do not establish precedent and generally cannot be cited when similar issues arise in other cases. French courts also lack the ability to strike down laws as being unconstitutional. That task is assigned to a quasi-independent Constitutional Council that can be called upon to determine the constitutionality of laws, although only after they have been passed by parliament and before they have been signed into law by the president. The Constitutional Council, which has become more active in recent decades, is not a law court but a political body appointed jointly by the president and the heads of the two chambers of the national legislature.

As befits a unitary state, France has a single unified court system, rather than multiple court systems in each of its provinces. Within the judicial system, cases can be appealed up to the highest judicial body, the Court of Cassation, which may review cases from all lower courts. The court does *not* decide cases itself but can remand them for retrial to a lower court different from the one from in each case originated, along with its reasons for doing so. The court also generally does not speak as a collective body; instead, the judges are fragmented into multiple panels that deal with different cases and usually do not take coordinated action as a single entity. By no means is the Court of Cassation analogous to the U.S. Supreme Court, nor can the French judiciary play anything like the role of the U.S. federal courts.

Impartiality and Independence

The idea that courts must act impartially is a long-standing principle of democratic politics; in a country in which all people are equal, the law should apply to all people equally. Yet, in practice, the line separating courts in nondemocratic and democratic systems may not always be so clear. Indeed, in the vast majority of cases that have no political implications, courts in nondemocratic countries may be perfectly capable of applying existing legal norms to routine issues such as traffic violations, contract disputes, divorce settlements, or personal assaults. The relevant line of division in such cases may well be not whether a country is democratic but the degree to which its judges and court personnel are susceptible to bribery or are vulnerable to threats of retaliation. Thus, in cases with no political implications, the legal system in a nondemocratic but capably governed country such as China may well be more impartial than that in a more democratic but less well-governed country such as Brazil.

On the whole, the courts in long-established democracies perform with greater impartiality and professionalism, but the correlation is inexact, and certainly no system is entirely free of bias and corruption. Further, in countries such as the United States, where judges tend to play the role of neutral arbiters, differences in wealth and education can become greatly magnified as the court does its work, because a greater burden falls on individual defendants who may lack the educational background to assist in their own defense or the economic means to hire highly qualified legal representation. In systems in which judges play a more active role, the quality of the defense becomes a less crucial factor.

The question of the independence of the courts is always relevant when a case has political implications. Such implications may arise when a case involves someone powerful or well connected, such as when a wealthy contributor to a political party or public official is charged with business fraud. Political implications may also develop when a case involves actions by government, such as when a court must adjudicate whether police officers used excessive force against protestors. In cases with political implications, a well-timed phone call to a judge, whether to exert pressure or make an overt threat, may be all that is needed to ensure a favorable outcome. In some countries, deference to the powerful may be so thoroughly ingrained that no such call is even needed; judges simply know how they must rule to preserve their personal and professional well-being. However, in one remarkable show of the increasing relevance and authority of the judiciary in 2007, the military dictator of Pakistan, President Pervez Musharraf, arrested and deposed that nation's chief justice, Iftikhar Chaudry who opposed Musharraf's attempts to expand his illegal power. Such confrontations have usually ended up with the opposition figure in exile, in jail, or worse. But Chaudry came to personify the desire of many Pakistanis for the restoration of democracy and the rule of law, sparking sustained protests by cadres of lawyers that ended in 2009 with Musharraf's resignation and Chaudry's reinstatement! Similarly, in the aftermath of the Arab Spring upheavals in Egypt in 2012, the nation's court system resisted a power grab by the newly elected president, Mohammed Morsi, who was forced to backpedal from a declaration that his actions were above review by the judiciary.

In the United States, the court system is generally considered both impartial and independent. A major source of independence among federal judges, including Supreme Court justices, is that, once nominated by the president and confirmed by the Senate, their terms extend for life or until they decide to retire (the possibility of impeachment by Congress also exists but is exceedingly unlikely). Federal judges thus also have no further accountability to the executive or the legislative branches and are largely free from the pressures of public opinion or concerns about reelection. However, many state, county, and municipal judges are elected, making them more similar to ordinary politicians. And even federal judges, because of the significant political role of the courts, are often initially chosen by presidents for their ideological views as much as their legal skills. In countries where the courts play a narrower role, judges are more likely to be selected for their technical competence and experience.

Courts as a Separate and Coequal Branch

Even when courts are both impartial and independent, it need not be the case that they are considered a completely separate and coequal branch of government. As seen in the case of France, courts in some democratic countries—indeed, throughout most of the countries of continental Europe and in their former colonies abroad—may be viewed as organs of the state, with an important but narrow technical role. In fact, France is the prototype of a *civil-law* system in which legislation is spelled out in great detail and specificity at the time that it is written by the legislature. The principal source of the meaning of law is the wording of the statutes as written by the legislature and, to a lesser extent, their explication in analyses by law professors. Prior rulings by other judges carry little weight because the codified laws are considered to contain all the answers that a judge needs to rule on any specific case.

This approach contrasts sharply with the *common-law* system that prevails in Britain and in many former British colonies, including the United States. In common-law systems, laws tend to be fewer in number and written with less detail. As cases arise, judges have much greater discretion to articulate the broader meaning of the law, indeed helping to write the law in some senses. Their rulings establish case law that establishes a precedent that can and must be cited when similar situations arise in future cases. Lower courts are bound by the rulings of higher courts, and even the Supreme Court tends to apply the principle of *stare decisis* ("let the decision stand") under which precedent should not be overturned without very compelling reasons. Table 7.1 provides an overview of the use of civil-law and common-law systems in sixty major democracies.

In recent decades, the civil- and common-law systems have converged to some degree, with civil-law judges becoming more likely to cite previous cases and legislatures in common-law countries producing more detailed codification of laws. And even in common-law systems, the extent to which judges should play a role in creating law remains controversial. Since the 1970s, there has been widespread criticism in the United States of so-called legislating from the bench by activist judges. Such critics, who tend to be from the conservative side of the political spectrum, feel that judges have in recent decades exceeded the scope of their roles by making expansive rulings, especially in the area of civil liberties and civil rights. These critics instead endorse the idea of deference to concept of "original intent." Under this doctrine, judges are bound to interpret laws in light of what was intended by the legislature that first passed such laws, be it Congress for federal law, a state legislature for state law, or the framers of 1787 in the case of the U.S. Constitution. This approach would move the U.S. judiciary closer to a civil-law system and weaken the ability of courts to be independent actors in the political system. Those preferring a more flexible system with a greater role for judges generally argue that the Constitution and the law should be interpreted as living documents whose meanings evolve over time and whose broad principles must be adapted to changing circumstances.

Another distinction between civil-law and common-law systems also significantly affects the role of judges. In common-law countries, an adversarial approach is employed in which judges act essentially as neutral arbiters standing between two parties and ensuring that proper legal procedures are employed. In criminal cases, in which a person is charged with breaking a law, those two parties are the prosecutor and the accused, the prosecutor bearing the burden to demonstrate beyond reasonable doubt the guilt of the accused, who is presumed innocent until proven guilty. (Civil cases, in which one person claims to have been economically harmed by another, are of less interest for present purposes because they involve action by private parties rather than by government.) In common-law countries, especially in the United States, the role of the judge is even further limited by the use of juries composed of ordinary citizens to determine the guilt or innocence of the accused.

In civil-law systems, the role of the judge is very different. Rather than use an adversarial approach, civil-law systems tend to employ the inquisitorial approach in which the goal is not for one side or the other to win the case but to find the objective truth in a situation. Before the start of an inquisitorial trial, an entire investigation has been conducted by a different judge to determine whether the case should even come to trial. If this high threshold has been met, then it is considered that the accused is quite unlikely to be completely innocent (although this should not give rise to an outright

Table 7.1 Civil and Common-Law Systems in 60 Major Democracies

Civil-Law Countries	Common-Law Countries	Mixed-System Countries
Argentina	Australia	Cyprus
Austria	Botswana	Guyana
Belgium	Canada	Israel
Benin	Ghana	Namibia
Brazil	India	South Africa
Bulgaria	Ireland	
Chile	Jamaica	
Costa Rica	New Zealand	
Croatia	Trinidad and Tobago	
Czech Republic	United Kingdom	
Denmark	**United States**	
Dominican Republic		
El Salvador		
Estonia		
Finland		
France		
Germany		
Greece		
Hungary		
Indonesia		
Italy		
Japan		
Latvia		
Lithuania		
Mali		
Mauritius		
Mexico		
Mongolia		
Netherlands		
Norway		
Panama		
Peru		
Poland		
Portugal		
Romania		
Serbia		
Slovakia		

(*Continued*)

Table 7.1 (Continued)

Civil-Law Countries	Common-Law Countries	Mixed-System Countries
Slovenia		
South Korea		
Spain		
Sweden		
Switzerland		
Ukraine		
Uruguay		

presumption of guilt). The goal of the judge in such an inquisitorial approach then is not to be a neutral arbiter between parties but to actively engage in the questioning process and to seek to resolve the question before the court. Thus, in criminal trials in civil-law systems, judges do not stand between the government and the accused but rather work on behalf of the government to determine whether the accused is guilty.

Judicial Review

As can be seen from this discussion, judges in common-law systems constitute a branch of government that is separate and coequal in that courts are not simply vehicles for propounding the intentions of legislators or of advancing the law enforcement goals of executives. But in the United States, the power of the federal courts goes much further; they also have the authority to strike down actions by Congress, the president, or the states that they deem to be unconstitutional. Although the nature and scope of judicial review is not explicitly included in the wording of the U.S. Constitution, it was discussed at the time of the founding and firmly established by the 1803 case *Marbury v. Madison* and has been widely accepted ever since. (State supreme courts also have comparable final say over the meaning of their respective state constitutions.)

Judicial review is fairly uncontroversial as it applies to the power of higher courts to review the rulings of lower courts. It is also understood that in a federal system, the highest national court must be able to overrule the courts of the provinces, states, or other federal units, at least on issues that involve federal questions. More controversial, however, is that federal courts can and do strike down laws passed by Congress and actions taken by the executive that violate some principle of the Constitution. For instance, in the 1996 *Lopez* case, the Supreme Court ruled that Congress exceeded its power under the interstate commerce clause by banning guns in schools that are administered by the states. In the 2006 *Hamdan* case, the Supreme Court specifically rejected the Bush administration's use of military tribunals to try terrorism suspects. In a landmark case in 2012, however, the Supreme Court restrained itself and narrowly declined to overturn the highly controversial Patient Protection and Affordable Care Act (aka the "Obamacare" health bill), one of the most far-reaching expansions of the federal government in decades.

Although such cases of overt judicial review are not very common, the will of the Supreme Court does sometimes trump that of the legislative and executive branches, serving as a major source of checks and balances. Indeed, the powerful role of the U.S. Supreme Court is a significant factor in explaining why the separation-of-powers system that has contributed to so many dictatorial presidents in Latin America has not done so in the United States. The institutional prestige of the Supreme Court has, for example, permitted it to intervene at two pivotal moments in recent political history when a constitutional crisis loomed. In 1974, during the Watergate affair, the Supreme Court broke a deadlock between Congress and President Richard Nixon over release of taped conversations made in the Oval Office, setting off a chain of events that led to Nixon's resignation. In 2000, with the outcome of the presidential election deadlocked in Florida, the Supreme Court stepped in with a ruling that effectively allocated the state's electoral votes to George W. Bush. In his concession speech, Al Gore accepted the ruling even as he signaled his disagreement with it. Without a Supreme Court capable of rendering an authoritative decision in these cases, American democracy might well have been threatened both in 1974 and 2000.

By comparison, supreme courts in less established democracies rarely have the same degree of authority, either tending to provide a justification for the outcome preferred by those in power or finding their rulings ignored (and their jobs and perhaps even their lives imperiled). Even robustly democratic countries, however, vary in the degree of judicial review that they afford their courts. In Britain, courts may provide redress if a law or regulation has been mishandled at an administrative level. But the long-standing principle of parliamentary supremacy means that they have no authority to strike down any law enacted by parliament or any action taken by the government (though European Union law has lately begun to impinge on parliament's ability to act completely unilaterally). Canada has put a unique twist on the issue of judicial review, giving its Supreme Court full powers of judicial review over federal and provincial parliaments in its 1982 constitution. However, due to objections from some provinces, the Canadian constitution includes the so-called Notwithstanding Clause. This provision allows the Supreme Court to make a ruling but empowers the federal or any provincial parliament to reassert a law "notwithstanding" the view of the Supreme Court that it violates the Canadian Charter of Rights and Freedoms. Such assertion of parliamentary supremacy has never been used at the federal level, although the province of Quebec asserted it twice to uphold laws favoring the use of French even after the Supreme Court ruled that both French and English have equal status. Despite the sparse use of the Notwithstanding Clause, its very existence restrains the Canadian Supreme Court in ways that the U.S. Supreme Court is not restrained.

As we have seen, France does not allow its courts any degree of influence in reviewing the constitutionality of executive or legislative acts; several neighboring countries, such as Belgium and the Netherlands, have similar systems. A number of other European countries, including Italy, Austria, and Germany, have established special constitutional courts with powers of judicial review. However, such constitutional courts can be difficult for citizens to access and often have limits on the range and types of issues they can address. Also, in these countries, only the official constitutional court can rule on constitutional issues, whereas in the United States all federal courts have this authority, with the Supreme Court having final say. Thus, judicial review can be and is applied by dozens of courts throughout the United States on a regular basis, greatly expanding its use and scope.

One of the clearest exercises of judicial power in the United States during the twentieth century was *Brown v. Board of Education*. Between 1896 and 1954, the brutal system of racial segregation that prevailed in the American South had the full endorsement of the Supreme Court under the theory that the equal protection clause of the Fourteenth Amendment permitted separate facilities for whites and blacks as long as they could somehow be construed as equal. In practice, though, equal provisions could be stretched to mean that blacks and whites were treated equally if both had access to schools, even if the black schools had untrained teachers, inadequate supplies, and poorly maintained buildings. In *Brown*, the Supreme Court recognized the reality that "separate is inherently unequal," opening the floodgates for a half century of social advances for minority and disadvantaged groups.

Despite some reservations, U.S. presidents from Eisenhower to Kennedy to Johnson took the ruling seriously enough to deploy federal forces to back up desegregation orders. Congress eventually also came around by passing the Civil Rights Act of 1964 to enforce the Fourteenth Amendment and the Voting Rights Act of 1965 to fulfill the Fifteenth Amendment's promise that race would not be a barrier to full citizenship. During the same era, the Supreme Court also redefined the scope of the Bill of Rights, vigorously reinforcing freedom of speech and the press, proactively protecting the rights of the criminals and accused, and articulating a right to privacy in areas of sexuality and reproduction.

The power of judicial review not only is significant for the system of checks and balances in the United States but also has implications for political participation. In many countries, there is little if any hope of effecting significant political change through the court system because courts either have limited power or are difficult to access for ordinary people. In the United States, the federal courts are a major point of access into the political system, one that is especially important for minority groups that are unlikely to be able to achieve their aims through the electoral process. Because the federal courts are entrusted with the authority to protect constitutionally established civil liberties and civil rights regardless of the will of the majority, minority groups have found it particularly effective to use the court system to advance their cause. However, this trend has gone some way toward reinforcing a popular antipathy in some circles toward "unelected, unaccountable" judges who are seen as imposing their own views rather than merely interpreting the law.

Despite its enormous powers, the U.S. Supreme Court does labor under a number of limitations. One restraint is that its jurisdiction is limited to actual cases and controversies and can be altered by act of Congress. Unlike constitutional courts in many other countries, the U.S. Supreme Court cannot issue advisory opinions in the abstract about whether a particular law would pass constitutional muster. Instead, it must wait for a law to be enacted, challenged in lower courts, and eventually appealed up to the Supreme Court. Then it must find a place for the case on its extremely limited docket. The Supreme Court rejects some 99 percent of the appeals that are made to it, meaning that many constitutional questions are ultimately decided by lower courts. Thus, the theoretical power of the U.S. Supreme Court to exercise judicial review is limited by its capacity as an institution, although it is generally still free to choose the cases it deems most significant. However, the limited institutional capacity of the Supreme Court does not diminish the judiciary's overall power of judicial review as much as it disperses that power widely throughout the federal court system as a whole.

The courts also face the reality that their rulings are not self-executing but rather must be carried out by Congress, the president, the bureaucracy, or, in some cases, the states. Thus, courts must exercise a certain degree of self-restraint, issuing rulings that are as persuasive as possible and that do not too sharply overstep the bounds of what the public or other political actors will be willing to accept and enact. For example, the expansive and historic ruling in *Brown* was followed by a much more tempered requirement that desegregation be carried out with all deliberate speed rather than on a fixed timetable. It then took until 1971 before the courts ordered more vigorous enforcement of racial integration through compulsory busing of students to achieve racial balance in primary schools. The subsequent history of integration efforts also reveals much about the limits of judicial power. It has largely succeeded in areas such as employment and access to public accommodations such as theaters, restaurants, and hotels. However, it has in many ways failed in housing and primary education, with minorities almost as segregated de facto today as they were under law fifty years ago. The courts in the United States play an extraordinarily important role, but they are but one of many political players and are far from the judicial tyrants that some have accused them of being.

Conclusion: Why It All Matters

No modern country could long endure without a functioning legal system. From traffic violations to homicides, real-estate transactions to adoptions, authoritative mechanisms for applying the law are essential to maintain social and economic institutions. Yet the political role of courts in maintaining democracy is much less clear. Some of the world's most robust democracies, from Finland to New Zealand to the Netherlands, maintain traditions of parliamentary supremacy that leave the judiciary decidedly less powerful than the executive or the legislative branches and essentially unable to check or balance them.

The United States is at the other end of the spectrum, as few other countries invest their court system with the scale and scope of power that the United States does. And although, on the whole, the role of the judiciary has been expanding throughout the world, it is unlikely that the U.S. court system could be successfully transplanted in full to other countries. Indeed, it remains one of the remarkable factors of American democracy that the two elected branches do not more often disregard Supreme Court rulings with which they disagree. This is in part a result of the self-restraint exercised by the Court in not overreaching in the scope and timing of its rulings. But such deference is also to the result of a particular reverence for the U.S. Constitution as being virtually synonymous with the state itself. Neither of these factors can simply be created out of thin air in other countries, which may have very different political histories and cultures.

Further Reading

Abraham, Henry J. *The Judicial Process: An Introductory Analysis of the Courts of the United States, England and France.* New York: Oxford University Press, 1993.

Huls, Nicolaas Jacob Herman, Maurice Adams, and J. Bomhoff. *The Legitimacy of Highest Courts' Rulings: Judicial Deliberations and Beyond.* The Hague, The Netherlands: T. M. C. Asser, 2009.

Jacob, Herbert, et al. *Courts, Laws, and Politics in Comparative Perspective.* New Haven, CT: Yale University Press, 1996.

Lasser, Mitchell. *Judicial Deliberations: A Comparative Analysis of Transparency and Legitimacy.* Oxford: Oxford University Press, 2009.

Web-Based Exploration Exercise

Visit the website of the supreme court of another country and examine the structure of that court and of that country's judicial system. Identify at least one similarity to and one difference from the U.S. system, and discuss their implications for the functioning of the judiciary. A comprehensive portal to the world's supreme courts can be found at www.globalcourts.com/mini-oversikt.html. The U.S. Supreme Court's website can be accessed at www.supremecourtus.gov.

Question for Debate and Discussion

In many ways, the U.S. Supreme Court is the most powerful court of law in the world. Given that judges are unelected and serve life terms, should the expansive powers of the judiciary be curbed? On the basis of the models used by other countries, how could the U.S. Supreme Court be reined in? What would be the advantages and disadvantages of such a change?

Part III

Political Participation

Chapter 8

Conventional and Unconventional Participation
Activism, Social Movements, and Interest Groups

Political participation is often conceptualized as spanning a spectrum from conventional modes of behavior, which are accepted by the norms of society and have the greatest sanction under the law, to unconventional modes of behavior, which stretch the boundaries of the acceptable and not infrequently cross over into the illegal. As depicted in Figure 8.1, the most conventional of all modes of political participation is holding elected or appointed public office.

Through officeholding, citizens can wield the power of the state itself, making this the ultimate "insider" strategy of participation; officeholding was largely the subject of the preceding three chapters, on the legislative, executive, and judicial branches of government. At one remove further from this ultimate "insider power" is the ability to choose officeholders through the electoral process and the exercise of the vote, which was a hard-won right for many groups in the United States. One step further away, neither established nor prohibited by the Constitution, is activity through the channel of political parties. These two modes, voting and political parties, are the subjects of the next two chapters. This chapter focuses on the forms of participation that are in the center and at the unconventional end of the spectrum, including violent protest, nonviolent activism, and interest-group activity.

The exact dividing line between conventional and unconventional modes of participation is not always entirely clear and varies from country to country, but the simplest marker is to ask whether a type of political participation can lead to arrest and punishment. In some nondemocratic countries, attempts to organize an election, create a new political party, or even form an interest group might be considered illegal. In more democratic countries, these types of political activity are widely accepted, but other types of more unconventional activity remain less tolerated. Peaceful protest marches, demonstrations, and other forms of activism are often highly restricted by the authorities, who may intervene forcefully if traffic is being disrupted or property is being damaged. Almost universally, regardless of whether a country is democratic or nondemocratic, the use of violence to achieve political aims will be met with countermeasures by police or military forces.

UNCONVENTIONAL					CONVENTIONAL
"Outsider" Strategies		⟶			*"Insider" Strategies*
Violent Protest	Nonviolent Activism	Interest Group Activity	Political Parties	Voting and Elections	Public Officeholding

Figure 8.1 The Political Participation Spectrum

Voting and political-party activity are less robust in the United States than in many other democracies, as we will see in the next two chapters, given that the United States has only two major parties and voter turnout rates are quite low. Such realities are, to some degree, balanced by a strong American tradition of interest-group activity and nonviolent activism via social movements and protest activities that originate among outsider groups and target structures of power. Thanks to institutional features including federalism, bicameralism, and separation of powers, there are a huge number of elected officials in the United States who can act as "points of access" into the political system for organized interests and for demonstrators alike. As long as politicians need to be reelected, they will need to be responsive to the mass public.

In the United States, unconventional political participation, including but not limited to the use of protests and demonstrations, has been most closely associated with marginalized or disempowered groups, which are often unable to muster the electoral majorities needed to elect politicians to office. Fortunately, violence to achieve political goals has not been a major factor in the United States since the Civil War, although it is a mode of political participation found throughout the developing world. Whenever citizens find that their voice is not effectively heard within the political system, they may find it necessary to turn to other means, ranging from picketing and demonstrations to violence and even armed insurrection.

Case Study: The Zapatistas and Indigenous Political Participation in Mexico

Mexico is a country with a long history of demonstrations, protests, and other forms of both violent and nonviolent political activism, usually targeting the long-ruling Revolutionary Institutional Party (PRI). By rigging elections, suppressing opposition, and distributing government funds to win political support, the PRI ruled Mexico for most of the twentieth century. By the 1990s, however, the party's many broken promises, corrupt practices, and authoritarian tactics began to generate serious opposition, especially in crushingly poor rural areas such as the state of Chiapas, in the country's far south. In 1992, indigenous groups staged demonstrations to mark the five hundredth anniversary of Columbus's arrival in the Americas, destroying the statue of a Spanish conquistador in one town. Protests intensified in 1993 when the central government removed traditional protections for peasant landholdings. Then a turning point arrived when Mexico acceded to the North American Free Trade Agreement (NAFTA), which many indigenous peoples viewed as benefiting large agricultural corporations to the detriment of small farmers.

On January 1, 1994, an armed left-wing group calling itself the Zapatista National Liberation Army (ELZN) seized control of four towns in Chiapas and essentially declared war on the PRI and, more broadly, the Mexican government. The initial confrontation was brief, with the Mexican army regaining military control within two weeks. But this proved to be just the opening gambit of the EZLN, whose name invoked the legacy of Emiliano Zapata, the foremost peasant leader of the Mexican Revolution. Reflecting not only the anger of dispossessed peasants but also the anxieties of a country reeling from a series of economic crises, the EZLN became a rallying point for anger at the authoritarianism of the PRI. Dozens more towns declared themselves to have Zapatista governments, and proreform forces in Mexico City and elsewhere rallied to support the EZLN.

Throughout the 1990s, however, the EZLN gradually evolved from a violent faction into a more peaceful social movement. It proved skillful in building political alliances both inside and outside Mexico, such as by convoking a forum of indigenous peoples that drew participants from throughout Latin America. In particular, the EZLN was also a pioneer in the use of the then-nascent Internet, sometimes depending on websites maintained outside Mexico, to build support and disseminate information—an action clearly intended to go beyond their largely illiterate base in Chiapas, where computers and even electricity can be scarce, to court a global audience.

In the process, one EZLN leader, a Marxist college professor turned revolutionary known as Subcommandante Marcos, made the transition from outlaw to folk hero, emerging as an iconic figure always seen in a ski mask and usually puffing on a pipe. The government eventually signed an agreement with the Zapatistas regarding indigenous rights and culture but failed to implement it meaningfully. Instead, it increased military pressure, covertly supported political assassination, and tacitly approved massacres by paramilitary groups. But each new action by the government drew greater attention from human rights organizations throughout the world, including many on-the-ground observers whose presence disrupted usual patterns of corruption and election rigging.

The activities of the EZLN contributed greatly to the downfall of the PRI in 2000, when for the first time in seventy-two years the presidency went to the candidate of another party, Vicente Fox. In an extraordinary turnaround, the Zapatistas formed a huge but peaceful convoy and traveled overland to Mexico City to attempt to promote greater reforms for the impoverished regions of the country. The Zapatistas converged in the *zocalo*, the city's main plaza, for one of the largest mass demonstrations in Mexican history. One of the group's leaders, Subcommandante Esther, in a signature Zapatista ski mask, even delivered an address to Congress. Reflecting the entrenchment of powerful interests in Mexico, however, the Congress passed only weak legislation.

Since then, the EZLN has de facto abandoned armed struggle, although it has still clashed with police at times at some rallies and demonstrations. Parallel to the 2006 Mexican presidential election, the Zapatistas openly sponsored a nationwide set of activities termed The Other Campaign to draw attention to issues left unaddressed by the major party candidates. They have forged coalitions with other progressive social movements and interest groups throughout Mexico and the world, evolving into something approximating a standard social movement, although violent clashes with police have still occurred at some demonstrations. After nearly twenty years, the EZLN has become increasingly institutionalized and established; if it has not (yet) emerged as a conventional interest group, it is at least a recognized and accepted player on the left wing of Mexican politics.

The Ultimate Unconventional Participation: Political Violence

By the standards of political violence throughout the world, the EZLN's seizure of villages was a fairly mild event, more a symbolic act than a true armed threat to the Mexican state. Sadly, political violence and even full-scale civil war are far more common and destructive in many other precincts of Latin America, such as in Colombia, which has been torn apart for generations by a complex struggle among multiple power centers. Such civil wars are generally of two types: those in which an insurrectionary internal force tries to topple the existing central government (or at least radically alter its policies) and those in which separatist rebels seek autonomy or outright independence for a particular region.

Well-established democratic countries such as the United States are largely insulated from the former type of civil war. As long as the democratic system is at least fairly representative of the broad majority of the population and power periodically alternates between competing factions, it is generally far more productive to channel disagreements into politics than into revolutionary conflict to topple the existing regime. Indeed, it has often been said that in democratic systems, "politics is a substitute for warfare." Of course, even in broadly democratic countries there will always still be some portion of the population—usually the extreme left or right wings—that believe that they cannot achieve their goals through the existing structures of the state and that may challenge the legitimacy of the state itself. Such extremists can certainly be deadly in their actions; a compelling example in the United States was the Oklahoma City bombing in 1995 in which the right-wing ideologue Timothy McVeigh bombed a federal office building to strike a blow against what he saw as a tyrannical U.S. government. Acts of political violence have also originated from the left in the United States, notably in the 1960s and 1970s, when armed revolutionary factions, such as the Weathermen, radicalized by the Vietnam War, planted bombs in a string of government facilities.

The second kind of civil war, focused on achieving independence for a particular geographic region, is more common throughout the world. When a portion of a country wishes to secede territorially from an established country and become a new independent state, central authorities tend to reflexively resist either over concern about loss of some economic input, such as diamonds or oil, or out of concern for the territorial integrity, historic continuity, or national honor of the state. Separatism most often arises among groups that are distinct from the national majority in terms of ethnicity, religion, language, or some other cultural or historical factor and that consider themselves oppressed on the basis of that difference. Separatist-oriented civil conflict can be hard for even democratic countries to resolve because minorities are likely to feel outnumbered and poorly represented in the political system, as has been the case among the Irish Republican Army (IRA) in Northern Ireland, Basque separatists in Spain, and even French-speakers in usually quiescent Canada.

In broad historical terms, the United States is, of course, no stranger to separatist civil war. Remarkably, however, the United States has not witnessed any large-scale violent insurrections on its soil since 1865. This can be traced partly to memories of the sheer trauma of the U.S. Civil War, which constitutes the major national tragedy of American history and remains prominent in the national consciousness. The U.S. Civil War also resolved lingering constitutional questions about the proper relationship of the U.S. states to the national government, providing legitimacy for the idea that the national government is clearly supreme and that the union is indivisible. But the successful avoidance of further separatism in the United States has also been the result of pragmatic political compromises of the kind that were not reached in time to avert the Civil War. Thus, in the period after the end of Reconstruction, in 1877, the southern states were returned to self-government through a negotiated settlement. Part of the price of peace, however, was that the southern states were allowed to enforce a system of racial segregation—in fact, outright subordination—of African Americans.

This pragmatic but unprincipled compromise may have resolved one political problem, but it prolonged another. It is noteworthy that the only other time any region of the country has come close to outright rebellion since 1865, the dispute also involved the states of the former Confederacy. During the civil rights movement of the 1950s and 1960s, both the population at large and elected officials mounted massive resistance to the racial desegregation ordered by the courts. Occasionally, the federal government had to resort to force in several southern states, such as the use of federal troops to integrate the high school in Little Rock, Arkansas, although the civil rights era never developed into anything approaching outright armed conflict. Indeed, in many ways the country once again reached a negotiated solution.

Officially sanctioned racial segregation of neighborhoods, workplaces, and schools was ended. But attempts to reach full integration of housing and education have fallen short, leaving in place striking gaps in socioeconomic status and life opportunities between whites and people of color.

Such an incomplete reckoning with the legacy of racism in the United States has contributed to what is arguably the principal form of political violence in the United States today. Observers disagree about whether to call such episodes riots, rebellions, urban insurrections, or simple mob violence. But their usual manifestation is the result of a long-simmering anger among poor, inner-city, racial, and ethnic minority groups that explodes periodically in a burst of street violence, arson, looting, and other forms of lawlessness. Such events occurred in cities such as Newark and Detroit in the late 1960s, for instance, sparked by the news that the Reverend Dr. Martin Luther King Jr. had been assassinated. By far the most prominent recent example in the United States occurred in Los Angeles in 1992 when the South Central neighborhood experienced three days of violence following the acquittal of four members of the Los Angeles Police Department accused of brutalizing a black motorist. The LA riots were forms of political violence in a different way than, say, the coordinated bombings by the Weathermen or the Oklahoma City bomber in that they were unplanned and unorganized and did not seek to advance a particular political message or goal. However, they were a reaction to the long-term grievances of populations that felt themselves to be marginalized by an unresponsive political system and oppressed by the brutal tactics of the LA Police Department.

Such bursts of violence are far from uniquely American. Among democracies, France offers archetypal examples of spontaneous, often violent urban unrest, given both its revolutionary tradition and its strong conception of every citizen relating directly to the state without group intermediaries. In late 2005, in the slums on the outskirts of Paris, for instance, groups of unemployed youths of North African descent torched cars and damaged property to protest their sense of exclusion from full participation in French society. Spontaneous uprisings of this type certainly can attract attention to an issue and may win some short-term concessions from the government, but their longer-term effectiveness is very much subject to doubt. The end result of such episodes seems often to be the destruction of the rioters' own neighborhoods, the devastation of local economies, increased pressure on the part of police and government, and the bolstering of law-and-order advocates in the next election cycle.

Nonviolent Activism

If political violence is always considered a form of unconventional political participation, nonviolent activism straddles the line between the conventional and unconventional. Peaceful protest may be sporadic or sustained, spontaneous or organized, but its goal is not to use force to enact change but rather to bring pressure to bear on the political establishment to enact reform. The example of the EZLN in Mexico is particularly interesting because it represents the coalescence of scattered groups of protestors into an armed force, which then transformed itself into a mostly peaceful activist movement and may be on its way to becoming a more conventional interest group. Despite a continued rhetoric of militancy and the symbolic maintaining of an armed presence, the Zapatistas present far less of a military challenge to the Mexican government than a political one. In reality, they pose no threat of fomenting secession in Chiapas state, much less of seizing control of the Mexican state. Indeed, violent but largely apolitical conflict with narcotraffickers has posed a fare more dire challenge to the Mexican state in recent years. But, as attested to by the Zapatistas' dramatic march on Mexico City, their mass rally in the city's main square, and their continued high profile online and in various other media, the Zapatistas have helped to promote the democratization of the country.

In countries with repressive governments, spontaneous protest activities may occur from time to time, but the police and other government forces are usually able to curb the emergence of full-scale movements. Such a scattered approach still tends to be common in nondemocratic countries, in which the citizens may hold targeted demonstrations to air a particular grievance but then are prevented by the police or other authorities from forming organized protest groups. For instance, landless farmers, displaced villagers, and others excluded from the advance of affluence in China regularly picket and demonstrate, but the government then uses arrests, threats, or economic incentives to defuse the situation. While such repression can quell protest in the short term, it runs the risk of bottling up discontent, which can explode into revolutionary conditions, as happened with the ousting of such dictators as the shah of Iran in 1979 and President Ferdinand Marcos of the Philippines in 1986. By contrast, nonviolent activist social movements, when allowed to function freely, can serve as safety valves for democracy, providing a forum within which grievances can be aired and demands made for reform.

With its comparatively open society, the United States has been a particularly fertile home for sustained and organized activist movements; examples stretch back to antislavery abolitionists, suffragists seeking the right to vote for women, the antialcohol prohibitionists, and labor union activists. The modern prototype of a protest movement in the United States is the African American civil rights movement, which itself drew upon and applied lessons learned during the struggle for the independence of India led by Mohandas K. Gandhi. The civil rights movement pioneered tactics including boycotts of segregated bus services, sit-ins at lunch counters that refused to serve black customers, pickets and demonstrations up to and including a mass march on Washington, and jail-ins designed to force authorities to arrest so many protestors that their capacity to function was strained. The civil rights movement also made savvy use of the courts, which can play an important role as protectors of minority rights. The desegregation orders issued in *Brown v. Board of Education* did not simply drop from the sky in 1954 but rather were the culmination of a half century of strategic litigation brought by the National Association for the Advancement of Colored People (NAACP). These and other tactics of nonviolent civil disobedience are especially well suited for use by social groups that are disadvantaged and discriminated against but that live in countries that are democratic enough to allow some latitude for citizen initiative.

Waves of successive protest movements have emerged in the United States and other democratic countries since the 1960s. Perhaps because of the strength of group identities in the United States, American activist movements have tended to be based around stable, long-term sources of identity such as race, gender, sexual orientation, and physical disability. Such U.S.-initiated movements have often had a major influence on protest politics among such groups around the world. For example, the many branches of the global movement for gay and lesbian equality almost all trace their roots to three days of rioting in New York City in June 1969, which ensued after police raided a gay bar called the Stonewall Inn. Every June, in commemoration of the Stonewall riots, hundreds of gay and lesbian communities throughout the world hold "pride marches," lively parades held on the main thoroughfares of major cities that bring people "out of the closet" and into public view while demonstrating significant numbers of supporters. Similarly, AIDS activism also traces many of its roots to New York City, where in 1987 the local gay community formed the direct-action protest group ACT UP, which in turn spawned chapters and affiliated organizations across the country and around the world.

Activism in the United States has more often been built around group identities and less often focused on broad ideologies or issues that affect the nation or the world at large than it is in other countries. For instance, environmental activism has been less extensive and coherent in the United States than in Western Europe, where green movements have become so well developed that they have evolved into full-scale political parties that have been part of governing coalitions in Germany, France, Italy, Belgium, Finland, and Ireland. Similarly, the nuclear-disarmament movement of the 1980s and subsequent peace movements garnered far more support in European countries than they ever did in the United States, except perhaps during times when American troops were actually in combat.

Likewise, aside from a few eras, such as the labor unrest of the 1930s, class-based protest movements have also not been very central to American history. The United States has seen much less "class warfare" calling for high tax rates to allow for massive income redistribution or for heavy government regulation of the workplace, such as by offering job guarantees, than have the wealthy nations of Europe. American labor unions have tended to focus not on broad societal objectives but rather on relatively narrow employment issues such as wages and benefits. Partly as a result, a disproportionate number of Americans continue to live in or near poverty, benefiting little from the economic dynamism that has made the United States the wealthiest country in the world.

Even traumatic events such as the aftermath of Hurricane Katrina in 2005 and the "Great Recession" of 2008–9, which vividly exposed the vulnerability of the poor and the limited scope of government services for them, appear to have done little to spur sustained protest or activism on behalf of poverty reduction. If anything, most of the grassroots energy of the "Tea Party" movement created in the wake of the massive government bailouts of 2008 and 2009 is directed *against* a more proactive role for government in addressing social ills. One major exception was the small but symbolically potent "Occupy Wall Street" movement of 2011. Although its message was diffuse and its policy impact uncertain, the Occupy Movement succeeded in highlighting the growth of income inequality through its slogan "We are the 99 percent"—and may have helped to doom the 2012 presidential prospects of Mitt Romney, who was decidedly part of the top 1 percent.

Protest movements among youths, so influential in other countries, have also been relatively muted in the United States. The youth empowerment movement of the late 1960s and early 1970s, focused mostly on college campuses, was highly influential in such areas as the lowering of the voting age to eighteen and increasing opposition to the Vietnam War. But this period was a historical outlier, the product of a radicalized era and a huge youth population caused by the demographic bubble of the baby boom generation. The eighteen-to-twenty-four-year-old demographic has long had the lowest level of voter turnout and has been notable for disengagement from politics. In fact, since the 1970s, most American college students have had little interest in large-scale challenges to the government or to social norms. Rather, the reigning paradigm of multiculturalism at American universities seems to have the effect of channeling student activism toward protest based on group-level identities of gender, race, or ethnicity rather than broader ideological issues.

Notably, however, one area of activism in which students, or more precisely younger people in general, have led the way has been in pioneering new forms of Internet-based activism. As seen in the example of the Zapatistas, the World Wide Web, by its very nature, has the ability to bridge social, geographic, and other divides. Over the past decade new forms of social solidarity, particularly around opposition to processes of globalization and corporate power, have sprung up under the decentralized leadership of youths around the world, adding a layer of generational solidarity that has often otherwise been missing. Within the United States, the most notable uptick in political engagement among youth in a generation was Barack Obama's 2008 presidential bid, which was based largely on the appeals to the "Netroots" for donations and campaign support. This trend was powerfully reinforced when the Obama reelection campaign made extensive use of Facebook, Twitter, and other social media to identify, motivate, and mobilize youth voters.

Interest-Group Activity

A final form of political participation to be considered in this chapter is that of established interest groups. Often derided as "special interests," such groups have long been viewed suspiciously in American politics. Indeed, when James Madison famously warned against the "mischief of faction" in *The Federalist 10*, he was mostly referring to what we would today consider interest groups (although also partly to political parties). Yet, in an environment of relative egalitarianism, freedom of association, and a diverse society and economy, interest-group formation has been inevitable, as Madison recognized. As the French aristocrat Alexis de Tocqueville noted during his travels in the 1830s, lacking innate hierarchies and expansive government, Americans were far more likely than Europeans of that era to form voluntary associations of all types. Today, as throughout American history, interest groups are more prolific in the United States than in other industrialized democracies. While many politicized interest groups are affiliated with social movements, they are defined by their far greater degree of organization and permanence. Indeed, the simplest litmus test by which to distinguish a more amorphous social movement from an interest group is to ask whether an entity has a physical headquarters, an executive director, a fixed phone number, or even just an organizational letterhead. The Southern Christian Leadership Conference and the National Organization for Women do, while the "civil rights movement" and the "women's rights movement" do not.

Interest groups focus on a wide array of issues. At any given moment, many may not necessarily be politicized, but, because of their potential to organize, they remain of interest to political scientists: consider groups of bird watchers whose interests are ornithological yet who might be quick to jump into the political arena if a particular avian habitat were threatened. Robust norms of freedom of association in the United States mean that nearly any group can, at least in theory, form at any time at the initiative of any of its members. In practice, however, group formation and maintenance requires a huge initial and ongoing commitment of money, time, effort, leadership, and rank-and-file engagement. Private-industry groups, such as professional or trade associations, are well positioned to sustain interest groups for purposes of lobbying lawmakers and otherwise advancing their agendas and thus have a tremendous impact. Many high-profile "public-interest" groups also flourish because of individual and corporate donations, from the Brady Campaign to Prevent Gun Violence to the National Rifle Association and from Planned Parenthood to the National Right to Life Committee.

Because the principal purpose of interest groups is to seek benefits from government, interest-group activity in the United States parallels the fragmentation of the U.S. governmental structure. Interest groups operate at the local, state, and national level, some mainly at one level, others at multiple levels. They may also target legislators, executives, and bureaucrats at all levels; a considerable number also engage in litigation strategies that involve various levels of courts. Further, because of the relative autonomy of American politicians from the control of political parties, interest groups must form connections directly with elected officials and their staffs, rather than simply with party leaders. All of these influences—plus the sheer size and diversity of the United States—have led to the creation of an unusually large and decentralized universe of interest groups in the United States. Such a system is in marked contrast to unitary states with parliamentary systems, in which the geographic and institutional concentration of power leads most interest-group activity to be focused on the executive branch of government and in the national capital.

Although many U.S. interest groups naturally ally themselves with one party or the other, they need not work through party structures. Public-interest groups concerned about, say, the environment or gun rights would find little utility in pressuring the national organizations of the Democratic or Republican Parties, as these have very limited direct influence on office-holders. Instead, interest groups must approach individual legislators or executives directly. To be effective in the United States, interest groups must have the funding, expertise, and support to offer a variety of resources to politicians, including expert advice during the legislative process, endorsements at election time, and get-out-the-vote activities of various types. A 2010 Supreme Court ruling in the case known as *Citizens United* unleashed an even greater avalanche of private spending in elections in 2012, but the results were less stark than many had predicted, with Democrats holding their own against Republicans and corporate interests less likely to enter the fray than independently wealthy tycoons.

The clearest and also perhaps the most pernicious linkage between interest groups and officeholders comes in the form of campaign donations to politicians who rely mostly on their own fund-raising abilities to fund expensive and near-continuous reelection activities. Interest groups that represent wealthy sectors in any country have clear-cut material advantages over those representing poorer and disadvantaged sectors. But in the United States, the skew is even more pronounced than in countries with parliamentary systems in which there are fewer offices open for election, campaigns are shorter, individual candidates have fewer fund-raising pressures, and the public sector often provides funding, free television time, and other resources during campaigns. Campaign financing is so important that it has been argued that some powerful interest groups in the United States are able to virtually dictate public policy in the areas of concern to them.

They do so, it is argued, by providing crucial financial and other support, such as endorsements to members of Congress who sit on key committees, enabling them to write legislation and to pressure the federal bureaucracy on the interest group's behalf. The result is that some powerful interest groups can come to dominate government decision making in specific small areas, forming what have been termed subgovernments or iron triangles. Such arrangements can be found in governments around the world, but they particularly flourish in a political system with weak parties, wide dispersal of legislative and executive authority and decentralized bureaucracies.

Despite these informal flows of influence, interest groups in the United States rarely have any sort of official status or standing awarded by the government. By contrast, a number of other countries employ a system sometimes called *corporatism* in which a small number of groups representing major social sectors play a more or less official role in government decision making. (This academic use of the term *corporatism* is only distantly related to the more recent popular use of the term to criticize the excessive influence of wealthy business corporations.) In Sweden, a single federation of labor is officially recognized by the state as the organization with which it negotiates wage levels. In Japan, a federation of economic organizations has played a major role in negotiating export policies. And in France, a national farmers' federation has worked with the government to modernize French agriculture. In each of these cases, the partnership between the state and a single representative of powerful interests has promoted social harmony, although sometimes at the risk of subsequent inflexibility in policy formulation.

When powerful economic interests have such a direct role in the work of government, it can be hard for the state to later extract concessions from them when economic circumstances change. This is less of a problem in authoritarian countries, such as China, where corporatist arrangements are sometimes created in order to provide expertise to state policymakers and then to help with carrying out the decisions of those policymakers with little or no questioning. By contrast, in the United States, interest groups function in a much more competitive environment, each struggling to have its influence felt. There is, for instance, no single labor association or single association of business interests that is formally empowered to speak on behalf of that entire sector of the economy or to participate in the work of government.

Another notable pattern in the United States is that labor unions are simply one type of interest group among many. Union membership in the United States has been declining for many years, but, even at its height, unions never played the central role in American politics that they have played elsewhere, especially in Western Europe, where class divisions have always been more pronounced. In some of those countries, labor unions formed the nucleus of political parties that have, in many cases, emerged as a major force in the politics of their countries. The British Labour Party was a particularly good example of that in the 1960s and 1970s when that country's Trade Union Congress essentially controlled the party, which in turn, often controlled government. In some other countries the linkages are not quite that direct, but governments sometimes provide official recognition of labor federations, which are given a role in policy formulation. By comparison, U.S. labor unions have generally been strong supporters of the Democratic Party but have formed just one part of that party's large electoral base.

Just as neither labor nor interest groups hold official status in the United States, neither do any religious groups or denominations enjoy the status of being the official religion of the state. Perhaps the classic example of an established church is in Britain, where the head of state, the king or queen, is also the head of the Church of England, and the nation's Anglican bishops officially hold seats in the House of Lords as "lords spiritual." The Catholic Church has also held official status as the church of the state in a number of countries, such as Spain and Ireland. The secularization of Western Europe has rendered these relationships largely obsolete, although the Catholic Church and various Orthodox Christian Churches still exert considerable sway in parts of Eastern Europe. The special status given to Islam in many Muslim countries is today a more relevant example. In a number of countries stretching from Nigeria to Malaysia, the state is often so committed to Islamic values that the Koran forms the basis of the law. Although Americans profess strong religious beliefs, which influence public discourse, religions as organized bodies are blocked from official status because of the First Amendment's requirement for separation of church and state.

Conclusion: Why It All Matters

Democracy tends to direct citizen input into conventional modes of political participation such as voting and involvement with political parties and interest groups. Unconventional means of participation can also have an impact on politics, however. At their best they serve as additional vehicles for democracy, but at their worst they can create instability and unrest. Since the American Civil War, the United States has largely avoided political violence on its territory, although there have been sporadic riots, uprisings, and other isolated incidents. Most unconventional participation takes the form of peaceful protest, particularly with regard to the grievances of particular groups, rather than challenges to the state or the basic order of society. Meanwhile, the activities of organized interests, although often considered suspect from the time of the founders down to today, remain an integral part of the American political system. As seen in the next two chapters, the U.S. political party system is unusually narrow and limited, and in a very real sense, these other forms of participation have flourished in order to fill in what might otherwise be participatory voids in U.S. politics.

Further Reading

Castells, Manuel. *Networks of Outrage and Hope: Social Movements in the Internet Age*. Cambridge: Polity, 2012.

Dalton, Russell J., and Mandred Kuechler, eds. *Challenging the Political Order: New Social and Political Movements in Western Democracies.* New York: Oxford University Press, 1990.

Della Porta, Donatella. *Social Movements, Political Violence, and the State.* New York: Cambridge University Press, 1996.

Klanderman, Bert, and Conny Roggeband. *Handbook of Social Movements across Disciplines.* New York: Springer, 2010.

McAdam, Doug, John D. McCarthy, and Meyer N. Zald, eds. *Comparative Perspectives on Social Movements: Political Opportunities, Mobilizing Structures, and Cultural Framings.* New York: Cambridge University Press, 1996.

Shigetomi, Shinichi, and Kumiko Makino. *Protest and Social Movements in the Developing World.* Cheltenham, UK: Edward Elgar, 2009.

Thomas, Clive S., ed. *First World Interest Groups: A Comparative Perspective.* Westport, CT: Greenwood Press, 1993.

Web-Based Exploration Exercise

Visit the websites of any three social movements and/or interest groups in the world that are engaged with related issues. Identify at least one of their issues and one of their tactics for influencing outcomes in their favor; then discuss the extent to which these issues and tactics would be relevant to the context of the United States. A useful listing of world social movements and their associated interest groups can be found at http://en.wikipedia.org/wiki/List_of_social_movements.

Question for Debate and Discussion

Protest politics is a common activity in the U.S. political system. What dimensions of the U.S. political system may help to channel citizens toward protest politics? What reforms could be introduced from other political systems that might reduce the occurrence of protest politics in the United States?

Chapter 9

Voting and Elections

Voting and elections are absolute prerequisites for democracy, the very definition of which is "rule by the people." *Direct* democracy, which refers to the practice of having the people vote directly on all matters of importance, is now extremely rare in the world. Only a handful of jurisdictions—and none at the national level—are still small and uncomplicated enough to allow for direct democracy. *Representative* democracy, by far the predominant form of democracy today, involves the election of individuals to public offices in which they are empowered to exercise authority on behalf of the people.

In order for a country to qualify as a bona fide democracy, elections must be free, fair, and competitive, and the right to vote and to run for office should be open to all or nearly all adult citizens. Beyond basic questions of electoral procedure and broad citizen participation, however, systems of voting and elections diverge greatly across democratic countries. Some countries place a very light burden on their voters, with elections being held only every few years and with a limited number of offices to fill. Others, perhaps most prominently the United States, have frequent elections with quite complicated ballots. Many countries facilitate the participation of their citizens in elections; others—including the United States—take a less proactive approach, leaving it mostly up to citizens' own initiative, with the predictable result of low voter turnout. Finally, the particular electoral system used can determine how votes are translated into seats and whether only the will of the majority prevails or election outcomes will reflect the wishes of a larger portion of the electorate.

Case Study: Voting and Elections in Israel

Israel has a robust, even combative democracy, but, in many ways, Israeli voting and elections are far more straightforward and streamlined than those in the United States. This geographically tiny country is a unitary state, meaning that there are no levels of government between the local and the national for which elections must be held. It also employs a parliamentary system with just a single chamber, the Knesset, which in turn elects both the prime minister and a ceremonial president. Further, there are no electoral districts—all 120 seats of the Knesset are filled by a single national election. Essentially then, Israelis must answer only a single question when they go to the voting booth in national elections: which party do they wish to support for power?

This question may sound like an easy one to most Americans, who are used to a two-party system, or even to many Europeans accustomed to having perhaps four or five parties. But in Israel, the political party system is highly fragmented along ideological, religious, and ethnic lines, with more than a dozen political parties contesting each election. Under Israeli election rules, each party gets the same percentage of seats as the percentage of the national vote that it wins (a system called proportional representation [PR]). The only limitation is that the party must receive at least 2 percent of the national vote to be apportioned any seats. In elections held in February 2009, the two largest parties were the centrist Kadima Party with 22.5 percent of the vote and twenty-nine seats and the right-wing Likud Party with 21.6 percent of the vote and twenty-seven seats. But in all, twelve parties in total received more than 2 percent of the vote and thus at least three seats in the Knesset. This level of multiparty fragmentation is so commonplace that no single party in Israel's more-than-fifty-year history has ever been able to establish a majority in the Knesset: all Israeli governments have been based on coalitions among multiple parties. In this particular election, although Kadima won the most votes and seats, it was Likud that was able to assemble a majority coalition and to form a government.

As for electoral law, all Israeli citizens over the age of eighteen are eligible to vote, including the significant number of Arabs and other non-Jews who are citizens. In order to facilitate wide-scale participation, election day is a national holiday, and special arrangements are made for active-duty soldiers, overseas diplomats, the hospital bound, and even prisoners to cast a ballot. Voter turnout routinely reaches the 80 percent mark, although it has dropped to about 65 percent in recent elections in part due to voter frustration with political scandals and an unusually confused political situation.

The picture of democracy and electoral participation in Israel is complicated, of course, by the long-term Israeli occupation of Palestinian territories. The Palestinian residents of the West Bank and the Gaza Strip are heavily influenced by the policies chosen by Israeli elected officials but have no say in electing them. However, in recent years they have had their own elections for the government of a quasi-autonomous Palestinian Authority.

Free and Fair Elections

As stated earlier, a minimal criterion for democracy is that elections must be free, fair, and competitive. Free elections require secret ballots along with protection from coercion and undue influence on how individuals vote. In the past in the United States (and still in some countries today), voters had to publicly request a color-coded ballot for one party slate or another when at the voting booth. This choice could then be recorded, and voters would often be in plain sight when carrying and casting their votes, the color of their ballot clearly visible. Whenever the secrecy of the ballot is compromised, individuals can be subjected to enormous pressure to vote a certain way from family members, communities, employers, or the government itself. In the United States today, as in most democratic countries, the use of secret ballots, usually in a curtained or otherwise isolated voting booth, largely removes such problems, although they are being considered anew in the context of policies to expand voting by mail and/or via the Internet.

The question of whether elections are fair raises a different set of concerns, which secret balloting can do nothing to ensure. Guaranteeing the fairness of an election rests almost entirely with the authorities who oversee elections to ensure that strict procedures are adhered to. Yet the United States has an extraordinarily decentralized, even chaotic system for administering elections. Unlike voting rights, which are largely regulated at the national level, elections are explicitly designated in the Constitution as a right and responsibility of the states. Indeed, there is no such thing as a national election in the United States—even the presidential election is really fifty-one separate elections, in each of the states and in the District of Columbia. Further, many states devolve much of the responsibility for administering elections to the county level, meaning that there are thousands of different policies and procedures in place throughout the United States. By contrast, centralized control of voting procedures allows fewer opportunities for fraud, although it by no means prevents it entirely. In one infamous incident in 1988, for instance, the central-government computers being used to tabulate the overall results of the presidential election in Mexico mysteriously crashed when the opposition candidate pulled ahead. When they were operational again, the candidate of the ruling party suddenly had a comfortable lead.

Unfair election practices can occur at three distinct points: before, during, and after the casting of ballots. Before votes are cast, unfair practices can include preventing certain voters from submitting ballots or allowing some individuals to vote more than once, usually under different names. During the balloting process, certain voting sites in areas known to support one candidate or another can be (intentionally or unintentionally) provided with inadequate staffs or equipment, creating long lines that discourage voters or make it impossible for everyone to vote before closing time. Even more overtly, voting machines can be rigged to under- or overcount votes for certain candidates. Finally, vote tabulations can be misrepresented, either by simply discarding some ballots, miscounting them, or misreporting the final count to election officials.

One vivid example of fraud took place in the 2004 presidential election in the former Soviet country of Ukraine, in which the sitting prime minister was running against a reform candidate. The state-run media heavily favored the prime minister, who was also an ally of the departing president, and opposition activists were harassed and arrested. In western regions of the country that favored the challenger, numerous voters were turned away at the polls, whereas in the central and eastern regions many people registered on the spot under odd circumstances, such as with large groups being brought in by bus to vote. Many unauthorized individuals, including police and local officials, were witnessed being involved with the counting process, and the reported voter turnout was suspiciously high, approaching an extremely unlikely 100 percent in some places. In response, thousands of Ukrainians with orange-colored banners occupied the capital city's main square for days demanding a revote, which the Supreme Court ultimately ordered. In the new vote, the challenger, Victor Yuschenko, won convincingly, leading many to call the entire episode Ukraine's "Orange Revolution." Sadly, the following years in Ukraine have left a much more muddled picture, demonstrating that elections alone can go only so far in promoting democratization.

In the United States, victory in the first two presidential elections of the twenty-first century hinged on the contested election in just a single state: Florida in 2000 and Ohio in 2004, states run at the time by Republicans. On both occasions, the losing side, the Democrats, alleged a wide range of violations of voting rights. These included the purging of African Americans (known to generally be staunch supporters of the Democrats) from the voting rolls in Florida and the questionable rejection of registrations of new voters (also mostly believed to be Democrats) in Ohio. Voter fraud is, however, most definitely a bipartisan issue: the Democratic Party machines in big cities regularly tampered with voting throughout the twentieth century and may even have helped throw the 1960 presidential election to John F. Kennedy over Richard Nixon. And in the past two races won by Democrats, the congressional elections of 2006 and the presidential election of 2008, the left-wing community activist group ACORN was widely criticized for voter registration fraud and other possible offenses. In 2012, much of the attention was on attempts by Republican-led state legislatures to enact voter ID laws that they said were intended to thwart fraud and that their detractors claimed were aimed at suppression of minority and other Democratic voters.

Competitive Elections

Even if elections are both free and fair, they cannot be said to fully reflect the will of the people if they are not also competitive—open to all, or nearly all, views held by the general public. Indeed, totalitarian states can, in a technical sense, hold elections that are free and fair but still not democratic if there is but one choice on the ballot. Such elections were quite common in countries of the former Soviet bloc, where citizens were required to vote but the only name on the ballot would be that of the designated candidate of the Communist Party. Some dictatorships still stage such "acclamatory elections" and then, in the elaborate fictions that they use to claim legitimacy, point to such election results as evidence of the support of the people; on the eve of the U.S.-led invasion of Iraq, Saddam Hussein staged an election in which it claimed he received 100 percent of the vote amid a ludicrous 100 percent national turnout.

An only slightly less undemocratic practice in Egypt led many to accuse long-time President Hosni Mubarak, a thirty-year incumbent, of considering himself a modern pharaoh. The Egyptian system allowed only one candidate to be presented to the people after nomination by the legislature—which was itself preserved under the control of a single party. Under international pressure during elections in 2005, Egypt undertook some reforms, but the ruling party still gained unfair advantage through other mechanisms, such as the government's control of mass media and its ability to use government funds to win over supporters. Ultimately, in 2010, Mubarak was toppled by street protests—only to find his successor as president, the opposition leader Mohammed Morsi, similarly accused of "pharaonic" tendencies.

In the theocratic state of Iran, the ruling clerics are empowered to invalidate the candidacy of anyone they deem to be opposed to the values of the revolution they supposedly safeguard, thus ensuring that any candidate they find unacceptable has no chance to compete for office. When even this failsafe seemed to be unable to secure their desired result in 2009, the regime falsified the vote to allow President Mahmoud Ahmadinejad to stay in power, triggering massive nationwide protests. Although the protestors failed to bring down Ahmadinejad, deep tensions and conflicts within the regime were made apparent.

As for the competitiveness of its elections, at first glance the United States would appear to meet this criterion easily. Beyond a few requirements relating to age, time and place of residence, and length of citizenship, almost all American citizens are eligible to run for almost all public offices (although presidential and vice presidential candidates must be native-born Americans). At a deeper level, however, it can be argued that U.S. elections are less than fully competitive.

One problem is that campaigning and media advertising, particularly for higher offices, can be prohibitively expensive, effectively excluding those who cannot raise funds from wealthy donors or organized interests or who are not wealthy enough to self-finance their own campaigns. In some other countries, many of the costs of campaigning are borne to a far greater extent either by political parties or through public resources allocated by the government, such as direct funding or free time on television. In parliamentary systems such as Canada and Britain, campaigns also tend to be much briefer. Unlike the enormously costly eighteen-month marathons that precede U.S. presidential elections, parliamentary elections can unfold within as little as a few weeks because the positions of parties and the qualifications of the leading candidates are generally already well known to the public at large.

Campaigns in the United States, by contrast, are highly candidate centered, with each office seeker left largely to his or her own means. This has the effect of greatly weakening the power of parties while greatly strengthening the influence of wealthy interests over candidates (and, later, officeholders). The demands of campaign fund-raising also help to further reinforce the powerful "incumbency effect" in the United States. Once in office, elected officials can use the resources and influence of their offices to raise funds to all but ensure renomination by their party and then reelection. In some elections over the past twenty years, more than 90 percent of House members who sought reelection won it.

Further, it is extremely unusual for anyone other than a candidate of either the Democratic or the Republican Party to win an election. Although these two parties aspire to be big tents that include voters and politicians with a wide range of views, some individuals whose views do not fit clearly within either party may find themselves unable to seriously compete for office. (The causes and consequences of the two-party system in the United States are discussed in more detail later in this chapter and in the next chapter.) In about 85 percent of congressional districts, only the candidate of one party has a realistic chance of winning the general election. Increasingly sophisticated software applications are now available to gerrymander electoral districts in the House and in state legislative chambers to cluster voters in such a way as to all but guarantee either a Republican or a Democratic victory.

However, one factor that makes U.S. elections genuinely more competitive than those of many other countries is the prevalence of primary elections, in which voters rather than political parties choose party nominees for the general election. Having an array of candidates representing differing views (as well as qualifications and personalities) can generate genuine electoral competition within parties. In practice, however, serious primary battles are usually found only when there is an open seat, that is, one that has been vacated by the incumbent. The existence of term limits for many executive offices means that open seats are fairly common in mayoral, gubernatorial, and presidential elections but much less common in congressional races or in elections for those state and city legislatures that do not have term limits. By contrast, the leaders of political parties in many other countries, particularly those with parliamentary systems, simply bestow their party nominations. In this way, such political parties can choose candidates who they feel will support the views of the party leadership—and can punish those officeholders who fail to support the party once they have been elected.

Primary elections can also have the somewhat counterintuitive effect of reducing the competitiveness of moderate candidates in favor of more extreme ones. Consider that in the United States, speaking in rough terms, the most conservative third of voters in the country are likely to be Republicans, the most liberal third are predominantly Democrats, and the moderate middle third are largely independents who have registered to vote but not as members of any party. (Relatively few Americans are registered with so called "third" parties.) Generally, it is the most ideologically driven and politically minded voters who turn out to vote in their party's primaries. Thus, the Republican nominees produced by the primary system will likely fall somewhere in the middle of the pack of the most conservative third of the country—making them more conservative than about five-sixths of the country. Similarly, the Democratic nominee is likely to be more liberal than all but one-sixth of the country.

When it comes time for all the voters in the general election to choose between the nominees of the Democratic and Republican parties, the moderate candidates who might otherwise appeal to them may have already been excluded from contention. This is not invariably the case because sometimes primary voters endorse the candidate they think is most likely to win the general election rather than an ideologically more "pure" candidate that they may most prefer in the primaries. Also, candidates generally "move to the middle" in general elections in order to appeal to centrist voters. Still, the trend toward marginalizing moderates is noteworthy.

Further, the two-party system also excludes minor-party candidates from meaningful contention. In only two elections since World War II (1968 and 1992) has a third-party or independent presidential candidate broken the 10 percent threshold, and no such candidate has gotten more than 20 percent since 1912; the results at other levels of government are scarcely better. Thus, many voters whose views are out of line with the views of the base of the Democratic and Republican parties are likely to find themselves without a clear candidate to support. Such was clearly the case with many supporters of Ron Paul in the 2012 Republican presidential primaries, who supported his libertarian views but did not find a natural home in either major party but felt that the small Libertarian Party had no chance of really influencing the election.

Voter Eligibility and Turnout

Another hallmark of democratic elections is a broad right to vote, sometimes called the electoral franchise. The story of U.S. political history is largely one of the expansion of franchise, so that almost all unincarcerated citizens over the age of eighteen are now able to cast ballots. This is a standard commonly applied in democracies around the world; the right to vote today is rarely abridged by law due to race, ethnicity, or religion. Gender is likewise declining as a reason for exclusion from the right to vote, although such barriers persist in a small number of states. The voting age is also usually set at around eighteen, although it may vary a few years in either direction.

The United States is typical in that voting rights are limited only to citizens. This is to some degree inherent in the logic of rule by the people, which generally defines who are and who are not part of "the people" by whether they hold citizenship. As with most countries, the United States has procedures by which people can become naturalized as citizens and also goes further by providing automatic citizenship to anyone born on American territory or to an American citizen abroad. Some countries have defined citizenship differently, often relying on ethnic descent; for example, generations of ethnic Koreans born in Japan were long denied citizenship—and thus political participation—in that country, although the law has been liberalized more recently. Others provide preferential naturalization procedures for some groups, as does Germany for people of ethnic German descent and Israel for those of the Jewish religion.

Even with full voting rights afforded to most adult citizens, Americans do face additional challenges to voting. Some of these are practical, such as the requirement to register to vote and to change one's registration after every move to a new residence. The burden of registration falls entirely on the American voter, unlike in some systems in which centralized government records can be used to register voters on the basis of their age and place of residence. Another practical barrier is that in the United States, unlike in many countries, Election Day is not a holiday, making access difficult to the polls for some people, such as those with long and inflexible work schedules, heavy child-care responsibilities, or poor transportation in sparsely populated areas.

Further, voting—unlike such civic responsibilities as serving on juries and paying taxes—is not a required activity. In this regard, the United States is in line with most of the rest of the world, but there are a number of countries, including such democracies as Australia and Brazil, where voting is compulsory. While voting rates do increase when nonvoting is punished by fines or other means, the wisdom of this practice has been questioned. Compulsory voting inevitably means that a large number of poorly informed people will be casting ballots, perhaps subject to misinformation, demagoguery, or even bribery. Civil libertarians have also argued that compulsory voting violates freedom of speech by forcing people to register a political opinion.

Another major barrier to voting in the United States is the frequency and complexity of elections in the United States. In this regard, the contrast with Israel is particularly enlightening; as seen in the case study, elections in Israel are as nearly opposite from elections in the United States as can be imagined between two democracies. Because Israel is a unitary state with a unicameral national parliament, there are no separate elections for executive office, no elections for an upper house of the legislature, no provincial-level elections, and not even any electoral districts (although there are occasional municipal elections). In the United States, voters must cast ballots for a wide array of positions, including president, U.S. senator, U.S. representative, governor, state senator, state assembly member, mayor, city council member, and, sometimes, also state attorneys general, judges, county officers, and a wide variety of other positions. Plus, many states also ask citizens to vote directly on questions of public policy, especially about taxing and spending, through

Table 9.1 Voter Turnout in 60 Major Democracies (based on most recent election for determining control of the executive)

Parliamentary	Semipresidential	Presidential
Australia (93.2%)	Finland (68.9%)	Argentina (79.4%)
Austria (81.7%)	France (80.3%)	Brazil (78.5%)
Belgium (89.2%)	Guyana[1] (72.8%)	Chile (86.9%)
Benin (84.8%)	Mongolia (73.5%)	Costa Rica (69.1%)
Botswana (76.7%)	Romania (58%)	Dominican Republic (70.2%)
Bulgaria (60.6%)	Ukraine (69.7%)	El Salvador (61.9%)
Canada (61.4%)		Ghana (72.9%)
Croatia (50.1%)		Indonesia (68.5%)
Cyprus (89.6%)		Mali (36.2%)
Czech Republic (62.6%)		Mexico (63.1%)
Denmark (87.7%)		Namibia (85.4%)
Estonia (63.5%)		Panama (68.5%)
Germany (70.7%)		Peru (82.5%)
Greece (62.4%)		South Africa[1] (77.3%)
Hungary (46.6%)		South Korea (70.1%)
India (58.1%)		**United States (57%)**
Ireland (70%)		Uruguay (89.1%)
Israel (64.7%)		
Italy (80.5%)		
Jamaica (53.1%)		
Japan (69.2%)		
Latvia (59.4%)		
Lithuania (35.9%)		
Mauritius (77.8%)		
Netherlands (75.4%)		
New Zealand (74.2%)		
Norway (76.3%)		
Poland (48.9%)		
Portugal (58%)		
Serbia (57.7%)		
Slovakia (59.1%)		
Slovenia (65.6%)		
Spain (68.9%)		
Sweden (84.6%)		
Switzerland (49.1%)		
Trinidad & Tobago (69.4%)		
United Kingdom (65.8%)		

1. An executive president is chosen by parliament for a term of office, so turnout rates refer to parliamentary elections.

questions, called referenda or initiatives, placed on the ballot. And citizens may be asked to do this as often as every year or two and then not once but twice, in both party primaries and in general elections. Residents of New York City, for example, were asked to go to the polls about twenty times in the decade of the 2000s.

The complexity and frequency of American elections are often viewed as exacting a heavy toll in terms of "information costs." In order to cast meaningful ballots, voters must not only know when and where to vote but also which positions are open, what these positions do, what the parties stand for, who is running, what their qualifications and records are, and what they have promised to do once in office. Absent any piece of that information, it becomes harder to cast a meaningful ballot. In a relatively high-literacy country such as the United States, this problem is not as acute as it would be in a developing-world context. But there are still considerable numbers of Americans with relatively modest educational backgrounds and many others for whom English is not their native language.

Finally, characteristics of the U.S. party system and government structure may also help to suppress voter turnout by reducing the perceived relevance of elections among citizens. The effective exclusion of minor parties and the similarities between Democrats and Republicans on many issues means that many voters do not find their own preferences well reflected by the candidates on offer. By contrast, in a multiparty system, various parties will offer widely divergent platforms that are more highly focused on a few key issues: Green parties will strongly highlight environmentalism, anti-immigrant parties will focus on border control, rural-based parties will emphasize the needs of farmers, regional parties will agitate for local autonomy, and so on. This panoply of choices provides much more vivid contrasts than the comparatively muddled and centrist platforms typical of two-party systems. Finally, separation of powers and federalism in the United States prevent sudden or sweeping changes in public policy, further reinforcing the idea that "nothing changes" after an election and leading some to ask themselves why they should even bother to vote.

Taken together, these factors help to explain why the United States has nearly the lowest voter turnout rates found in large and/or populous democracies. Table 9.1 lays out voter turnout rates in sixty major democracies for the most recent election that determined control of each country's executive. As can be seen, the U.S. voter turnout rate was 57 percent, which placed it lower than in about five-sixths of the democracies. It is worth further noting that voter turnout in the United States is at its highest in presidential election years, dropping even further when only congressional and state and local offices are up for election.

The political significance of the issue of voter turnout has sometimes been questioned, especially in long-established democracies such as the United States. It could well be argued that low voter turnout means that people are relatively content with the political system and that if they were more worried, they would turn out to vote in higher numbers. And, indeed, this was the case in 2004, when voter turnout jumped to 60 percent and then again in 2008 to 63 percent, only to slump back to 57 percent in 2012. Still, low voter turnout can be cause for concern insofar as some groups are far less likely to vote than others, particularly disadvantaged groups such as ethnic and racial minorities and those with low levels of education and income, although the two Obama presidential campaigns have made progress in mobilizing these underrepresented groups.

Although no single cost associated with voting may prove decisive, the cumulative impact of high costs can suppress the turnout of groups that also do not see their own issues and concerns—or their own group members—reflected among the candidates for office and the political parties. When the pool of such alienated citizens grows too large, it can be destabilizing to the political system if they come to feel that they do not have meaningful access to the political system and then turn toward unconventional forms of participation, such as the disruptive protest and political violence discussed in more detail in chapter 8.

The Winner-Take-All Electoral System

One of the most anomalous features of elections in the United States is also one that many Americans view as virtually synonymous with democracy itself: the idea that there can be one and only one winner in an election. In general elections under a two-party system, one candidate usually garners an absolute majority of the vote, and that person takes whichever office is at stake. At an instinctual level, Americans tend to view such an outcome at face value. Democracy is equated in the popular mind with majority rule, and the simplest definition of a bare majority is 50 percent of the votes, plus one vote.

When each election can produce one and only one winner, it is hard to argue against such a bare-majority rule. If the winner of the election in, for instance, the Fifth Congressional District in Wisconsin is a Republican who receives 60 percent of the vote, it is hard to argue that his or her Democratic challenger should take office instead. But what of the 40 percent who voted against the Republican? There is a good chance that their concerns will be largely overlooked, perhaps for years or decades at a time. This becomes even more problematic when all or part of that 40 percent has some concerns very distinct from those of the 60 percent majority, such as when they are ethnic, racial, or religious minorities or are geographically, economically, or ideologically distinctive in some way.

In the U.S. system, called the single-member plurality system, the just outcome is, of course, for the candidate who wins the most votes (the plurality) to take office, for example, to be the single member of the House from a congressional district. But there is nothing in the concept of democracy itself or even in the U.S. Constitution that demands that the single-member plurality system be used in House races. It is actually only a 1967 law passed by Congress that requires the states with more than one House seat to carve themselves into different congressional districts. Thus, a state whose population gives it ten house seats currently runs ten different elections in ten different districts with ten different winners, each of whom then individually goes to Washington. But constitutionally, the same state could just as easily have one election throughout the state for all ten seats; that is, it could make itself not a *single-member* system but a *multimember* system producing not one but ten election winners.

A number of U.S. states have in the past chosen their House members in this manner, and a variety of cities, counties, and school boards choose all or some of their legislators without the use of districts. (In this case, they are usually called at-large members.) Multimember districting of this type is also used in the majority of democracies in the world today. Indeed, it is for the most part only Britain and former British colonies, such as the United States, Canada, India, and a number of Caribbean island countries, that employ the strict single-member system.

Certainly, the linkage between a particular representative and a distinct, relatively small geographic area does enable legislators to know and serve that small area well and for their constituents to know exactly which single legislator represents them. Indeed, this was the primary rationale for first introducing a single-member plurality system for elections to the House of Representatives, the institution of national government that is closest to the people and the only one that was originally directly elected by the people. But this approach can also promote local, parochial interests over broader regional or national interests. It can also effectively deny minorities a voice in government unless they happen to be geographically concentrated enough to form the majority in some electoral districts.

Under a multimember system, there is no longer a requirement that there be a single plurality winner who takes all (i.e., the one and only seat available). While one seat is not divisible, ten seats are, and this makes it possible to move toward a system of proportional representation. Under this system, the focus shifts from individual candidates to parties, which create a party list of as many candidates as there are seats up for election in any given constituency, ranked in the order that the party prefers. Thus, in our example, if 60 percent of the voters of a state with ten House seats voted for the Republican Party, then the top six names on the Republican Party list would become part of the Wisconsin delegation to the House of Representatives, as would the top four names on the Democratic Party list. Rather than being entirely shut out of power, the 40 percent of the state who voted Democratic would be represented by 40 percent of their congressional delegation. (This simple example assumes round numbers, but there are various mathematical formulas available to determine how to convert votes into seats.)

Table 9.2 Voting Systems for Election of National Legislatures in 60 Major Democracies

Proportional Representation (PR)	Single-Member Plurality (SMP)	Mixed System (SMP + PR)
Argentina	Botswana	Germany[3]
Australia	Canada[1]	Hungary
Austria[3]	Ghana	Japan
Belgium	India[2]	Lithuania
Benin	Jamaica[1]	Mexico
Brazil	Trinidad & Tobago[1]	New Zealand
Bulgaria	**United States**	South Korea
Chile	United Kingdom[1]	
Costa Rica		
Croatia		
Cyprus		
Czech Republic		
Denmark		
Dominican Republic		
El Salvador		
Estonia		
Finland		
France[3]		
Greece		
Guyana		
Indonesia[3]		
Ireland[3]		
Israel		
Italy		
Latvia		
Mali		
Mauritius		
Mongolia		
Namibia[3]		
Netherlands[3]		
Norway		
Panama		
Peru		
Poland		
Portugal		

(Continued)

Table 9.2 (Continued)

Proportional Representation (PR)	Single-Member Plurality (SMP)	Mixed System (SMP + PR)
Romania		
Serbia		
Slovakia		
Slovenia[3]		
South Africa[3]		
Spain		
Sweden		
Switzerland		
Ukraine		
Uruguay		

1. Members of the upper house are appointed or hold hereditary seats.
2. Members of the upper house but not the more powerful lower house are elected via proportional representation.
3. Members of the upper house but not the more powerful lower house are elected indirectly, such as by provinces.

By many counts, proportional representation better reflects the wishes of the electorate than the single-member plurality system. It is perhaps for this reason that some element of proportional representation is used in most democratic countries. As we saw, the system used in Israel is highly representative, with any party that garners more than 2 percent of the vote getting a proportional number of seats in the Knesset. Israel is unusual in that all 120 seats of the Knesset are allocated through a nationwide vote. More typically, each province or electoral district of a country is apportioned a certain number of seats on the basis of its population (as is the case in the United States). This system has led to an exceptional proliferation of political parties in Israel, with more than thirty parties running in the 2009 election. Indeed, multi-member proportional representation systems strongly tend to reduce the incentive for the maintenance of a two-party system, a theme discussed in greater detail in the next chapter.

In parliamentary systems, in which executive power arises from control of the legislature, it is also possible for executive authority to be distributed across multiple parties, such as by offering significant ministerial positions in the cabinet to representatives of smaller parties. The smaller parties can also extract concessions from the larger parties in terms of the government's agenda, further enhancing their role. Under the U.S. system, however, multimember districting would have little or no bearing on the election of executives, such as the president, governors, or mayors, in which one and only one executive office exists. Such elections are by their very nature single-member offices and thus cannot be subject to proportional representation.

Still, by increasing the number of parties that are able to contest legislative races, proportional representation in the United States could help to expand the number of viable candidates for executive office. Further, there are also other electoral reforms that could enhance the competitiveness of executive elections in the United States. A simple solution would be to have two-stage elections, with the first stage open to all parties and candidates. If no one gets an absolute majority of the votes, then a runoff is held between the two highest vote getters. Some version of this system is already widely in use for executive elections as diverse as the primary for mayor of New York City, the governorship of Louisiana, and the presidencies of France, Argentina, Ghana, and Indonesia, among others.

A variation on this theme is called instant runoff voting or the single transferable vote. Under this system, voters list two or more candidates in their order of preference. The candidate with the lowest number of votes after the first tabulation is dropped from the election. All of those who selected that candidate as their first choice would have their votes transferred to their second-choice candidate for another tabulation. In that way, votes for small parties are not "wasted" as they are under the current U.S. system, because the voter's preferences are still being accounted for. This process is continued until one candidate has an absolute majority of votes.

This instant runoff system directly addresses the criticism that voting for minor-party candidates is pointless since they almost certainly will not win and that such voting may even indirectly contribute to the election of the voter's least favorite candidate. A striking example comes from the year 2000, when many more left-wing voters might have cast their vote for the Green Party candidate, Ralph Nader, in an instant runoff election, secure in the knowledge that if Nader were eliminated, their second choice, presumably the Democrat Al Gore, would then receive their vote. Under current rules, those left-leaning citizens who voted for Nader rather than Gore prevented Gore from winning enough votes in the Electoral College to defeat Nader's ideological opposite, the Republican candidate, George W. Bush.

Peculiarities of the U.S. Presidential Elections

No discussion of U.S. voting and elections would be complete without an examination of one of the most unusual yet influential of all electoral features: the institution of the Electoral College. Indeed, it is hard to overstate the peculiarities of this method of selecting the president, a method that is neither entirely direct nor entirely indirect. Fearful of allowing the people to directly choose an executive, the founders created instead a nebulously defined intermediate institution of electors. Mindful of states' rights, they gave the power to determine how electors are chosen to the legislature in each state. And eager to capitalize on their hard-won compromise balancing the interests of both large and small states and southern and northern states in Congress, they simply imported that same formula into the method for selecting presidents, with each state having the same number of electors as it has members of the House and the Senate combined.

As democracy became more widely established in the early 1800s. Every state in the union eventually decided that their electors would automatically be allocated on the basis of the popular vote in that state. But in order to maximize their impact on the election, all except two states decided to employ a system in which whoever receives the most votes in that state gets all of that state's electoral votes. This has long had the effect of giving the victors in presidential elections a far larger share of the electoral vote than the popular vote, but for more than a century the winner in the popular vote at least was always the winner in the electoral vote.

That changed, of course, when Al Gore won the popular vote by more than a half million votes but received four fewer electoral votes than George W. Bush as a result of the contested election in Florida. This anomalous outcome brought closer scrutiny of the Electoral College and some of its other oddities. It was noted, for instance, that voters today still do not actually cast their ballot for a particular candidate for president but rather vote for a slate of electors who have pledged to formally cast their electoral votes in support of a particular candidate. Because the electors are chosen by the political parties, they are considered to be reliable when it comes time to cast their electoral vote the way they pledged, but it is not clear how effectively electors can really be bound to do so; indeed, in 2000 one Democratic elector cast a blank ballot (rather than one for Gore) as a protest.

And there are still other peculiarities. It is entirely possible that, had the outcome of a recount gone to Gore, the Republican-controlled Florida state legislature could have used its constitutional authority to appoint a slate of electors of its choosing regardless of the popular-vote outcome. And the closeness of the election also brought about reminders that if no candidate received an absolute majority of 270 of the 538 electoral votes, then it would be up to the House of Representatives to choose the president. Not only would this be something of a violation of the general principle of separation of powers, but each state's entire House delegation would collectively cast just one vote, drastically inflating the influence of low-population states.

Certainly, no one would design the Electoral College today, yet it persists. As we have seen, it is enormously difficult to amend the Constitution, particularly around issues that might weaken the position of the low-population states. Defenders of the system have argued that the Electoral College system has some benefits, such as forcing a presidential candidate to amass support throughout many areas of the country. Others have noted that the winner-take-all system focuses campaign time and energy disproportionately on higher-population, so-called swing states such as Ohio and Florida in which a relatively large pot of electoral votes can potentially be won by either candidate, unlike staunchly Republican Texas or solidly Democratic New York. But what is definitely clear is that the Electoral College is one of the most anomalous of all institutions of American democracy.

Even without the Electoral College, U.S. presidential elections would still be unusually long, arduous, and unpredictable. As early as two years before the election, contenders begin to emerge from one or both of the major political parties, especially when no sitting president will be running for reelection. These presidential aspirants then embark on a more than year-long marathon of policy speeches, campaign stops, and media appearances, all under the searing scrutiny of the national press. They must also undertake relentless fund-raising efforts to garner the tens of millions of dollars needed to mount a viable national campaign. Soon, the rise and fall of poll numbers, fund-raising, endorsements, and many other factors contribute to a horse-race mentality, with some candidates seen to be gaining ground and others falling behind. And all of this comes before they ever get to the first of the party primary elections (or, in some states, caucuses) used to allocate each state party's electoral support to specific candidates.

Because different states hold their primaries on different days over the course of several months, the horse-race mentality intensifies until one candidate captures enough support to be assured of that party's nomination. The formal nomination is bestowed at a coronation-like national party convention during the summer before the election. At this point, the nominees must simultaneously try to patch up relations with the rivals they had fought throughout the primaries, shore up the support of the base voters within their party, and also begin reaching out to the centrist voters needed to win in November. Then the campaign is resumed with a focus on the other major party's candidate in the general election, often characterized by intensely negative campaigning. And then maneuvering to win over the peculiar institution of the Electoral College takes center stage.

By contrast, elections in parliamentary democracies are far quicker and more predictable and are usually much less about personalities than about support for the specific public policies of different parties. Because parliamentary elections do not occur on a clearly fixed schedule and because they have no primary-election phase, the entire process can be collapsed into just a few weeks; in Britain, for instance, they must, by law, occur within seventeen working days of the prime minister calling for a general election. Such a truncated timetable is possible because potential prime ministers, having worked their way to the leadership of a major party, are usually already well-known, long-established politicians on the national stage. For better or worse, parliamentary systems rarely produce a prime minister who is an outsider to the existing political elite.

On balance, the U.S. system does allow for a great deal of competition, a long timetable during which the people can scrutinize the candidates, and a rough-and-tumble debate over opposing values and views. It can also sometimes allow talented newcomers, such as Barack Obama, a window of opportunity and can bring fresh perspectives to office. Because of their length and complexity, U.S. presidential elections can have many twists and turns and seem to hinge on trivial incidents and personal foibles that have little to do with the candidates' fitness for office, political skills, or views of public policy. Few would argue that the arduous and expensive American way of electing its chief executives consistently produces the best possible results.

Conclusion: Why It All Matters

Elections are essential to democracy, but electoral systems also shape the form that democracy will take in any particular country. The winner-take-all system used in the United States is a rarity, with most countries of the world using some form of proportional representation (PR) so that elections more closely reflect the wishes of voters. The use of PR can have significant implications for democratic practice, such as increasing voter turnout and providing a broad array of voices in government. One of its major impacts is the promotion of multiparty rather than two-party political systems, a theme discussed in greater detail in the next chapter.

Further Reading

Baldini, Gianfranco, and Adriano Pappalardo. *Elections, Electoral Systems and Volatile Voters*. Basingstoke, UK: Palgrave Macmillan, 2009.

Franklin, Mark N. *Voter Turnout and the Dynamics of Electoral Competition in Established Democracies since 1945*. New York: Cambridge University Press, 2004.

Gallagher, Michael, and Paul Mitchell. *The Politics of Electoral Systems*. Oxford: Oxford University Press, 2005.

Moser, Robert G., and Ethan Scheiner. *Electoral Systems and Political Context: How the Effects of Rules Vary across New and Established Democracies*. Cambridge: Cambridge University Press, 2012.

Norris, Pippa. *Electoral Engineering: Voting Rules and Political Behavior*. New York: Cambridge University Press, 2004.

Powell, G. Bingham Powell, Jr. *Elections as an Instrument of Democracy: Majoritarian and Proportional Visions*. New Haven. CT: Yale University Press, 2000.

Web-Based Exploration Exercise

Examine the voting system of any three other countries other than the United States, at least one of which uses a proportional representation system in its elections. Identify and discuss any one similarity and one difference with the

U.S. system of elections. A useful website for information about elections worldwide can be found at http://www.idea.int/uid/countryview.cfm.

Question for Debate and Discussion

Low voter turnout is an unusual and even somewhat embarrassing feature of politics in the United States, which has often held itself to be a model of democratic practice. To what extent and in what ways is lower voter turnout problematic? Are there features of other political systems that could usefully be adapted to the U.S. system in order to increase voter turnout? Would it be worthwhile to carry out such changes?

Chapter 10

Political Parties

Political parties are a vehicle for political participation that is central to American democracy, yet they are entirely unmentioned in the Constitution. Indeed, James Madison, in *Federalist 10*, famously warned against the "mischief of faction" in which groups pursuing their own goals undermine the collective good. Yet it would be hard to imagine how the U.S. political system would function in the absence of political parties to provide broad alternatives to the electorate—indeed, there cannot truly be said to be a single functioning democracy in the world that does not have at least two political parties that compete for power via free and fair elections.

A particularly unusual feature in the United States is that since 1800 there have been two and only two major parties at any one time—and that since 1860 these have been the same two parties: the Democrats and the Republicans. Although their geographical bases and their ideological positions have shifted over time, these same two major parties have provided stable, predictable choices for the American electorate and organizing structures within American government. No president since the unanimously elected George Washington has hailed from a minor party, nor has either house of Congress had more than a smattering of nonmajor party members. As of this writing, 533 of 535 seats in Congress, forty-nine state governorships, and all but a handful of seats in the nation's ninety-nine state legislative chambers are held by either Democrats or Republicans.

The monopolization of power in the United States by just two parties is such a fact of political life that many Americans might be surprised to learn that such a long-term two-party system is a true anomaly in the world. Indeed, far more common are countries in which two centrist parties predominate—one somewhat left of center and one somewhat right of center—but a variety of other smaller parties regularly affect the outcome of elections and win some offices. Some of these are so-called two-party-plus systems, while others are true multiparty systems of four or more parties. The number of parties can have a major effect on the politics of a country in terms of both how voters are represented by their elected officials and how political views are translated into public policy.

A Hypothetical Case Study: Electoral Systems and the Number of Parties

As discussed in the previous chapter, the number of parties in a political system that can actually contend for power is largely determined by characteristics of the electoral system. The single-member plurality electoral system used in the United States thus is a major reason for the two-party system in the United States. Recall that under this system each election can result in one and only one winner—whichever candidate gains more votes than any other candidate. The French political scientist Maurice Duverger has argued that most modern democracies have broad electorates that are divided by class, region, religion, ethnicity, and a number of other factors. Such countries, states Duverger's Law, naturally gravitate toward creating a multiparty system unless, as in the United States, the country's electoral system "punishes" the proliferation of parties.

To understand the connection between electoral systems and the number of parties, it may be helpful to consider a hypothetical case study focusing on two dimensions of political disagreement that can be found in most countries: between conservatism and liberalism over economic issues and over social issues. Suppose that 40 percent of the country has economic conservatism as their major policy concern. They might form an Economic Conservative (EC) Party favoring low taxes, probusiness policies, and limited government regulation of the economy. Another 30 percent of the country might be economic liberals, whose EL Party supports social welfare programs that redistribute income, policies that favor labor unions, and heavy government involvement in economic issues. Suppose that the remainder of the electorate is more focused on social than economic issues, with 20 percent being social liberals (SL) and the remaining 10 percent being social conservatives (SC). The resulting SL Party and SC Party likely would be in conflict over such social issues as abortion, prayer in schools, and gay rights.

Now imagine an election to a national legislature in which each of the four parties fielded its own candidate and garnered a percentage of the vote exactly equal to its support among voters, but under two different electoral systems: single-member plurality and multimember proportional representation. In the single-member plurality system, the EC Party, with its 40 percent total, has a plurality of the votes and wins the one seat being contested in that particular election. Ironically, the 60 percent of the population that voted *against* the EC Party have no representation. In effect, the smaller parties have been punished by the single-member plurality system. So what would happen next?

Upset at their exclusion from power and seeking a new electoral strategy, the second-place finisher, the EL Party, might very well seek an alliance with another party. Its most likely alliance would be with the SL Party, which shares some of its basic ideology of equality and fairness even if not all of its specific policy preferences. The merger of the 30 percent of voters who are

Party	Percentage of Vote	Result under the Single-Member Plurality System (1 seat per electoral district)	Result under the Multimember Proportional Representation System (10 seats per electoral district)
Economic Conservative Party	40%	1 seat won	4 seats won
Economic Liberal Party	30%	0 seats won	3 seats won
Social Liberal Party	20%	0 seats won	2 seats won
Social Conservative Party	10%	0 seats won	1 seat won

Figure 10.1 Breakdown of a Hypothetical Four-Party Election

economic liberals and the 20 percent of voters who are social liberals into a new Unified Liberal Party would bring their percentage of the vote to about 50 percent, meaning that they would be assured the most votes in the next election. Naturally, the economic conservatives would note this development and begin to court the social conservatives, with whom they share a concern about individual responsibility and social order. Together, they would be able to create a new Unified Conservative Party to meet the threat of the Unified Liberal Party.

By the next election, we will have seen Duverger's Law in action, and the country will have created a two-party system, with each party fighting to win just a small advantage over the other by winning over persuadable, mostly centrist swing voters. The new, larger parties will have to orient themselves toward a broader set of concerns and accept greater ideological variation among their members. Rather than having the sharper focus of the smaller parties, the new, larger parties will likely be big tents that can accommodate a majority of the country's electorate. (By now, some readers may have noted that this case study is not *entirely* hypothetical; a large coalition of economic and social conservatives is not a bad way to describe the U.S. Republican Party, while the U.S. Democratic Party might well be considered a broad umbrella organization of economic and social liberals.)

The results of the exact same election would play out very differently under a system of proportional representation with multimember districts. Under this system, there would likely be multiple legislative seats up for election, say ten for the sake of simplicity and round numbers. Under this system, the EC Party would take four seats (40 percent), the EL Party three seats (30 percent), the SL Party two seats (20 percent), and the SC Party one seat

(10 percent). Thus, none of the principal parties would be denied representation; they would each send at least one member to the legislature where they could make speeches, introduce legislation, and engage in debates that clearly represent the views of their voters. If this were a parliamentary system, they might even have the opportunity to join in a coalition government, perhaps holding a cabinet position in a ministry that is very important to their voters. While parties might make a strategic decision to join a governing coalition so as to benefit their members, there would be little incentive to lose their individual organizational and ideological identities by merging into two large parties. Thus, a multiparty system would become established, perhaps even adding additional parties over time.

Single-Party Systems

Before we consider the merits of a two-party versus a multiparty system, it is worth noting that a number of nondemocratic countries have only a single functioning party, with all other parties either formally outlawed or prevented from gaining power through various legal and extralegal means. The party in such situations may play a leading role in the society, usually on the basis of some elaborate religious, nationalistic, or other ideological justification. Formal membership in the party may be extended to the most prominent and powerful people in the country, forming a ruling stratum that dominates the entire country. Such has often been the case in Communist countries, but similar dynamics can be found in a number of other countries, such as Syria, with its dominant Baathist Party, and formerly, Iraq. Suffice it to say that in these cases the word *party* has a rather different meaning than that used in democratic countries, closer to that of a regime with a monopoly on power than of a group that contends for power via the ballot box.

Two-Party-Plus Systems

As the hypothetical case study suggests, the roots of the American two-party system are largely a function of the electoral system used in the United States, but this is not the sole explanation. The single-member plurality system has indeed led to rigid two-party structures in a number of other former British colonies, such as the relatively small island nations of Jamaica, Barbados, the Bahamas, and Malta. However, larger and more diverse countries that make use of the single-member plurality system do not exclude minor-party participation quite as much as does the United States. Some of these countries, notably Britain and Canada, have been termed two-party-plus systems. In these countries, only the two major parties in each country have any real hope of forming a parliamentary majority, but at least one other small party continues to win seats in parliament and to meaningfully influence political debate, though they rarely enter into the governing coalition.

Table 10.1 Party Systems in 60 Major Democracies

Multiparty systems	Two-Party-Plus Systems Top two parties together hold between 80% and 95% of seats in the national legislature	Two-Party Systems Top two parties hold >95% of seats in the national legislature
Argentina	Australia	Ghana
Austria	Botswana	Guyana
Belgium	Canada	Jamaica
Benin	Croatia	Mongolia
Brazil	Dominican Republic	Trinidad & Tobago
Bulgaria	France	**United States**
Chile	Greece	
Costa Rica	Hungary	
Cyprus	Japan	
Czech Republic	Mauritius	
Denmark	Namibia	
El Salvador	New Zealand	
Estonia	Poland	
Finland	South Africa	
Germany	South Korea	
India	United Kingdom	
Indonesia		
Ireland		
Israel		
Italy		
Latvia		
Lithuania		
Mali		
Mexico		
Netherlands		
Norway		
Panama		
Peru		
Portugal		
Romania		
Serbia		
Slovakia		
Slovenia		
Spain		

(Continued)

Table 10.1 (Continued)

Multiparty systems	Two-Party-Plus Systems Top two parties together hold between 80% and 95% of seats in the national legislature	Two-Party Systems Top two parties hold >95% of seats in the national legislature
Sweden		
Switzerland		
Ukraine		
Uruguay		

Control of parliament in Canada, for instance, has for generations alternated between a center-left party, the Liberals, and a center-right party, the Conservatives (under various party names). However, there are two other parties that regularly win seats in the House of Commons. One, the socialist New Democratic Party (NDP), unexpectedly won enough seats in the 2010 election to become the second-largest party in parliament and thus became the "Official Opposition." Since 1990, the country has also had a regionally based party representing French speakers at the national level. In Britain, control of parliament alternates between the Tories, the conservative party, and the Labour Party, traditionally based upon the support of labor unions. Before the rise of Labour after World War I, the Liberal Party was one of the two major parties; since then, rather than vanish, it has remained a significant third force in British politics. The party has continued to hold a significant number of offices in local government, and had a major breakthrough in 2010 when it won enough seats in parliament to force the Conservative Party to accept it as a junior coalition partner. Meanwhile, a small number of regional parties also regularly elect candidates from Scotland, Wales, and Northern Ireland.

Since both Britain and Canada use the single-member plurality system, it seems clear that the electoral system cannot be the sole explanation of the preponderance of the two major parties in the United States. In understanding why minor parties are so marginalized in U.S. politics, at least three additional factors should be considered. The first is that most developed countries have a greater range of ideological differences than the United States. The British Labour Party and the Canadian NDP have both traditionally been socialist parties, meeting the need for the party system in those countries to stretch from laissez-faire market capitalism all the way to redistributive socialism—too great a reach for just two parties. The historical failure of socialism in the United States (for reasons discussed in chapters 11 and 12) has resulted in a much narrower spectrum of views that could be considered mainstream.

Second, the Scots, Welsh, and Northern Irish consider themselves separate nations from the majority English in Britain, and the Quebecois view themselves as a distinct society within Canada, providing added impetus for the maintenance of ethnolinguistically based minor parties. The United States, however, is indisputably one nation. From time to time, regional candidates in the United States have attempted to form separate parties, as when Southern Democrats ran for president in 1948 and 1968 as the candidates of breakaway parties focused on states' rights, winning thirty-nine and forty-six electoral votes, respectively. But these have been short-lived and ultimately ineffective efforts. Further, the Democratic and Republican Parties in the United States are more decentralized than are parties in other countries. Thus, Republicans in New England or Democrats in the Deep South, who may be at odds with the leadership of their national parties, have a great deal of latitude and flexibility in how they conduct their affairs. This further diminishes the temptation for regional parties to break away from the national party as might occur in more rigidly centralized party systems.

Finally, minor parties in a parliamentary system have some hope of entering into a coalition to share in executive power, but in the United States the president is elected separately, and the presidency is an office held by only a single individual. The rules of the Electoral College make it even more difficult for a minor-party candidate to be a contender because most states allocate their electoral votes such that the winner of the plurality takes all of that state's electoral votes. Thus, minor-party candidate H. Ross Perot won 19 percent of the popular vote for president in 1992 and 8 percent in 1996 but received zero electoral votes both times because he never won a majority in an entire state. With control of the executive firmly out of reach, it is especially difficult for any third party in the United States to gather much steam on a national basis, further deterring the emergence of a two-party-plus system in the United States. Similar factors make it difficult for third parties to establish a foothold even at the state level, from which they might grow into national contenders for power, although independent candidates have occasionally been successful in winning governorships.

Multiparty Systems

In contrast to two-party and two-party-plus systems are those in which four, five, six—or even more than a dozen—parties regularly contend for power. At the lower end of this spectrum are countries that have a relatively high threshold for entry into parliament, thus minimizing the role of more extreme parties. In Germany, for instance, a party must receive 5 percent of the national vote to be allocated any seats in the Bundestag under proportional-representation rules. This has had the effect of diminishing the electoral appeal of extreme parties, most notably the far-right Republikaner Party and the former Communist Party of East Germany, both of which have been excluded from or marginalized within the Bundestag. Further, Germany uses a mixed electoral system in which each voter casts two votes, one for a seat to be decided under the single-member plurality system and a second for seats allocated on the basis of proportional representation using party lists. The use of the single-member plurality system to choose half of the Bundestag serves to reduce the number of parties, just as it does in Britain and Canada. Despite these factors, Germany still generally has four or five parties that might be considered significant players. This has led to a great deal of stability in German politics, with control alternating between the Christian Democrats and the Social Democrats, often in coalition with a smaller party and sometimes in a so-called "grand coalition" with each other.

Once the threshold for entry into parliament is lowered even further, the number of parties proliferates. As seen in the previous chapter, Israel has only a 2 percent threshold and a pure proportional representation system. In 2009, twelve parties won seats in the Knesset, showing far more diversity and variation than are found in most other countries. Three of the largest parties represented more or less the classic span of left-wing, centrist, and right-wing parties (Labour, Kadima, and Likud), but other parties drew support specifically from Israeli Arabs, Russian Jewish émigrés, and Jews of Sephardic, or Mediterranean, ancestry. Ideologically, the parties ranged from the unabashedly Communist to the stridently nationalistic. Further instability is added to the Israeli party system by the frequent appearance of new parties and disappearance of old ones. In fact, the party that won the most votes in 2006, Kadima, was contesting its first election that year.

The same threshold of 2 percent and pure proportional representation also prevails in Italy, with even more fragmented results in that country's 2006 elections. Nine parties on the left won more than 2 percent of the vote, including two separate Communist parties, as did five parties on the right, including one party with fascist roots and another sympathetic to separatist impulses in the wealthy north of Italy. The electoral situation in Italy was not quite as chaotic as it may seem, however, because many of the parties had formed various electoral alliances prior to the vote, so that protracted post-election coalition negotiations were not needed. Still, the end result was a razor-thin margin for the left, which was bitterly contested for a time, and the government fell after a vote of no confidence just nine months later. The long history of unstable party coalitions in Italy has seriously hampered the ability of the government to tackle violence, corruption, and inequality in that country. Amid economic crisis in 2010, the country had to virtually ignore its usual political structure to install a technocratic prime minister to manage government fiscal policies.

In the case of both Israel and Italy, the fragmentation of the party system both reflects and reinforces preexisting ideological, socioeconomic, religious, regional, and other tensions in those countries. However, multiparty systems do not necessarily lead to greater discord. The Nordic nations, for instance, have multiparty systems but also have political cultures in which either broad coalition governments are created with little rancor, or minority governments can be allowed by the opposition to rule without being brought down by early votes of no confidence. Clearly, the relative ethnic homogeneity and socioeconomic equality of the citizenry in such countries as Norway, Sweden, and Denmark helps to promote a sense of national cooperation.

Somewhat counterintuitively, however, multiparty systems can also be used to bridge differences within highly diverse countries. Two of the most ethnically divided long-term democracies in Europe are Belgium, with two major linguistic communities, and Switzerland, with three. Yet both of these countries have also created formal and informal power-sharing agreements across political parties that foster consensus over conflict. In all of these examples, it is probably the case that consensus building has been greatly aided by economic prosperity and social tranquility and also by a high degree of decentralized power through robust federalism. Switzerland, which has a unique seven-member executive, has gone so far as to establish the so-called Magic Formula, in which a set number of the seven slots go to representatives of particular parties and language groups. In Belgium, linguistic communities can block legislation that might affect their fundamental interests, though even this has not quelled separatist impulses that may someday split the nation into its two major regions of Wallonia and Flanders.

Sadly for the most divided and unstable countries of the world, it seems that such consensus arrangements, sometimes called "consociational democracies," must evolve naturally within a country and cannot be imposed from outside. Attempts to establish a delicate consociational political balance among the Christians, Sunni Muslims, and Shiite Muslims of Lebanon broke down in 1975 into a bloody fifteen-year civil war. A consociational solution would have been ideal in the case of Bosnia, as discussed in chapter 2, but deep-seated animosities have at least thus far prevented any such creative solutions there. In Iraq, however, the consociational arrangements established under the 2005 constitution for power sharing among the Sunni Arab, Shiite Arab, and Kurdish populations has had some limited success, but remains a work in progress.

The U.S. Two-Party System in Comparative Perspective

What does it mean for the U.S. political system that the same two political parties have vied for power for more than two-thirds of the country's history? Certainly, one major impact has been a much greater degree of stability than exists in the many countries where new parties are created, splinter, merge, or vanish on a regular basis. Although their geographical bases and their ideological positions have shifted over time, the same two major parties have for nearly 150 years provided stable, predictable choices for the American electorate and useful organizing structures within American government.

The downside of stability, of course, can be inflexibility, inertia, and even stagnation. With the same two parties all but assured of dominance, it can be hard for new voices and new ideas to enter the U.S. political system. In particular, minor parties in the United States struggle to make an impression of any kind. Throughout continental Europe, for instance, environmentalism-oriented Green Parties have flourished, but the U.S. Green Party has struggled to elect even a few state legislators. Not entirely coincidentally, the two major parties have been promising for generations to advance research on clean alternative fuel sources with little real progress, nor has the major challenge of global warming been seriously addressed by the United States.

Similarly, the Reform Party that emerged with the presidential candidacy of H. Ross Perot in 1992 and 1996 rose meteorically and fell just as quickly, garnering less than 1 percent of the vote in 2000 and splintering thereafter. Although the Reform Party was unable to mount a challenge to the two-party system, it did manage to influence the national agenda. After Perot won 19 percent of the popular vote in 1992, both the Democrats and the Republicans quickly repositioned themselves to capture the Reform Party's signature issue, which was concern about the federal deficit. The once seemingly unconquerable issue of the budget deficit was suddenly resolved in the mid-1990s, a time when the country was awash in surpluses. There were other factors contributing to this shift, such as high tax revenues from a robust economy, but the electoral challenge posed by the Reform Party was certainly a contributing factor. Thus, the experience of the Reform Party is typical in that minor parties are more likely to alter the positions of the major parties than to achieve any direct impact or win offices themselves. Critics charge, however, that once the groundswell of support for a particular minor party has been coopted, its fragile institutions undermined, and its threat dissipated, politics as usual is restored; consider the return of budget deficits after 2001.

The U.S. two-party system has also been faulted for denying voters the opportunity to support a party that clearly reflects their own views. The larger the number of parties in a country, the narrower the set of issues on which each party tends to focus. To return to the hypothetical case study described earlier, if a country had four parties based on economic conservatism, social conservatism, economic liberalism, and social liberalism, each of those parties would be fairly tightly focused on a core set of issues and concerns. Both during elections and in government, the economic conservative party would emphasize policies that benefit business and promote economic growth. The social conservative party would focus on topics that they see as contributing to a decline in social order and traditional values. The economic liberal party would stress the need to protect labor unions and redistribute income. And the social liberal party would concentrate on minority rights and diversity concerns. Although any of these parties might have to compromise to some degree if it entered into a coalition to create a parliamentary majority, the individual parties would not lose their separate organizational structures or their basic priorities. When the number of parties proliferates further, as in Israel and Italy, then each party can become even more specialized, such as by focusing on the concerns of specific ethnic groups, religious beliefs, or regions.

However, when a country has only two parties, both must be "big tents" large enough to encompass the views and garner the support of at least 50 percent of the electorate. Such parties can become vague and unfocused in their platforms, trying to appease an overly broad array of conflicting views. Thus, voters are less likely to see their own views clearly articulated by either of the parties and must tolerate the presence within their party of views with which they may strongly disagree.

Exactly such a muddled situation has emerged on the incendiary issue of illegal immigration in the United States. The economic conservative wing of the Republican Party has sought to maintain a steady supply of inexpensive labor, proposing various guest-worker programs. Social conservatives within the Republican Party, in contrast, tend to see illegal aliens as lawbreakers who should be punished. A parallel debate has also developed within the Democratic Party, with economic liberals, who are often allied with labor unions, concerned that low-cost labor may undermine the wages of American workers. Meanwhile, social liberals in the Democratic Party often view undocumented immigrants as a vulnerable minority in need of social services and protection from exploitation. American voters thus cannot look to a single party that clearly reflects their own views on the issue of immigration, whereas in a multiparty system they might be offered clear policy alternatives by several parties. The result has largely been infighting, political paralysis, and an incoherent policy that fails to monitor immigrants, defend the borders, maximize economic benefits, or protect human rights.

The two-party system in the United States is also related to the striking narrowness and rightward tilt of the American ideological spectrum (a theme that is discussed from a historical perspective in chapter 11). Critics from both the right and the left have argued that the Democratic and Republican Parties can barely be distinguished from each other. Ralph Nader, a perennial leftist presidential candidate, called his major party opponents "Republicrats," while George Wallace, an archconservative presidential candidate in 1968, famously declared that there "isn't a dime's worth of difference between the parties." While these are overstatements, they do underline the reality that the Democrats and the Republicans are clearly distinguishable on only a relative handful of issues, such as abortion, taxation, and some elements of foreign policy. Both parties are in basic agreement on the majority of public-policy issues. Such similarity between the two major parties is in marked contrast to the broader political spectrum found in multiparty democracies. As noted earlier, the parties represented in the Italian parliament stretch from the far left, essentially old-style Communism, to the far right, with some roots in Mussolini-era fascism. Further, the leaders of such parties in Western Europe are often household names, not the obscure, marginalized figures of their ideological counterparts in the United States.

In addition to being relatively similar on many issues, both the Democratic and the Republican Parties are more conservative than most parties in the developed world. A useful comparison can be made between the United States and France, where politics stretch much further to the left. It has credibly been argued that presidential candidates of the center-left party in the United States, the Democrats, would be considered center-right candidates in France—and some Republicans would be considered candidates of the far right. This leftward tilt of the political systems found in France is largely emblematic of that found throughout Western Europe (and is discussed further in the case study in the next chapter).

A final characteristic of U.S. parties that bears reiteration here is that they are weaker than parties in countries with parliamentary democracies. As discussed in the previous chapter, party leaders in parliamentary democracies typically have several major sources of strength lacking in the United States: they control nominations during elections as well as upward career mobility from backbencher to ministerial position. The decentralization of the party system in the United States is also a factor. In many countries, particularly unitary states, there is likely to be one powerful national organization for each party, with local or provincial branches simply carrying out the wishes of the national party. In the United States, however, there are separate party organizations in every state that are quasi-independent and only partly subject to the demands of the national party organization. An example would be Montana, in which, in the 2012 election, local Democrats won statewide races for governor and senator but President Obama lost by some fourteen points to the Republican challenger, Mitt Romney.

The U.S. parties also have limited sway over the rank-and-file members of the party. In this sense, the Republicans and Democrats are good examples of so-called cadre parties in that most political activity is undertaken by a relatively small core of leaders and activists. In the United States, the party identification of voters can be quite a significant factor in the way that they view political issues and how they vote, but some voters still regularly cross lines to support candidates of the opposite party. Such cadre parties are in contrast to mass-membership parties, most notably Labor parties, in which membership in a labor union and in the party is simultaneous. In such mass-membership parties, rank-and-file members may be much more influential in the setting of party policy positions than they are in cadre parties. But, in turn, these parties can make much more compelling ideological and psychological claims on the loyalties of their members.

Despite these weaknesses, the two major U.S. parties do still have an exceptional measure of clout in that they have long been the only electorally viable parties, and on some levels they collude to maintain their long-term claims to power. For instance, the two parties have used their long-standing monopoly on power to make it difficult for third parties to emerge, such as by creating demanding rules for access to the ballot and high thresholds for public financing and participation in campaign debates. In this regard, the Democrats and Republicans fare better than many of their counterparts in other separation-of-powers systems. Political parties are particularly weak in most of Latin America, where the separation-of-powers system is combined with the use of proportional representation in legislative elections. Thus, not only do Latin American parties lack the tools to impose party discipline that are found in parliamentary countries, but they also experience the fragmentation into multiple parties that comes from the use of proportional representation. This weakness of the party system is another contributing factor in the political instability commonly found in Central and South America.

Conclusion: Why It All Matters

Political parties represent important collective vehicles for citizens who share political views. The type, number, and activities of parties may vary widely from country to country but always conform to the institutions and processes of their countries, while also significantly shaping the politics and government of those countries. The long-term two-party system found in the United States is quite unusual in comparative terms, but at this point it is also an integral part of the American political scene and is firmly anchored by its winner-take-all electoral procedures.

The U.S. two-party system can, paradoxically, contribute to both consensus and polarization. In terms of consensus, having two large, elite, essentially permanent establishment parties leads both parties to strongly support the status quo, reinforcing the relative narrowness of the American political spectrum and the fundamental similarities between the two major parties while marginalizing other voices and new ideas. At the same time, on those key wedge issues on which the two major parties *do* substantively differ—a list that usually includes tax rates, the degree of government regulation of business, unilateralism in foreign policy, abortion, and support for social diversity—partisan battles become all the more shrill and unreasonable, since the parties have to find some way to appeal to their respective bases while also clearly differentiating themselves for swing voters. By contrast, multiparty systems offer a greater opportunity for a variety of political viewpoints to be aired but, when taken to an extreme, have led to coalition governments in some countries that are often fragile and fleeting and that are just as likely to lead to rancor and political paralysis, particularly in poorer and more recently established democracies. It may well be there is a happy middle ground to be found, such as in a country with three, four, or perhaps five viable parties, in which real competition takes place yet effective government coalitions can be formed.

Further Reading

Bogaards, Matthijs, and Françoise Boucek. *Dominant Political Parties and Democracy: Concepts, Measures, Cases, and Comparisons.* London: Routledge, 2010.

Dalton, Russell J., David M. Farrell, and Ian McAllister. *Political Parties and Democratic Linkage: How Parties Organize Democracy.* Oxford: Oxford University Press, 2011.

Gunther, Richard, Jose Ramon Montero, and Juan Linz, eds. *Political Parties: Old Concepts and New Challenges.* New York: Oxford University Press, 2002.

Hazan, Reuven Y., and Gideon Rahat. *Democracy within Parties: Candidate Selection Methods and Their Political Consequences.* Oxford: Oxford University Press, 2010.

Ware, Alan. *Political Parties and Party Systems.* New York: Oxford University Press, 1995.

Webb, Paul, David M. Farrell, and Ian Holliday, eds. *Political Parties in Advanced Industrial Democracies.* New York: Oxford University Press, 2003.

Web-Based Exploration Exercise

Visit the websites of significant political parties in any two countries outside the United States (a significant party can be defined as one with more than one member of a national legislature). Identify at least one similarity and one difference between the way in which those parties present themselves to voters via their website, and compare them with the Democrats and Republicans in the United States. A useful website for accessing world political parties can be found at www.gksoft.com/govt/en/parties.html.

Question for Debate and Discussion

The single-member plurality system and other factors in the United States serve to effectively exclude minor parties from electoral competition. On the whole, is the effect of such exclusion on politics and public policy in the United States positive or negative? What features of other political systems could be adapted to the U.S. political system to expand voter choice among political parties? What might be the disadvantages of such changes?

Chapter 11
Public Opinion and Political Values

Unlike voting behavior, protest actions, or the activities of political parties and interest groups, public opinion is not in itself a form of political participation. However, the views of the public on a range of issues and the political values that undergird those views greatly influence other forms of political behavior. These help to determine, for instance, for whom citizens vote, whether they engage in other political activities, and whether they vote at all. Further, in an era of near-constant polling of every type, public opinion surveys have become a de facto form of political participation, albeit a passive one based on the initiative of newspapers, government officials, and other actors who collect information from the mass public. This is especially true in countries, such as the United States, with vigorous free presses and frequent competitive elections. But even closed, authoritarian governments must take the pulse of public opinion, if only to figure out how to promote the cooperation and dampen the resistance of their populations.

In the short run, public opinion can be volatile and appear unstable. Responses to public opinion polls vary over time and according to specific circumstances. For instance, after the September 11 terrorist attacks, concerns about security rose sharply in U.S. polls; likewise, financial worries routinely increase in times of economic recession, as in 2008. Such shifts are fairly easily explained and common among populations around the world. Of greater interest for present purposes are broader and deeper patterns of beliefs, values, and opinions in the United States and how those compare with those in other countries.

It is notoriously difficult to generalize about the political opinions held by any group, much less by entire countries. Indeed, the very attempt to identify and define the political culture of a country runs the risk of descending into overly broad judgments and casual stereotyping, and it certainly can never represent the views of every member of that country. Thus, for instance, the oft-noted tendency of the Japanese to be group oriented and Americans to be individualists obscures the fact that Japanese are, of course, all individuals and that Americans gather together in groups of all types. To say that people in Iran support the commingling of religion and government while those in the United States prefer the separation of church and state overlooks those Iranians who might prefer a more secular state and those Americans who are ready to embrace theocracy. But over time and across surveys, it does become possible to generalize about the values, beliefs, and opinions of countries in the aggregate and to see how they are similar to and different from those in other countries.

Case Study: The World Values Survey

One of the largest, most comprehensive, and most influential studies of comparative political values and public opinion is the World Values Survey, led by the political scientist Ronald Inglehart and colleagues in the 1990s. Between 1990 and 1993, with several follow-up studies since then, the World Values Survey asked some 350 questions of thousands of respondents in dozens of countries representing 70 percent of the world's population. The societies varied widely in terms of geography, culture, politics, and economics, ranging from democratic to authoritarian regimes, from laissez-faire capitalist to central-directed socialist economies, from the wealthiest to some of the poorest countries. The survey's often-cited results provide a basis for standardized examination of dozens of topics relating to politics, economics, and social issues.

The single most compelling product of the World Values Survey has come to be known as the Inglehart Values Map, which is presented in Figure 11.1. (The map and accompanying discussion can be accessed at www.worldvalues survey.com/library/set_illustrations.html.) Depending upon their responses to particular questions, the forty societies in the study are placed on the map according to an X coordinate on the horizontal axis and a Y coordinate on the vertical axis. The X coordinate is fairly straightforward, relating to *survival* values (emphasizing the struggle for economic and physical security) versus *well-being* values (focusing on more subjective standards of self-expression and quality of life).

The Y coordinate refers to the source of authority cited by the respondents in their answers: whether it was traditional or secular-rational. Those who were on the traditional side cited obedience to religious authority and strong adherence to the standards of behavior expected by the family, community, and nation. As might be expected, the traditionalists believe in absolute standards of morality; uphold traditional views of divorce, abortion, euthanasia, and related social issues; and are highly nationalistic. Those on the secular-rational side embody the opposite set of values, stressing individual achievement and personal liberty with a heavy emphasis on the role of an active state and comparatively less deference to the expectations of religion, families, or communities.

The remarkable result of the mapping of the forty societies provides visual confirmation that they cluster together in highly predictable ways. The

154 The American Anomaly

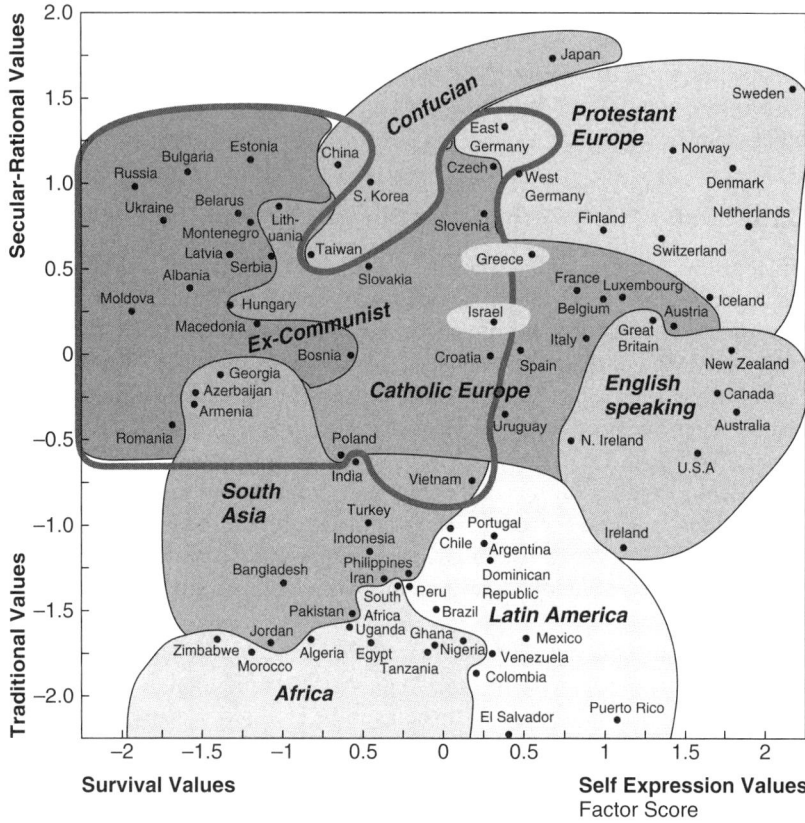

Figure 11.1 The Inglehart Values Map. Reprinted from Ronald Inglehart and Christian Welzel, *Modernization, Cultural Change and Democracy*. New York: Cambridge University Press, 2005.

Inglehart Values Map strongly suggests that the political values held by people around the world are closely related to their specific geographic, historic, economic, and religious experiences and traditions. For instance, the countries of South Asia, Latin America, and Africa each form distinctive clusters, and all three regions—representing the survey's sample from the developing world—strongly advocate traditional values over secular-rational values. Similarly, the Confucian countries of East Asia, the formerly Communist countries of Eastern Europe, the traditionally Catholic countries of Europe, and the traditionally Protestant countries of Europe all also cluster, generally favoring secular-rational authority over traditional authority.

As might be expected on the dimension of survival versus well-being, the poorer countries of the world reflect a much greater emphasis on survival than the wealthier countries, with the countries of Africa and South Asia nearly all emphasizing fundamental economic and physical security. Populations of formerly Communist countries also tend to heavily emphasize survival values, even though most are objectively wealthier than countries in the developing world. The economic and political uncertainty and upheaval of the 1990s in Eastern Europe and the former Soviet Union, including the loss of the cradle-to-grave social programs provided by Communism, seem to have raised great anxieties about physical and economic security. Latin American countries, many of which are somewhat wealthier than some African and Asian countries, modestly veer in the direction of values focused on well-being. Western European countries all fit clearly on the self-expression side of the map.

So where does the United States fit into all of this? On the dimension of survival versus well-being—essentially the economic dimension—the United States is much like the other countries of the wealthy world, placing right in the middle of the European countries and closest to such other wealthy nations as Austria, Switzerland, Iceland, and Norway. Most Americans, like Western Europeans, are not consumed with the question of how they will get by on a day-to-day basis but focus instead on quality-of-life issues.

Strikingly, however, the United States rates traditional sources of authority more highly than *any* other established wealthy country and more highly than all but three countries of the developed world (the devoutly Catholic and traditionally poor European nations of Ireland, Poland, and Portugal). On the spectrum of traditional values versus secular-rational values, the United States places midway between the two polar opposites of Japan and El Salvador; its position on the map puts the United States rather far from most of the countries of Europe and closest to Uruguay, Romania, India, and Vietnam. When both axes are considered, the United States falls within a clear cluster of English-speaking countries alongside Australia, Canada, and New Zealand, with Britain and Ireland slightly further away. This clustering clearly suggests a significant role for history, culture, geography, legal inheritance, and even language in the making of public opinion.

U.S. Public Opinion in Comparative Perspective

As the World Values Survey suggests, the United States is among the most typical of developed nations in some ways and among the most atypical in other ways. The ways in which the United States is typical—its emphasis on well-being values over survival values—are fairly easily explained and unsurprising. Inglehart and his colleagues refer to the positioning of the United States—and virtually all other countries of the developed world—as reflecting a shift from industrial to postindustrial societies. The unprecedented affluence of the developed world has meant that most people do not find basic material existence needs to be more compelling than "postmaterial" values such as control over one's work circumstances, the importance of leisure pursuits, and general life satisfaction. The economies of the developed world are so prosperous that they provide many opportunities for jobs that pay well enough to satisfy basic human needs. The existence of a social safety net for those in economic hardship further allows most people in Europe and North America to avoid being preoccupied with simple survival. Given this basic security, people's minds naturally gravitate to higher-order concerns such as psychological well-being, personal fulfillment, and opportunities for self-expression.

Income inequality certainly continues to persist in the developed world in general, and in the United States in particular. However, only the most unfortunate citizens in the developed countries—such as the homeless—experience levels of material deprivation comparable with those of great masses of people in the developing world. That is to say, the poor in Western Europe or North America may experience relative deprivation in areas facing substandard education, shoddy housing, and limited disposable income. But, despite the use of the same word, poverty in the United States is categorically different from poverty in a developing-world context. This is made manifest by the willingness, even eagerness, of millions of undocumented immigrants to leave their own countries to occupy even the lowest rung of the socioeconomic ladder in the developed world. Mexicans coming to the United States, Algerians moving to France, Turks arriving in Germany, or Vietnamese relocating to Australia—all of these offer striking testimony to the immensity of the disparities between the poor and the rich countries of the world.

While it is not difficult to explain why Americans are unlike those in the developing world, it is rather more challenging to explain the ways in which Americans are unlike those in other wealthy democratic nations. As noted, the United States emphasizes traditional over secular-rational values more than almost any other developed nation. To some extent, this difference should not be overstated; Americans are only midway on this scale and are notably more secular-rational than the peoples of nearly all developing countries. And significant swaths of the American population, mostly registered Democrats and ideological liberals, hold views not too far removed from the European mainstream. Still, some of these differences are real enough to offer some sharp contrasts with Western European and other developed countries and often are the basis for miscommunication and mistrust between the United States and its allies. Many of these issues have been cogently analyzed through various surveys conducted by the Pew Global Attitudes Project (www. pewglobal.org), whose data form the basis of the discussion in the next section. Public opinion and political values in the United States particularly stand out in the areas of strong religiosity, moral values informed by religion, and deep patriotism and national pride but profound skepticism about an activist role for government.

Religiosity and Moral Values

As might be expected from the Inglehart Values Map, Americans are strikingly more religious than people in most other developed countries. In fact, the

United States is the *only* country in the world that is democratic, wealthy, and highly religious, making for a truly anomalous combination. In the United States, 94 percent of the population indicate a belief in God, whereas only 61 percent in Britain and 50 percent in Germany did so. Most Americans (58 percent) state that a belief in God is necessary for a person to be moral; only 30 percent of Canadians and 13 percent of French agree; a similar majority of Americans (59 percent) call religion very important in the lives, while 27 percent of Italians and 21 percent of Germans hold this view. Rates of membership in organized religious bodies and attendance at worship services are also higher in the United States than anywhere else in the Western world. The religiosity of Americans has some clear impact on their opinions on a variety of issues. Americans are generally more likely than people in other developed countries to view prostitution, abortion, suicide, and euthanasia as being never justifiable. Just 60 percent of Americans but 81 percent of British and 87 percent of Germans agree that homosexuality should be accepted by society.

While Americans may be more progressive on these social issues than most developing-world populations, the relative prudishness of Americans is an object of some wonderment and even scorn on the part of Europeans. Likewise, the idea that an American president could be threatened with removal from office for a sexual dalliance with a young woman baffled many in Europe; as one American comedian noted at the time, the French would probably impeach their president if it were discovered that he *didn't* have a mistress. And, indeed, when former French President François Mitterrand died, his burial was attended by his wife and their sons as well as his long-term mistress and their grown daughter. Mitterrand, who was elected twice as president, was also an openly avowed atheist, a religious sensibility that a majority of Americans say would disqualify someone from their vote for U.S. president. More recently, less than a year into his first term, the wife of President Nicholas Sarkozy left him for the man with whom she had had a public affair in 2005. After a quick divorce, Sarkozy married an Italian supermodel he had known for less than six months—and the main reaction from the French public was the proverbial Gallic shrug.

As might be imagined, many of the religious and moral issues that are the subject of heated debate in the United States have been largely resolved in Western Europe. Access to abortion services, contraception, and comprehensive sex education is largely uncontroversial. Assisted suicide for the terminally ill, same-sex marriage, and use of soft drugs such as marijuana are less universally embraced, but there is a strong, clear trend toward broader acceptance of these issues. Some issues that regularly arise in American politics debate—such as whether to teach evolution, creationism, "intelligent design," or all of these in public schools—would be considered akin to debating flat-earth theories in most of Europe.

Thus, it is clear that Americans are quite anomalous on religion when compared with the populations of most other developed nations. In fact, however, it is *those* nations that are anomalous when viewed in world context: 80 to 97 percent of respondents from fourteen African and South Asian countries rated religion as very important, while figures for most South American respondents were between 60 and 80 percent. Also, European populations are much less religious than they were even two generations ago, with their withdrawal from religion occurring mostly since the time of World War II.

Thus, the real question may not be why Americans are religious but why Europeans have become so secularized in recent decades. The answer in most of the formerly Communist countries of Central and Eastern Europe seems fairly clear cut—forty years under the sway of authoritarian governments that discouraged religion and promoted atheism have disrupted traditional patterns of religious devotion in most, although not all, places. The decline of religion in most of Western Europe—and also in other Western countries such as Canada, Australia, and New Zealand—appears rather more challenging to explain.

One line of reasoning holds that the rise of robust government welfare programs in Western countries undermined the traditional role of religious bodies in distributing charity. From this perspective, church attendance declined as people needed neither the material resources formerly distributed by churches nor, amid postwar conditions of peace and prosperity, the spiritual comfort that religion can provide. In the United States, by contrast, nongovernmental actors, and in particular religious institutions, still play a major role in providing services. It is also striking that some of the most ardently religious communities in the United States are those that still face social and economic difficulties, notably African Americans. Likewise, the most thoroughly secularized European countries, those in the Nordic countries, also have the most elaborate social welfare systems.

Another line of reasoning argues that the established, state-supported churches in many of those countries seemed stodgy and dull in comparison with the profusion of religious denominations within the United States. Official churches that in the nineteenth and early twentieth centuries were supported by tax dollars or that received other types of public support did not need to fill the pews in order to survive. Over time, they grew to be inward looking and uninspiring, a drab obligation on occasions such as weddings and funerals rather than a vital part of people's lives. The United States, by contrast, was founded by many people who were seeking liberty from such hidebound and oppressive established churches, and as such a wall of separation was introduced between church and state by the First Amendment. The result was a far more competitive market in the United States, where many different religious traditions developed, emphasizing distinctive theological perspectives and worship styles and thus engaging a broader swath of society. The presence of so many different religious bodies has also fostered a spirit of tolerance in the United States, in which many people hold their own beliefs strongly but respect the rights of others to have different religious convictions (as long as they have religious convictions of some sort).

On religious, social, and moral issues in the United States, there are definitely also libertarian strains that prefer the noninterference of government in the people's personal lives, as well as some secular and progressive strains whose views are not dissimilar from those of Western Europe, including some elements of the media and educational elite. Indeed, one American political commentator, Fox News's Bill O'Reilly, has built a career on condemning "secular progressives" in the United States and finds himself with the type of huge, receptive audience that would be unthinkable in most developed countries.

National Pride but Skepticism about Big Government

Another strikingly consistent finding in comparative public opinion polling is that Americans reveal levels of national pride and patriotic fervor much more like those of people in the developing world than those in the developed world. When asked if they are "very proud" to be citizens of their countries, 71 percent of Americans agreed, but only 45 percent of British and 38 percent of French and Italians did so. (By contrast, 87 percent of Filipinos, 72 percent of Nigerians, and 67 percent of Indians shared this sense of national pride.) Americans appear to have a clearer sense of where they are in the world, and that is at the top. The enormity of the American economy, the power of the American military, the influence of American political ideas, the popularity of American films, television, and music—all of these lead many Americans to reflexively assume their country and its culture to be "the best." Even before the rise of American power in the twentieth century, there was a well-established strain in American political thought that the country had a special destiny. Unencumbered by the corruption and stagnation of the Old World, many thought that the United States would play a special role in the world by offering a religiously inspired image of the nation as a "city on a hill" and the "last, best hope of mankind." The global economic, political, and military setbacks experienced by the United States since 2001 have only partly diminished these long-term views. (For more on the concept of "American exceptionalism," see the brief bibliographic essay at the end of this book.)

Notably, however, these feelings of national superiority do not particularly translate into a desire among the public to export American ways to other countries or for the United States to be a superpower wielding hegemonic control over the planet. When American poll respondents were asked to rank a list of foreign policy concerns, promoting democracy abroad was in last place, as over fifty percentage points behind such pragmatic concerns such as combating terrorism, eliminating weapons of mass destruction, and protecting energy supplies. Eighty-three percent endorsed focusing on national problems over international concerns. Why, then, if the American people are not especially eager to build a modern American empire, does the United States play such an overwhelming role in international affairs? As discussed in chapter 13, the answer may have as much to do with the logic of international relations as with the opinions, processes, and institutions of U.S. politics and government.

Another striking pattern is that, despite strong feelings of patriotism about the United States as a nation, Americans are deeply skeptical of "big government." Far more Americans see "big government" as a major threat to liberty (64 percent) than "big business" (26 percent) or "big labor" (8 percent). When asked whether government should leave people alone to pursue their own goals or should offer guarantees to everyone in need, 58 percent of Americans endorsed self-determination, but only 43 percent of Canadians, 36 percent of French, and 24 percent of Italians had the same response. Part of this is rooted in a belief in self-reliance that are among the highest in the developed world. Just 32 percent of Americans agree with the statement that "success in life is determined by forces outside our control," whereas 68 percent of Germans, 66 percent of Italians, and 48 percent of Britons do so.

Although the size of the U.S. government, and its commitment to the "general welfare" of its citizens has grown dramatically over time, the nondefense sector still remains far smaller than most of its counterparts in the wealthy industrialized democracies. And although many Americans register approval for specific government programs, such as Medicaid, they remain largely skeptical of or even outright hostile to public policy designed to provide social services and to try to even out social inequalities. This skepticism played out powerfully in 2009, when Barack Obama and congressional Democrats met with fierce political resistance to their (ultimately successful) proposals for nationwide comprehensive health-care reform. Much the same pattern has repeated itself throughout U.S. history. As a result, when compared with most developed nations, the United States has only a quite modest commitment to promoting socioeconomic equality, as discussed in more detail in the next chapter.

Conclusion: Why It All Matters

Comparative public opinion polls reveal that the United States is quite unusual in its political values and views, although it is not necessarily the most unusual country. Pew researchers have calculated an Exceptionalism Index that shows differences in public opinion in countries around the world. On this index, the Japanese, with a score of 338, were far more exceptional than Americans, as to a lesser extent, were Argentines (240) in South America, Jordanians (236) in the Middle East, and Angolans (235) in Africa. Still, with a score of 220 on this index, Americans stood out among the Western democracies (for instance, France scored 102, Germany 98, and Britain 77). In terms of political views and values, Americans are not entirely dissimilar from citizens of other developed nations. But on a handful of issues, including religion, the role of government, and national pride, they are quite anomalous indeed.

Public opinion can be placed alongside three other major influences—constitutional framework, the institutions of government, and processes of political participation—as a key factor in determining who is elected to office, what public-policy positions they take, and what the overall role of government will be in the United States. Yet public opinion is a complex and multilayered phenomenon in which incremental evolution in response to change is undergirded by long-term, historically conditioned political values. It reveals stable long-term patterns and yet can be highly responsive to whatever issues, from armed conflict to tax rates to the "culture war" to crime to inflation, happen to seem most urgent at the moment. The last two chapters of this volume, on domestic policy and foreign policy, then, may best be considered as the ultimate outcome of public opinion, along with all of the other issues raised in the earlier chapters of this book.

Further Reading

Dalton, Russell J. *Citizen Politics: Public Opinion and Political Parties in Advanced Industrial Democracies*, 5th Edition Washington, DC: Congressional Quarterly Press, 2008.

Inglehart, Ronald, and Christian Welzel. *Modernization, Cultural Change, and Democracy: The Human Development Sequence.* Cambridge: Cambridge University Press, 2005.

Kohut, Andrew, and Bruce Stokes. *America against the World: How We Are Different and Why We Are Disliked.* Pew Global Attitudes Project. New York: Henry Holt, 2006.

Web-Based Exploration Exercise

Visit the website of the Pew Global Attitudes Project (www.pewglobal.com), and examine the findings of any two polls on a related topic. Compare and contrast views in the United States with those in other countries, looking for common trends and divergences.

Question for Debate and Discussion

We have seen that both political values and political institutions in the United States are rather anomalous when viewed in comparative perspective. To what extent and in what ways do you think that American political values have shaped political institutions, and vice versa?

Part IV
Public Policy and Policymaking

Chapter 12

Domestic Policy
Socioeconomic Regulation, Civil Liberties, and Civil Rights

It has almost become a cliché that the United States has some of the developed world's most expansive and entrenched political freedoms, particularly in the realm of civil liberties and civil rights, yet has a social welfare system that is one of the developed world's least well established—one that is even considered miserly by no small number of critics. As with most clichés, this is a point that can easily be overstated. In fact, political freedoms found in most of the developed world are on par with those in the United States, although national customs and constitutional practices vary from country to country. And while the U.S. social safety network does contain some significant gaps, modern American society is hardly the dog-eat-dog, Darwinian struggle portrayed by some detractors on the political left. In fact, the combined efforts of national, state, and local governments, along with an active charitable sector, have led to the provision of substantial, if incomplete, social services to the vast majority of citizens in the United States. At the same time, no country, however well developed its social welfare system, is completely immune from poverty and inequality.

Still, observations about the expansive nature of American political freedoms and the limited range of American social protections certainly contain a kernel of truth and in fact may be the single most salient feature of U.S. domestic public policy when viewed from a comparative perspective. Both of these features share common root in a skepticism of "big government" that promotes a degree of libertarian thought and policy that is rare in the developed world. While citizens of most modern social welfare states embrace the concept of "positive liberty," the concept that the state should foster the well-being of the individual and of society, Americans remain more attached to the idea of "negative liberty," which is sometimes formulated as the "right to be left alone."

Case Study: Political Rights and Social Protections in Denmark

Perhaps the starkest contrast with the United States can be found in one of the oldest established states of Europe and a long-standing American ally: the kingdom of Denmark. For centuries feared as the home of marauding Vikings, Denmark and its Scandinavian cousins, Sweden and Norway, have over the course of the past two centuries evolved into the most peaceful and prosperous nations in the world. Today, Denmark is among the top five countries globally in terms of per capita GDP, yet it also boasts the most equal distribution of income of any country and the highest minimum wage on the planet. Comparative studies reveal Denmark to be among the world's least violent and least corrupt nations, and its citizens are ranked by social scientists as the "happiest" in the world (which many Danes modestly attribute to having a sober and realistic view of the world). Strikingly, and probably not coincidentally, the Danish state also controls a higher proportion, nearly 50 percent, of GDP than any other state in the world.

With only a modest portion of the national budget going to defense spending, vast sums are available to support the social welfare and development of Denmark's 5.5 million people. The Danes introduced embryonic welfare programs as far back as the 1890s in response to strong pressure from trade unions, but it was during the period of prosperity and consensus following World War II that the modern welfare state became fully entrenched. Today, Danes can truly count upon the assistance of government from cradle to grave. Family-leave policies are capacious, offering parents full pay for half a year and then eligibility for 60 percent of the unemployment wage while they are caring for children up to the age of eight; heavily state-subsidized day care is also readily available. At the other end of life, substantial retirement pensions are universally available, extensive in-home services are provided for the elderly, and supportive nursing care is guaranteed to those who become incapacitated. In between childhood and old age, the state is similarly active. Education and health care are free for all, disability and unemployment pay is high and available for long periods of time, and subsidized food and housing are provided to the poor. Of course, the cost of all this is considerable: the list of Danish superlatives includes tax rates that are the highest on the planet and that can exceed 60 percent of personal income. Indeed, it has been remarked that it is just as difficult to become very rich in Denmark as it is to become very poor.

Such a heavy equalizing role for the state can run the risk of dampening the free-market economy, but the Danes have successfully employed capitalist competition alongside social consensus—a policy dubbed "flexicurity"—to achieve consistent growth rates, a flexible, well-trained workforce, and high per-worker productivity. The country's business sector is consistently profitable while offering well-paid jobs and excellent working conditions, and Danish industries are among the most environmentally sustainable in the world. The notion that an expansive role for the state must automatically impinge on personal and political freedoms is also not borne out by the case of Denmark. The country has a vigorous multiparty system with voter turnout approaching 90 percent and more women officeholders than all but a handful of other democracies.

On the question of civil liberties and civil rights, it is notable that one of Denmark's most significant recent forays onto the world stage resulted from the publication of inflammatory cartoons about the Prophet Mohammed in a Danish newspaper. The controversy resulted in death threats and protests in Muslim countries around the world but also prompted a strident and uncompromising defense of freedom of expression from the Danish government and from most of Danish society at large. However, some observers saw in this controversy evidence of a nearly monocultural and highly secularized society that was insensitive to minorities and incapable of assimilating immigrants, particularly an ever-larger number of Muslims. With an aging population already straining resources for social welfare programs, Denmark may soon be forced to either scale back its social policies or promote continued and potentially disruptive immigration. No country is without challenges, and the greatest facing Denmark in the years ahead will likely be maintaining the seemingly idyllic society it has already built.

Socioeconomic Policy

While the overall landscape of social protections in Denmark is certainly quite different from that in the United States, not all of its features are entirely unfamiliar. The U.S. educational system provides free and universal services until age eighteen, with subsidized public colleges and universities as well as student loan programs available after that point. Other "socialized" services are also familiar to Americans on the local level, whether in the form of public libraries and parks or government-run police forces or fire departments. At the state and national level, the major social welfare systems created during the two great waves of twentieth-century liberalism—Social Security retirement income in the 1930s and Medicaid/Medicare health insurance in the 1960s—persist to the current day, as do provisions such as the federal minimum wage and the right to form labor unions.

On the whole, though, Americans lead lives that are rather more precarious than people in most other developed nations experience. Unemployment benefits, which range up to 90 percent of lost income for up to four years in Denmark, are at lower levels and expire more quickly in the United States. In the 1990s, aid to poor families in such forms as cash transfers, housing allowances, and food stamps—a collection of programs commonly called "welfare"—was sharply reduced in terms of amount, eligibility, and duration. Most notoriously, the U.S. system has proven unwilling or unable to provide affordable, universal health care to all Americans, a feat that has long since been achieved in most other places. In the United States, millions of people have no health coverage and no access to health care outside hospital emergency rooms, and millions more are denied coverage due to preexisting conditions or risk being driven into bankruptcy by incomplete coverage. At the same time, the large majority of Americans do have access to health insurance, usually through employers, and are generally satisfied with the quality of the medical services they receive. In 2010, a landmark health-care reform law was enacted, but it remains to be seen whether it will succeed in providing anything approaching truly universal coverage.

American workers also have fewer protections from a government that tends to prioritize the rights of businesses and the free market, nearly as much in times of rule by Democrats as by Republicans, despite the latter's probusiness credentials. In most comparably wealthy countries, the minimum wage can be more than double its level in the United States, while unemployment and disability compensation is provided at a higher rate and for a longer period of time—sometimes indefinitely. Most European workers also have a shorter work week, longer vacations, fully paid parental leaves, and far more job security. Thus, many Americans were baffled in 2006 when French students stormed the streets of Paris because of a law that would have allowed employers to fire employees under age twenty-five, which hardly sounds radical to American ears. Framed as an assault on employment guarantees, however, the protests quickly succeeded, and the French government withdrew the bill; a similar provision that was pending in Germany was also quickly withdrawn.

Yet there was a reason that the French government pursued legislation to give employers greater flexibility in hiring and firing personnel. Many European welfare states have at times found themselves with moribund economies experiencing unimpressive growth rates and unable to produce enough good jobs for populations that are highly educated and have a strong sense of entitlement. Further, European governments are far more likely to own or control large portions of the market for utilities, communication, transportation, housing, and other sectors, which can be both expensive and economically inefficient. In France, for example, the state has at times since World War II nationalized the electricity, gas, mining, telecommunications, railway, and even, briefly, banking sectors, though in recent years there has been a greater trend toward reprivatization.

By comparison, minimal government ownership, relatively light regulation, and low tax rates in the United States since the 1980s have generally fueled higher rates of economic performance, promoted low unemployment rates, and opened up opportunities for entrepreneurship and individual success. American businesses have far greater flexibility to offer innovations and meet the changing demands of the marketplace, even when that means wholesale layoffs or the slashing of benefits provided to workers. Similarly, U.S. public policy tends to heavily apply solutions oriented toward the private sector, such as helping the poor with tax credits rather than giving them direct subsidies or providing vouchers for private housing rather than constructing and managing extensive public housing complexes. However, with the sharp economic downturn of 2008, such promarket policies proved to have significant downsides, leaving millions of Americans exceptionally vulnerable to unemployment, housing foreclosure, and personal bankruptcy. Many European social democracies proved more resilient in terms of protecting the welfare of their citizens, and their already heavily regulated economies needed fewer massive stimulus bills, government takeovers, and other emergency interventions. At the same time, severe recessions in some of the weaker Mediterranean economies have begun to clearly point out the limitations of the EU model.

Skepticism of Big Government

In sum, although differences in social and economic policy between the United States and other developed nations are not a question of night and day, the United States is unquestionably an outlier—and has been throughout its history. So the question inevitably arises: why does the United States have such a great deal of skepticism of big government? The theories abound, some assessing closely related historical patterns of development, others examining quite divergent lines of reasoning.

For example, some commentators have pointed to the legacy of slavery and racial subordination in the United States, which did not exist as such in Europe. Because poverty is concentrated among racial and ethnic minority groups, it is argued, the white majority has been more willing to dismiss poverty as a problem affecting others rather than to see it as their concern. In fact, many government welfare programs introduced as part of the New Deal were deliberately structured in ways that disadvantaged African Americans. The heavy emphasis on racial and ethnic divisions in the United States has also dampened the development of class cohesion among working-class whites, blacks, Latinos, and other groups, thus weakening the ability of the labor unions to press for income redistribution.

A very different line of argumentation about small government in the United States focuses on the role of defense spending by the United States, especially during the Cold War, between 1947 and 1991. Protected under the nuclear shield of the United States, the countries of Western Europe paid relatively little for their own defense and were able to redirect their tax revenues toward building welfare states. In the aftermath of World War II, most European countries were burdened by destruction and deprivation, even as they found themselves withdrawing from their overseas empires and relegated to marginal status in the conflict between two superpowers. As such, European governments' main claim to legitimacy shifted from military prowess and national glory to the improvement of their citizens' everyday life circumstances, leading to the flourishing of the welfare state. The United States, strapped with the leading role in the Western military alliance, could not afford to simultaneously develop its social programs—consider the collapse of the mid-1960s War on Poverty under the weight of spending on the Vietnam War. Thus, in a vicious circle, Americans have tended to see little of the return on their investment in their daily lives that is so obvious to European taxpayers, generating further hostility toward any attempt to raise taxes in the United States.

Still another factor is that, ideologically, the United States was born out of a revolution and was based on the rejection of the power of the state in favor of individual liberty. The founders of the American republic were almost fanatical about the need to avoid tyranny or the excessive power of government over the individual. This obsession led to deliberately decentralized and divided institutions of government in the United States. This is, of course, a major theme of chapters 4–7 of this book and need not be reviewed in great detail here. Suffice it to reiterate that change does not come swiftly, easily, or comprehensively in a government characterized by federalism, separation of powers, symmetric bicameralism, and judicial review. Indeed, problems have long gone untouched or have been handled with inadequate half measures; examples include lagging educational achievement, an ever-increasing national debt, and the challenges of climate change.

However, the single most influential line of reasoning about the American preference for self-reliance can be characterized as the settler-frontier-immigration thesis. Although each of these strands is a distinct part of the American experience, collectively they created a country in which opportunities for self-reinvention and individual success were limited only by each person's own efforts. Many early settlers had fled from repressive kings and clerics and thus were only too glad to be free of government and church meddling in their lives. By virtue of circumstance, the earliest settlers were also left almost entirely to their own devices, with no preexisting government to either help them or hinder them. Social mobility became the norm: with no indigenous aristocratic hierarchy held over from feudalism, individuals were free to improve upon the circumstances of their birth. Much the same was true for those who participated in the subsequent nineteenth-century westward migration, which came to be viewed as an all-purpose solution to poverty: if things were bad, you could always build your own fortune by moving west. Finally, the self-reliance mentality was perpetuated among the huge waves of Southern and Eastern European immigrants who entered the country between the 1880s and 1920s. Many of these "tired, poor, huddled masses" were attracted to the United States as the land of opportunity where hard work and diligence could secure a better future, particularly for the next generation. For all of these and other reasons, as discussed further in chapter 8, class conflict and the ideology associated with it—socialism—have never become strongly established in the United States.

Taken together, the settler-frontier-immigration experience promoted a political culture that views government more as a threat to individual liberty than as its guarantor. This has been a long-term, even permanent feature of

American political thought from the Revolutionary Era, when Thomas Jefferson declared, "that government is best that governs least," to the 1980s, when Ronald Reagan famously proclaimed that "government is not the solution; it is the problem." At the same time, the United States developed a robust voluntary sector, or civil society, with a diverse array of private associations, religious bodies, and for-profit businesses providing many of the services for which Europeans look to their governments. Even the New Deal of the 1930s, which dramatically expanded the role of the federal government in the economy, was more of an attempt to save capitalism from its own excesses than to promote socialism. Similarly, the so-called Obamacare healthcare reform act enacted in 2010 is based on existing market mechanisms rather than introducing a European-style single-payer system.

With regard to such broad historical patterns, Canada offers an intriguing what-if case study in the development of American political culture. Both countries had somewhat similar experiences of European settlement, westward migration, and subsequent waves of immigration. However, Canada never experienced a revolution but has undergone slow, evolutionary political change. Whereas the American Declaration of Independence called for "life, liberty, and the pursuit of happiness," the Canadian founding documents of 1867 promised "peace, order, and good government." Rather than structuring their politics to overthrow monarchy and defend against tyranny, Canadians developed a quieter political culture of deference to rightful authority and concern for the common good. Even as the Canadian federation expanded toward the Pacific Ocean, Canada never really experienced a "Wild West." Instead, its government authority—best symbolized by the Royal Canadian Mounted Police, often called the "Mounties"—accompanied or even preceded westward migrants. Later, immigrants were actively courted to help build up the underpopulated Canadian landmass and then integrated into the social and political life of the country. Today, Canadian political culture stands more or less halfway between that of the United States and that of Western Europe. It demonstrates less of a commitment to socialism than its major colonizers, Britain and France, but more support than is found in the United States for activist government.

Civil Liberties

If the United States has trended away from the "positive liberty" and activist government social policy more widely embraced throughout the rest of the developed world, it has always tightly embraced the values of "negative liberty" or freedom from government interference. This has not always and everywhere been applied, of course, with women, African Americans, and other ethnic minorities long oppressed by both state and society and other groups, such as gay and lesbian people, still treated unfairly under the law. Yet the abstract idea of individual liberty retains a tremendous resonance for most

Americans, even among those who might be also inclined toward activist government. When Franklin D. Roosevelt expanded the social safety net, he described it not as leveling inequality but as providing even more freedom, specifically "freedom from want" and "freedom from fear."

The United States was comparatively early in terms of articulating civil liberties (i.e., individual freedoms *from* government), such as freedom of religion and expression, due process guarantees in legal proceedings, and protection from unreasonable search and seizure. It was also a pioneer in establishing civil rights (i.e., group protections *by* government), enshrining equal protection of the law in the Constitution in the period 1865–70, after the Civil War. Today, however, civil liberties and civil rights are to be found among all developed democratic nations. For example, the European Union's Charter of Fundamental Rights, to which all member states must agree, includes a panoply of protections that easily matches anything in the United States, ranging from prohibitions on torture and slavery, to the right to privacy and to property, to freedom of thought, conscience, religion, and expression. Backed by the European Court of Justice and by various national courts, these protections have real force throughout the European Union, providing freedoms at least as thoroughly as is the practice in the United States.

Still, the United States does stand out on a few issues of civil liberties and civil rights, most notably in the near-absolute nature of the First Amendment. The broad scope of protections for free speech, press, and peaceable assembly—all viewed as essential underpinnings for a free society—are as close to absolute as any liberties or rights anywhere in the world. To a striking extent, the U.S. government lacks the power to limit free expression; except in very narrow instances that would create an imminent threat to national security, the U.S. government has no power of "prior restraint," or the ability to control what is published in the media. Of course, those who knowingly publish falsehoods can be sued for libel by aggrieved parties after the fact, but elected officials and other public figures have relatively little protection under libel law, given that the public has a stake in their activities. Even highly unpopular forms of political expression have been repeatedly upheld by courts. Communists and neo-Nazis alike have the same right to march and demonstrate as others, and the burning of the U.S. flag has been ruled a legitimate means of political expression.

By contrast, the governments of many countries in the world to some degree control the content of their media, either formally under law or informally by extralegal pressure. Many authoritarian nations impose stringent filters on the computer servers operating within their borders to prevent Internet users from accessing certain types of information and also try to control access to television satellite dishes. In China, for example, this is called the Golden Shield Project, though it has been more widely dubbed the "Great Firewall of China" by outsiders. But even in established democracies, freedom of expression may not be as firmly established as in the United

States. For instance, some democratic nations declare certain sensitive subjects out of bounds: Germany prohibits denial of the Holocaust, Turkey has outlawed public acknowledgments of the early twentieth-century Ottoman slaughter of Armenians, and France has prohibited denial of both events. And in Great Britain, libel law is far more accommodating to those who bring lawsuits, basically reversing practice in the United States by requiring an author to prove the veracity of a claim rather than the petitioner to establish its mendacity. Across the developed world, government policies designed to carry out surveillance activities and to collect data about citizens were dramatically expanded in the 2000s in the name of antiterrorism policies, generally with less open debate, public scrutiny, and political opposition than has taken place in the United States.

However, the inherently global reach of the World Wide Web seems to be moving other countries in the direction of U.S. practice with regard to freedom of expression. Recently, German officials have been repeatedly censoring the online collaborative reference work Wikipedia because German law prohibits reporting on a person's criminal conviction once his or her prison term has been served. In France, vague rules about offending "the dignity of the state" through excessive criticism or ridicule of government officials are being tested by the bare-knuckled nature of Internet commentary. Both countries, however, seem to be fighting a losing battle against the flow of online information, and the issue is even challenging China, whose censorship has put it at odds with the Web giant Google. Meanwhile, in Britain, reforms are under way to tighten up the standards for proving libel allegations in the name of freer flows of information. Likewise, in more authoritarian countries, it remains unclear how much governments can any longer control the flow of information, as seen by the use of cell phone cameras and Twitter during the prodemocracy protests first in Iran in 2009 and then the next year as part of the "Arab Spring."

Despite the lack of government regulation of media in the United States, a few caveats are in order. While the classic civil libertarian response to hateful or harmful speech may be "more speech," that is to say, increased discussion and deliberation, not every individual or group has equal access to the means of communication. Certainly, when views are held by large majorities—be they religious, racial, ethnic, ideological, or otherwise—such views have a tendency to predominate to an extent that can silence and marginalize the minority. Likewise, the very separation between the press and the government has left most media in the hands of private, profit-seeking interests, increasingly large corporate conglomerates. The news media in the United States have, at times, been considered almost a fourth branch of government, assuming a stance of watchful opposition to the other "branches" and a studied distance from political parties and candidates. Yet, ironically, the very tradition of "journalistic objectivity" in the United States can have the effect of diminishing rather than expanding public discourse by reinforcing a manufactured "conventional wisdom." In countries in which the media are more openly partisan and ideological, there may often be more opportunities for vigorous political debate about fundamental questions of politics and government and less of an impulse toward a (largely manufactured) societal consensus. Of course, the news media in the United States, as throughout the world, are now in rapid flux because of the Internet and other advances in information technology. Long-standing business models and professional standards are rapidly disappearing, and the media are moving toward an uncertain future in which their traditional role as watchdogs of democracy is in jeopardy.

Beyond freedom of expression, other civil liberties also have a high degree of protection under the U.S. Constitution, sometimes in ways that are baffling to foreigners. One such liberty is the right to keep and bear arms under the Second Amendment, which thwarts attempts to control access to firearms. Although the founders may have been more concerned about maintaining viable state militias, individual gun ownership is now an established liberty in the United States. Americans also have a far-reaching right to freely express their religious views, but at the same time the strict separation of church and state has been vigorously enforced by courts in recent decades. By contrast, in many countries, certain religious traditions, such as Roman Catholicism in Latin America and Islam in Arab countries, enjoy a special status, which may curb the rights of those who adhere to nonmajority religions. In France, an official policy of secularism has led the government to ban the wearing of veils and head scarves by Muslim women in many public settings, a policy widely viewed as an affront to religious freedom in many other democracies.

The U.S. Constitution, as interpreted by the courts, also provides strict procedures for due process of law, to the extent that evidence gathered by police in violation of the Fourth Amendment protection against "unreasonable search and seizure" can be excluded from court proceedings. Under this "exclusionary rule," many individuals who might well be judged guilty of crimes in court systems less concerned about safeguarding individual rights have been acquitted. Nonetheless, the United States is a global outlier in the ways that it uses its criminal justice process to achieve social and political goals. While many countries deal with substance abuse as a public health problem, the United States has declared a mostly unsuccessful "war on drugs." Partly as a result, the United States incarcerates a far larger percentage of its population than any other democracy in the world, as reflected in Table 12.1. In fact, the United States incarcerates proportionately more people even than *any* other country, with the prison population heavily composed of impoverished and poorly educated African American and Latino men, a demographic that represents about 14 percent of the U.S. population but more than 60 percent of the incarcerated population. Further, the United States and Japan are also the only industrialized democracies to retain the death penalty; by contrast, disavowal of the death penalty is a requirement for membership in the European Union.

Table 12.1 Incarceration Rates for 60 Major Democracies

000–150	151–300	301–450	451–600	601–750
Australia	Argentina	Botswana		**United States**
Austria	Brazil	Chile		
Belgium	Costa Rica	Israel		
Benin	Czech Republic	South Africa		
Bulgaria	Dominican Republic	Ukraine		
Canada	El Salvador			
Croatia	Estonia			
Cyprus	Guyana			
Denmark	Jamaica			
Finland	Latvia			
France	Lithuania			
Germany	Mauritius			
Ghana	Mexico			
Greece	Mongolia			
Hungary	Namibia			
India	New Zealand			
Indonesia	Panama			
Ireland	Poland			
Italy	Romania			
Japan	Serbia			
Mali	Slovakia			
Netherlands	Spain			
Norway	Trinidad & Tobago			
Peru	Uruguay			
Portugal	United Kingdom			
Slovenia				
South Korea				
Sweden				
Switzerland				

Figures are rates per 100,000 population.

Civil Rights

While civil liberties are concerned principally with interaction between the state and the individual citizen, civil rights focus more on relationships between groups within society, particularly between privileged majority groups and disempowered minority groups. As such, civil rights differ from civil liberties in that they are concerned not with limiting the power of government but rather with using that power to curb societal discrimination, ensure equal protection before the law, and promote socioeconomic equality.

The management of relations between majorities and minorities is a recurrent theme throughout the politics of nearly every country in the world, with almost as many different configurations as there are countries. Some cases are unique, such as the elaborate caste system in India and the burakumin outcast group in Japan. Elsewhere, some consistent patterns can be discerned, such as the economic and political preponderance of colonizers over indigenous populations even many centuries after initial colonization, as throughout South America. Still other patterns occur in multiethnic societies in which one ethnic group dominates, as in Malaysia or Iran, or in which multiple groups vie for power, as in Afghanistan and Nigeria.

The U.S. experience with civil rights incorporates elements of several of these patterns. Certainly, the central narrative on the issue of civil rights in the United States has been the maltreatment of people of African descent, who were first enslaved, then segregated, and who to the present day experience greater socioeconomic deprivation as a group than any other.

The devastating institution of slavery was established throughout the Americas in tropical and subtropical areas in which slave labor could be used to produce cash crops such as cotton, tobacco, and sugar. As slavery was progressively abolished, mostly during the mid-nineteenth century, new forms of discrimination and subordination were established. One slave society, Haiti, won its own independence but then was alternately isolated and marginalized or invaded and occupied by the United States, a country built on the backs of slaves. Some other former slave areas remained under colonial status, with islands such as Jamaica and Barbados not achieving independence until the 1960s but thereafter being under the control of the black majority. In areas with exceptionally large slave populations, most notably Brazil, the population fused into a new racial mixture, although those with the darkest complexions have remained disadvantaged. Further afield, in South Africa, whites maintained the brutal system of forced racial separation known as apartheid; it was not until the mid-1990s that the nation embraced democratic black-majority rule.

In the United States, neither racial mixture nor black self-rule came to pass. Rather, a strict, pathological system of racial subordination and segregation was imposed for the century between the passage of the Thirteenth Amendment, which abolished slavery in 1865, and the enactment of the Civil Rights Act of 1964 and the Voting Rights Act of 1965. Since then, racial discrimination has been illegal, and advances have been made in curbing the most invidious forms of bias in areas including housing, education, employment, and public accommodations such as restaurants, theaters, and parks. Yet programs designed to overcome the legacy of historical discrimination, such as the integration of public schools and affirmative-action programs in higher education and employment, have been steadily rolled back since the 1980s even though their goals remain unfulfilled. The election and reelection of Barack Obama as president, along with the prominence of black people from Colin Powell to Oprah Winfrey to Condoleezza Rice demonstrates that there are no limits on the success that individual African Americans can achieve. However, as a group, they remain the most socially and economically disadvantaged demographic by nearly every measure, from income and accumulated wealth to incarceration rates and death by homicides.

With regard to the civil rights of native populations, the American experience reveals resonances with that of other nations and sharp divergences from the experiences of others. In countries that had large populations of native peoples, such as Mexico or Guatemala, the predominant pattern was one of class oppression and exploitation, with the development of a large landless peasantry. But in areas with comparatively sparse native populations, as North America and Australia, the main pattern was one of increasingly violent displacement, relocation, warfare, and cultural destruction of native societies. In this regard, the U.S. experience falls on the middle of the spectrum. Certainly, it was more brutal than what occurred in Canada, where a slower and more orderly westward expansion allowed native "First Nations" to maintain their identity and cultural integrity to a much greater degree. Yet the U.S. experience did offer at least some degree of recognition and respect to native societies, with whom the federal government struck numerous treaties allowing tribal self-government and, at least in theory, recognizing land rights. In Australia, the Aboriginal population was regarded as not only uncivilized but nearly subhuman by the first European colonizers there. The British Crown also declared Australia *terra nullius* ("no man's land"), thereby sweeping aside any Aboriginal claims to the lands they had occupied for millennia. It was not until 2008 that the Australian government issued a formal apology for abuses against Aboriginals, in particular the "Stolen Generations" of indigenous children taken from their homes in order to be made "civilized."

Yet another source of majority-minority tensions in the United States has resulted from immigration, which has formed the basis for the vast majority of the American population. Most new immigrant groups have initially found themselves at the "bottom of the heap," but Europeans were accepted far more quickly and completely into the dominant "white" majority than Asians or Latinos. For many decades, U.S. immigration and naturalization policy specifically discriminated against Asians, excluding them from entry and prohibiting foreign-born Asians from ever acquiring citizenship. Likewise, Latinos, particularly Mexicans and Mexican Americans, in the border regions were frequently subjected to forms of segregation similar to those that faced African Americans. Sometimes characterized as "intermediate" groups in the hierarchies of American racism, some Asian and Latino ethnicities (such as Japanese and Cubans) have experienced significant upward mobility, while others (such as Hmong and Central Americans) have faced racial, cultural, and linguistic discrimination and marginalization similar to those imposed on African Americans and Native Americans.

As remedial steps against the persistence of inequality and discrimination, the United States has enacted a variety of laws and programs to benefit African Americans and Native Americans, as well as members of other ethnic and racial minority groups such as Asian Americans and Latinos. In common with nearly all established democracies, it has put in place antidiscrimination laws to deter bias in such areas as education, employment, housing, and public accommodations, including shopping malls and restaurants. Similar laws have been extended beyond race and ethnicity to parallel categories, including religion, gender, age, and marital status. However, in keeping with the general skepticism of activist government, attempts to take more proactive steps to overcome the legacy of discrimination, such as busing of schoolchildren to achieve racial integration in primary and secondary schools and the use of affirmative-action policies in employment and higher education, have been and remain highly controversial.

If the United States has been more proactive than some other developed countries with regard to civil rights on the basis of race and ethnicity, however, it has done less than many other democracies to guarantee equality on the basis of gender. Though they actually form a majority of the U.S. population and of voters, women have also been historically subjected to forms of subordination and second-class citizenship (with women of color especially oppressed as "double minorities"). Though there has been considerable progress on this front, the United States has not been a leader in terms of guaranteeing women's equality. For reasons explored in chapter 2, the U.S. Constitution includes few explicit minority protections, relying more on a broad interpretation of the equal protection clause of the Fourteenth Amendment. More recent attempts to make gender protections more explicit, notably the Equal Rights Amendment to guarantee women's equality, have failed to be enacted. Other practices to promote gender parity for government positions, political party leaderships, corporate boards, universities, and other institutions are much more common in other parts of the developed world, and this is reflected in the still comparatively low number of women in positions of leadership in the United States.

The concept of civil rights protections has also been extended to other group identities that have historically experienced social disapproval or disadvantage. On the issue of sexual orientation, the U.S. federal government has done little beyond including gay and lesbian people in federal hate crimes statutes; in fact, until quite recently most actions at the federal level, such as banning "gays in the military" and barring recognition of same-sex marriage, had reflected continuing hostility towards gay and lesbian people. However, more progressive legislation has been enacted by many state and city governments and, even at the federal level, civil rights on the basis of sexual orientation have been gaining a firmer foothold through executive actions by the Obama administration. In the expanding logic of civil rights, protections have also begun to be expanded most recently on the basis of gender identity, protecting those who are transgendered or otherwise "nonconformist" with regard to traditional gender roles. Likewise, people with disabilities have also received a variety of statutory and policy protections that prohibit discrimination and require access ramps, sign-language interpretation, and other forms of accommodation. In all of these cases, as with civil liberties, the challenge facing the United States and all other democracies is how best to create public policy that balances freedom and equality as well as majority rule and minority rights.

Conclusion: Why It All Matters

Politics in the United States is often described in terms of sports metaphors, with races, contests, frontrunners, odds-on favorites, finish lines, victories, and defeats. Yet while the Superbowl or the World Series are ends in themselves, what happens on Election Day matters only in terms of what happens next—how actual governance and policymaking will be impacted depending on who takes office. For this reason, the issues covered in this chapter on domestic policy and in the next, on foreign policy, are in many ways the most substantively significant of the book: they are ultimately why the study of politics and government matters so much.

With regard to domestic policy, it can be easy to overstate the differences between the United States and other industrialized democracies. It is certainly the case that there has been a general propensity away from activist "big government" and toward free-market approaches in the United States, trends rooted deeply in patterns of historical evolution but also in the institutional inefficiencies of American government that make it difficult to enact major new public policies. However, at a substantive level, domestic policy in the United States should be viewed along a spectrum with other developed countries. Although its social welfare system is far less developed than that in the Nordic countries and a few other wealthy northern European countries, the United States does in fact have a social welfare infrastructure that would be the envy of most developing nations. American practices with regard to civil liberties and civil rights are also comparable to those of other countries with the exception of a few areas of "outlier policy"—freedom of expression is more absolute than in most countries, and the United States has resorted in recent years to the overuse of the criminal justice system to address social ills.

However, if the U.S. on the domestic front is not so dissimilar to other developed countries, on the international stage it places a unique role, which is the focus of the next chapter.

Further Reading

Alesina, Alberto, and Edward L. Glaeser. *Fighting Poverty in the US and Europe: A World of Difference.* Oxford: Oxford University Press, 2004.

Cochrane, Allan, John Clarke, and Sharon Gewirtz, eds. *Comparing Welfare States.* Newbury Park, CA: Sage, 2001.
Principe, Michael Luis. *Bills of Rights: A Comparative Constitutional Analysis.* Dubuque, Iowa: Kendall/Hunt, 2010.
Garfinkel, Irwin, Lee Rainwater, and Timothy M. Smeeding. *Wealth and Welfare States: Is America a Laggard or Leader?* Oxford: Oxford University Press, 2010.
Rothgang, Heinz. *The State and Healthcare: Comparing OECD Countries.* Basingstoke, UK: Palgrave Macmillan, 2010.

Web-Based Exploration Exercise

The constitutional basis for different types of civil liberties, civil rights, and social protections varies greatly from country to country. Visit the website "Human & Constitutional Rights" (www.hrcr.org/chart/categories.html), and choose any three categories of constitutional provisions. How does the situation in the United States compare with the situations in any two other countries of your choosing? What are the major differences? Why do you think such differences exist? What impact do you think they have?

Question for Debate and Discussion

When compared with most other developed countries, the United States has a minimal network of social welfare programs. This chapter lays out a number of possible explanations for this discrepancy deriving from broad historical patterns. Given the entrenchment of these precedents, how likely do you think it is that the United States will ever expand its social welfare programs? What are the arguments for and against such an expansion? Under what circumstances might expanded policies be enacted?

Chapter 13

Foreign Policy
The United States in the World

The first and second centuries of American foreign policy could scarcely be more different, reflecting the very different place of the United States in the world over time. When the U.S. Constitution took effect, in 1789, the fledgling nation was looking westward across the North American continent rather than eastward, back toward the intrigues of the Old World. Thomas Jefferson warned against "entangling alliances," and George Washington devoted much of his farewell address to extolling American geographic isolation as an opportunity rather than an obstacle to its development. The framers of the Constitution deliberately made it difficult for the new country to enter treaties by demanding ratification by a two-thirds supermajority of the Senate and assigned the power to wage war to the president while reserving declarations of war to Congress.

And so, after the United States ended its Revolutionary-Era military pact with France in 1794, it would not enter again into another military alliance until the formation of NATO in 1949. U.S. forces fought wars in the early nineteenth century, but only with the country's immediate neighbors: against the Canada-based British during the War of 1812, against various Native American peoples on the frontier, and against Mexico along what is today the U.S. southern border. True, as early as 1823, James Monroe enunciated his famous doctrine declaring that the United States would consider any new European colonization or even intervention in the Western Hemisphere to be acts of aggression against the United States. But the central events of the century were distinctly parochial concerns: the U.S. Civil War and the westward expansion.

By the 1890s, however, with the "War between the States" behind it and the expansion having reached the Pacific, an increasingly self-confident United States began its rise to global prominence. Defeating Spain in 1898, it acquired de facto colonies in the Philippines, Puerto Rico, and Cuba; shortly thereafter it also took over Hawaii and Samoa, and via treaty, asserted control of the Panama Canal Zone. Theodore Roosevelt extended the Monroe Doctrine, and by the early twentieth century the United States was able to wield the "big stick" that would put force behind its assertions of power. U.S.

forces played a critical role in World War I, after which President Woodrow Wilson emerged as the architect of a new structure of international relations.

But it was truly in the World War II era that the American role in the world became almost the exact opposite of that of its isolated, inward-looking early years. Although the Soviet Union bore the brunt of the battle against Nazi Germany on the eastern front, American participation was decisive in opening the western front and also in the defeat of the expansionist empire of Japan in the Pacific theater of war. After World War II, with most of its natural competitors in ruins, the United States experienced a level of military might and economic prosperity unmatched in human history.

Nonetheless, for some forty years, the country was locked in the tense Cold War with its fellow superpower, the Soviet Union, and it fought several smaller, "hot" war conflicts in Korea and Vietnam and more covert actions in many other places. Fortunately, fears of nuclear confrontation with the Soviet Union never came to pass, and the second century of U.S. foreign policy ended in triumph when European Communism collapsed under its own weight in the period 1989–91. At that time, many commentators spoke of a "unipolar world" in which global ideological conflict had essentially been resolved and "globalization" would proceed under a benign American hegemony. Such speculation came to a crashing halt on September 11, 2001, because of the terrorist attacks of that day and the subsequent open-ended American military incursions into Afghanistan and Iraq.

While Islamist fundamentalism and terrorism undoubtedly pose an ongoing danger to the United States, they do not present the ideological challenge once offered by Communism or the existential threat created by the Soviet nuclear arsenal. Still, it is clear that history is far from at an end, and the unipolar moment of the 1990s (if it ever really existed) is being replaced by the more conventional arena of multipolar competition among Great Powers. The European Union, though not quite a state (see chapter 3), already exceeds the United States in population and economic output and offers an alternative model for political and social organization. Buoyed by high prices for oil, Russia has rebounded significantly since its low point in the 1990s and is asserting itself regionally and globally. India, the world's largest and most culturally diverse democracy, has a society that is youthful, forward looking, and increasingly self-confident in ways that the United States and Europe have not been for many decades. Yet if any one global contender seems that it might eclipse the United States in the twenty-first century, it is the world's most populous and fastest-growing nation: the People's Republic of China.

Case Study: The Foreign Policy of China

Except for their shared status as large, powerful countries, the United States and China are about as different as two countries can be: one, a young state founded on democratic principles but little shared ethnic identity; the other the most ancient of nations, governed by an authoritarian Communist Party and drawing on a Han Chinese civilizational identity stretching over millennia. Long accustomed to seeing itself as the very center of the world, as the "Middle Kingdom," China eschewed engagement with international relations for much of its history, treating foreign states as subordinates and supplicants. This changed in the nineteenth century, when the European empires asserted their control over trade routes and strategic locations. Just since World War II, China has gone through nearly as many upheavals and changes in its foreign relations as the United States has in its more than two centuries. Throughout this period, Chinese foreign policy has been driven by two major engines: ideological views rooted in its revolutionary past and pragmatic considerations of its current national interest.

After decades of internal disorder, civil strife, and foreign occupation, in the late 1940s the Communist Party, under Chairman Mao Zedong, drove its chief rival, the Nationalist Party (Kuomintang), from the mainland to the island of Taiwan and proclaimed the new People's Republic of China (PRC). Initially, the new state acknowledged the paramount role of the Soviet Union in the leadership of global Communism, deferring to the will of Josef Stalin and his commissars. But as it gained strength, the PRC began to chafe at its subordinate role and eventually broke with the Soviets, particularly after they repudiated the crimes of Stalin—a move that Mao felt could undermine his own equally brutal dictatorship. During this period, the PRC was largely isolated from the rest of the world, marginalized diplomatically by the West and yet estranged from the Communist bloc; at one point, its only avowed ally was tiny Albania.

Nonetheless, the Chinese also fomented the spread of Communist revolution throughout Southeast Asia, supporting insurgents in Korea and Cambodia. At home, the country experienced chaos during the bizarre Cultural Revolution, during which Mao encouraged Chinese youths to form roving armed bands which violently attacked and degraded supposedly counterrevolutionary forces. Yet, at the same time, the regime opened diplomatic relations with the United States and the military regime in Pakistan in order to achieve a strategic balance against its bordering rivals, the Soviet Union and India. Scarcely a decade after some of the most far-reaching Communist social engineering experiments in history, the post-Mao Chinese Communist Party began a radical reorientation toward a market-based, export-driven economy, giving issues of foreign trade a central role in foreign policy.

Chinese foreign policy is at its most conventional and most intransigent with regard to its territorial integrity, which has long been a principal consideration of sovereign nation-states defined by inviolable boundaries. China invaded and annexed the formerly independent country of Tibet in 1950 and has since exerted enormous diplomatic efforts to assert its sovereignty and minimize the impact of Tibet's religious leader, the charismatic Dalai Lama.

Likewise, it went to great pains to reclaim the two comparatively small southeastern territories of Macao and Hong Kong, which had been colonized by, respectively, Portugal and Great Britain. More recently, China has been framing civil insurrections among the Muslim Uighur people of far western Xinjiang province as part of the global battle against Islamist terrorism. But no foreign policy issue is of more urgent concern than the status of the island of Taiwan, to which the Kuomintang fled in 1949 and whose government long claimed to be the legitimate government of all China. On the issue of Taiwan, the territorial and ideological strands of Chinese foreign policy experience their ultimate convergence, with a flourishing, democratic, and quasi-independent Taiwan compromising the territorial integrity of the state while challenging the ideology of the regime.

Beyond these issues of *realpolitik* and traditional sources of "hard power," China has also been forging a new and unique role on the global stage through the exercise of "soft power," sometimes called a global "charm offensive." The Chinese government offers foreign aid and, through state-owned companies, makes extensive investments throughout the developing world. The Chinese often add in "prestige projects," such as dams, highways, or sport stadiums, all while turning a blind eye to local corruption (or even promoting it) and imposing none of the labor, environmental, or other standards demanded by potential competitors from Western democracies. Such policies have situated China as a friend to the ruling classes of foreign nations, an ironic position for a country that is still nominally Communist and that claims one of history's great revolutionaries as its founder. At the same time, China has become the world's largest creditor nation, buying up more than $800 billion of U.S. debt. This move helped to maintain the interdependent relationship between American consumers and Chinese manufacturers, but it has also given the PRC new leverage over the United States by virtue of the creditor-debtor relationship. This was clear during President Barack Obama's 2009 visit to China, in which the president displayed less of the sometimes high-handed tone taken by former U.S. presidents, partly because of his personal style but also partly because of increasing American reliance on the Chinese economy.

A subject of fierce debate in the United States, particularly in conservative foreign policy circles, is exactly what China is up to. Is it merely pursuing its interests while capitalizing on its unique ability to provide "no-strings-attached" foreign aid and investment? Or is the growing Chinese global profile and role a conscious part of a master plan to supplant the United States as the next global hegemon? One major problem in reaching conclusions is the lack of transparency in so much of the Chinese foreign policymaking process. Formally, it is the Chinese Foreign Ministry that manages international relations, while the Defense Ministry oversees the military. But, as in all fields, the government is "guided" by the decisions and priorities set by the Communist Party, within which various shadowy factions and power centers may compete. Increasingly, the People's Liberation Army has also developed an independent voice and considerable influence. And so exactly who determines foreign policy and why and when certain decisions and activities are undertaken often baffle even experts. Without a clear and binding constitutional structure and always shielded from the scrutiny of the electoral process or of a free press, the thought patterns and decision-making processes of Chinese leaders remain hard to discern in even the short term.

China—or at least some of the players in its Communist Party, military, and bureaucratic leadership—may indeed have longer-term designs to achieve global preeminence, but a more likely scenario is that the leaders of the PRC are mostly concerned about maintaining their domestic monopoly on power by forestalling political liberalization. Thus, they must uphold their end of the central bargain they have made with the Chinese people: they will provide a constant expansion of the economy and improvements in standards of living if the Chinese people will put aside demands for democracy. While Taiwan and Tibet remain potential flashpoints, Chinese foreign policy seems overwhelmingly focused on gaining leverage in resource-producing countries in Africa, Asia, and Latin America, while expanding new opportunities for exports and trade with the developed world. All of these factors should help to establish China as a reliable and respectable partner in business—and limit the ability of the United States or anyone else to obstruct its goals.

Foreign Policymaking in the United States

Two of the major themes that emerged in this examination of China also resonate as major issues in the study of U.S. foreign policy: the mechanics of the policymaking process itself and the complex balance between the role of ideology (broadly defined) and pragmatic concerns about national interest. This section examines how U.S. foreign policy is made, while the next considers the major influences on the content of foreign policy itself.

While the U.S. foreign policymaking process is nowhere near as shrouded and convoluted as in China, it nonetheless is far less open to public scrutiny than the making of policy on the domestic front. Indeed, huge amounts of policy-relevant information are classified in the name of "national security," leaving the citizenry (and sometimes even Congress and the federal courts) only to guess at what information government decision makers have at their disposal, and to trust in the good faith and competence of those decision makers. Unquestionably, some degree of secrecy is necessary in order to prevent foreign governments and hostile nonstate actors from taking advantage of the free press and open society that generally prevail in the United States; much the same restrictions on national security-related information can be found in every democracy. Still, the potential for abuse is enormous, as demonstrated by episodes such as the Gulf of Tonkin Resolution, in 1964, when Lyndon Johnson's administration trumped up a minor naval skirmish in

Vietnam as a cause for escalation of the war. It also seems clear that the administration of George W. Bush, at least to some extent, willfully distorted the case for the invasion of Iraq in 2003 and then committed human rights abuses under the cover of national security.

While the George W. Bush administration pressed claims of executive power to an extreme, the U.S. president has traditionally had tremendous latitude in the roles of chief diplomat and commander in chief, far more than on the domestic front. Much of this emanates from the long-established patriotic notion that "politics ends at the water's edge" and that the United States must speak with a single clear voice in international affairs. The federal courts, up to and including the Supreme Court, interpret this notion quite stringently, generally refusing to second-guess presidential decisions in military and foreign affairs on the grounds that they are issues largely beyond the institutional capabilities of the judiciary to oversee. One of the darkest episodes in the history of the Supreme Court was its decision in *Korematsu v. United States* (1944) to uphold Franklin D. Roosevelt's authority to place some 120,000 Japanese Americans, citizens and noncitizens alike, in internment camps on the grounds that they posed a security risk after the bombing of Pearl Harbor. More recently, the Supreme Court has rarely taken up cases relating to the wars in Iraq and Afghanistan or the more nebulous "War on Terror." And when it has, the cases generally have related directly to a core judicial function, such as due process guarantees (as in the case of accused detainees held without access to lawyers or trial) or the issuance of search warrants (as in the case of domestic surveillance activities).

Ostensibly, Congress should have a much greater constitutional role in the making of foreign policy. With regard to military affairs, Article I, Section 8, clearly provides Congress with a broad range of powers including the power "to declare war . . . to raise and support armies . . . to provide and maintain a navy . . . to make rules for the government and regulation of the land and naval forces . . . [and] to provide for calling forth the militia to execute the laws of the union, suppress insurrections and repel invasions." In some areas, Congress has retained its prerogatives, notably its control over the Uniform Code of Military Justice, which regulates all aspects of life for members of the armed forces. In 2007, the new Democratic majority in Congress considered trying to halt the war in Iraq by using its power to cut off further funding. With troops already entrenched in combat, this turned out to be an untenable position, but Congress is able to use its appropriations authority to influence military policy in less dramatic ways. For instance, once U.S. troops had been removed from Vietnam, Congress used its appropriations authority to prevent a reengagement after the Communist victory in 1975. The withdrawals of U.S. troops from Iraq and Afghanistan have been driven almost entirely by presidential rather than congressional priorities.

Where Congress has seen the most dramatic ebbing of its power over military affairs, however, has been in the de facto abandonment of the formal "declaration of war" as a necessary basis for initiating sustained overseas military operations. Between 1789 and 1942, Congress declared war on five occasions, always at the request of the president. With regard to a number of far smaller military engagements, such as repelling attacks by Barbary pirates on U.S. ships and a small-scale intervention into the Russian Civil War, Congress specifically authorized limited presidential action. However, despite huge and costly wars in Korea, Vietnam, the Persian Gulf, Iraq and Afghanistan, and myriad smaller actions, Congress has not formally declared war since World War II. Instead, presidents have claimed far greater latitude for action on their own initiative and authority for significant engagements and have not even bothered to seek congressional support for numerous shorter incursions in places such as Grenada, Panama, Somalia, Haiti, Bosnia, and Kosovo. In its most notable attempt to reclaim its military authority, Congress passed the War Powers Resolution of 1973, providing presidents with a ninety-day limit on actions undertaken without congressional approval. But presidents have never recognized such a limit on their commander-in-chief role, and the federal courts have refused to engage the issue, leaving the extent of the president's unilateral war-making power murky and subject to abuses. For example, in 2011, President Obama used military force beyond the ninety-day limit in Libya without seeking congressional approval.

Following the literal wording of the Constitution, Congress—or at least the Senate—should also be able to exert considerable influence over U.S. diplomacy and foreign affairs. However, congressional power is, in fact, even more limited than in the military sphere. No one can become secretary of state or a U.S. ambassador without confirmation by the Senate, but such confirmation is only very rarely withheld and even then may not be decisive. In 2012, senatorial opposition to the naming of UN Ambassador Susan Rice as the next secretary of state ultimately scuttled her prospects, leading her to withdraw from consideration. While various standing committees of both houses of Congress are empowered to conduct oversight activities, they suffer from relatively limited capacity and the straightjacket of secrecy about national security issues.

Comparably limited in its modern application is the requirement that all international treaties receive the support of a two-thirds supermajority of the Senate. Even with this senatorial authority, it was still the sole province of the president to negotiate and sign treaties, which combined with the power to appoint and receive ambassadors, has amounted to control over foreign policy. But in recent decades, full-scale treaties have been used less and less often as instruments of foreign policy, increasingly supplanted by coordinated congressional-executive agreements (passed by a simple majority of both houses of Congress) or sole-executive agreements (enacted on the basis of the president's own Article II powers). The latter two types of agreements are not established by the Constitution but rather reflect the evolution of the foreign policymaking process into circumstances that are at a distant remove from those contemplated at the time of the founding. Still, the diminution of the Senate's power in the area should not be entirely disregarded. Certainly the most famous incident in American history was the Senate's refusal to ratify the Treaty of Versailles after World War I, which would have allowed American membership in the League of Nations. In 1996, the Clinton administration signed the Comprehensive Nuclear-Test Ban Treaty, and, although a simple majority of fifty-one Senators voted for ratification in 1999, it fell well short of the required two-thirds and was not ratified.

Overall, then, how does the foreign policymaking process in the United States compare with that of other countries? In nondemocratic states, for reasons discussed in chapter 5, policymaking is carried out entirely by the executive branch, often in ways explicitly intended to reinforce the regime's hold on power. In one extreme case, the military regime in Argentina had no specific reason to launch its 1982 invasion of the British-controlled Falkland Islands, known as Las Islas Malvinas to Argentines. But with their grip on power slipping and their legitimacy eroding, the generals (who had already dissolved the Argentine Congress) made a unilateral decision to try to rally the nation through an appeal to patriotism around Argentina's long-standing claim to the islands. Ironically, though, a quick and humiliating military defeat by Britain led to the fall of the military regime and the restoration of democracy in Argentina.

More recently, in Russia, the regime under Vladimir Putin has conducted foreign policy with a view not only to restoring Russian greatness but also to promoting the interests of billionaire business oligarchs with whom it is allied; the Russian parliament has become mostly a rubber stamp for the wishes of the executive. Iranian foreign policy, particularly with regard to its controversial nuclear program, seems to be driven mostly by the need of the regime of the Islamic Republic to suppress internal dissent and build public support by standing up to the West and, in particular, to "the Great Satan," as the United States is known. With the regime in charge of deciding who can and cannot run for seats in the legislature, it is guaranteed an acquiescent parliament.

In democratic countries, the legislature plays a more important role, though still one that is distinctly secondary to the executive. While it is true that in parliamentary democracies the legislature can remove the executive more or less at will, in practice the executive is so dominant that the request of any sitting prime minister for ratification of a treaty or authorization of a military action is quite unlikely to be denied. However, the knowledge that any parliamentary motion *could* fail and therefore trigger a vote of no confidence and bring down the government probably restrains some actions by parliamentary executives. For example, in the run-up to the 2003 invasion of Iraq, Chancellor Gerhard Schroeder of Germany was under enormous pressure to commit forces to the multinational invasion force. However, he refused to even contemplate it, in part because the junior partner in his coalition government, the Greens, made clear that they would bring down the government if there was any such participation. At the same time in Britain, Prime Minister Tony Blair sought parliamentary support to participate in the deeply unpopular invasion of Iraq. The motion passed, but only because of the support of members of the opposition, since many of the members of his own party voted against it and two senior members of his cabinet resigned on principle. Though Blair prevailed in the short term, the invasion and its mishandled aftermath led directly to Blair's being forced to step aside from the prime ministerial position in 2007.

In countries with separation of powers, it is, of course, more likely that the executive might be refused a declaration of war or ratification of a treaty, particularly if the legislature is under the control of the opposition party. However, few legislatures anywhere will refuse a well-founded request from the nation's commander in chief to authorize military action. For example, when presidents in El Salvador, the Dominican Republic, and Honduras decided to participate in the 2003 invasion of Iraq, they secured the support of their legislative branches despite the deep suspicion in those countries of anything resembling imperialistic impulses on the part of the United States. Likewise, most legislatures will also ratify treaties negotiated in good faith by their presidents, particularly since such votes usually require a simple majority rather than the two-thirds supermajority necessary in the U.S. Senate. It is striking that of 187 countries whose executives signed the Kyoto Protocol on climate change, 186 of them—whether they are democratic or authoritarian, parliamentary or presidential—went on to ratify the protocol; only the United States has not done so, because of lack of sufficient support in the Senate. The United States also remains one of just seven UN members not to ratify the Convention on the Elimination of All Forms of Discrimination against Women—even though President Jimmy Carter signed it all the way back in 1980.

In all democracies, the power of the executive to act unilaterally in foreign and military affairs is further constrained by a free press, by openly expressed public opinion, by the role of the organized interests, and, ultimately, by the power of the ballot box. For instance, the publication by the *New York Times* of the top-secret "Pentagon Papers" about illegal U.S. actions during the Vietnam War contributed to the collapse of public support for the war and the hastening of withdrawal. For nearly three decades afterward, U.S. public opinion had a constraining effect on the use of force abroad, until the invasions of Iraq and Afghanistan—which may well have much the same effect over the next few decades.

Vocal interest groups in society can also shape the direction of foreign policy. By pressuring Congress, domestic economic interests have ensured that when the United States provides aid to foreign countries, it is domestic U.S. companies that must provide the aid supplies. American farmers have won price supports for their farms, even in contravention of various free-trade agreements. A coalition of American Jews and biblically oriented fundamentalist Christians has been key in maintaining the U.S. commitment to Israel, while Armenian Americans have influenced U.S. policy toward their homeland's historic nemesis, Turkey. And although successive U.S. presidents have expressed an interest in lifting the antiquated economic embargo on Cuba, opposition from the anti-Castro Cuban American community has successfully blocked any such change. It is certainly no coincidence that Cuban Americans have influential concentrations in the major Electoral College states of New Jersey and Florida or that it has been legislators from Los Angeles, home to large Armenian American populations, who have been most responsive to that community's concerns. Indeed, at the end of the day, politicians must be concerned about their prospects for reelection or, in the case of second-term presidents, about keeping their party in the White House and protecting their legacy.

U.S. Foreign Policy: Realist and Idealist Perspectives

Within the discipline of political science, foreign policy is generally folded into the subfield known as international relations, which focuses on the ways in which the states of the world interact with one another at the diplomatic, military, political, and even social levels. International relations is a vast field, encompassing topics as diverse as nuclear disarmament, narcotrafficking, human rights, environmentalism, humanitarian aid, global public health, and international finance. Most of these topics are beyond the scope of this book and, hence, of this chapter. Therefore, this last section is designed to act as a bridge between the themes of *The American Anomaly* to the subfield of international relations by considering the two major academic perspectives on foreign policy: the *realist* and the *idealist* schools of thought.

Foreign policy realism emphasizes the idea that countries are driven primarily by competition for power, resources, territory, and other advantages and that makers of foreign policy should primarily be concerned with pragmatic questions of national interest. From this perspective, anyone seeking to understand U.S. foreign policy should look less to the internal institutions of policymaking or the ideals of the American regime and more to the basic logic of international relations. Realism argues that in a competitive, even cutthroat, global environment, countries of *all* types consistently try to maximize their power with relation to other countries and to seek out whatever political and economic benefits their power can secure for them.

For example, as seen earlier, China was politically unstable and economically weak for most of the twentieth century, unable to project power commensurate with its size and population. Today, politically unified and economically robust, it is vigorously reasserting itself in Asia and across the globe by using its international position to enhance its top priority of rapid economic development. Britain and France, once among the greatest of world powers, seek to maximize their former power by maintaining small nuclear arsenals, preserving links with their former colonies, and holding tight to their veto-bearing permanent memberships on the UN Security Council. Recovering from the collapse of the Soviet Union, Russia is using its oil wealth and its remaining military strength to reestablish a sphere of influence in neighboring countries. Even Japan and Germany, occupied and humbled after World War II, have begun to move toward a stronger military posture.

And it is not just the so-called Great Powers that show a propensity toward expanding their national strength whenever possible. The small European countries of the Netherlands and Belgium became significant colonizers when their economic and military advantages enabled them to conquer less developed peoples in Africa, Asia, and the Americas. These countries may be among the most peaceful and progressive in the world today, but in the seventeenth and eighteenth centuries they proved themselves as capable as any country of practicing repression and committing atrocities. Likewise, the former Yugoslav republic of Serbia—about the size and population of Ohio—waged several wars in the 1990s against its neighbors, going so far as to commit genocidal ethnic cleansing in an unsuccessful attempt to become the dominant power in the Balkans. Is there something uniquely aggressive about the Serbs, or are their actions largely explicable in terms of the logic of international relations? History suggests the latter.

Given its unparalleled might, it would thus be quite strange if the United States did not play a major, even dominating, role on the world stage. As laid out in chapter 1, the United States is very unusual in its combination of national assets, including the scope of its economy, the breadth of its geographic size, the size of its population, the power of its military, the fearsomeness of its nuclear arsenal, the magnitude of its wealth, and the global reach of its popular culture. Such extensive and varied sources of power have given the United States the capacity to act more decisively, unilaterally, and effectively than any other country in the world, probably in all of human history. The disparity between U.S. military spending and that of all other democracies, except embattled Israel, is clearly laid out in Table 13.1. Indeed, it is the unique place of the United States in the global arena that may be the greatest American anomaly of all.

During the long Cold War, U.S. foreign policy focused on such realist objectives as protecting its territory and that of the allies, winning over new supporters, and containing the expansion and influence of Communism. When necessary, the U.S. government was certainly willing to resort to ruthless means. When a Marxist, Salvador Allende, was elected president of Chile, the CIA engineered a coup that ushered in fifteen years of brutal military dictatorship. American intervention in Guatemala unleashed a three-decades-long civil war that killed two hundred thousand people, and in Nicaragua the United States backed right-wing *contra* rebels against the validly elected but stridently leftist Sandinista government. When Prime Minister Mohammad

Table 13.1 Military Spending as a Percentage of GDP for 59 Democracies*

0.0–1.0	1.1–2.0	2.1–3.0	3.1–4.0	4.1–5.0	5.1+
Austria	Australia	Botswana	Chile	**United States**	Israel
Argentina	Belgium	Cyprus	Namibia		
Benin (2008)	Brazil	France			
Costa Rica	Bulgaria	Guyana			
Dominican Republic	Canada	Greece			
	Croatia	India			
Ghana	Czech Republic	Portugal			
Hungary		Serbia			
Indonesia	Denmark	South Korea			
Ireland	El Salvador	United Kingdom			
Jamaica	Estonia	Ukraine			
Japan	Finland				
Mauritius	Germany				
Mexico	Italy				
Panama	Latvia				
Spain	Lithuania				
Switzerland	Mali				
	Mongolia				
	Netherlands				
	New Zealand				
	Norway				
	Peru				
	Poland				
	Romania				
	Slovakia				
	Slovenia				
	South Africa				
	Sweden				
	Uruguay				

* Statistics are unavailable for Trinidad and Tobago; all figures are 2010.

Mossadegh of Iran drifted too far to the left for American comfort, the United States fomented his overthrow and then supported autocratic rule by the hated shah—leading to the 1979 revolution and the continuing enmity of the Iranian revolutionary regime. The United States even supported the brutal Iraqi dictator Saddam Hussein in the 1980s in his war against Iran.

Indeed, there may be no better emblem of the opportunistic quality of much of American foreign policy than the photo of the meeting between Saddam and Ronald Reagan's special emissary—none other than Donald Rumsfeld, who as U.S. defense secretary would help to lead the 2003 invasion of Iraq. The basic realist orientation of U.S. foreign policy toward dictators during this era was sometimes encapsulated in the phrase "he's a son of a bitch, but he's our son of a bitch."

After the demise of the Soviet Union, in 1991, U.S. foreign policy became ever more unfettered. Some even took to saying that the United States was no longer simply a superpower but a "hyperpower" on an entirely new scale, perhaps even a "new Rome" with a reach that was illimitable and a force that was unstoppable. The collapse of Communism was even said to have brought about the "end of history" in the sense that there could be no further fundamental challengers to the U.S. model of liberal democracy and capitalism. More than any other nation in the history of the world, it could truly claim to be a global hegemon, and its foreign policy increasingly reflected an unwillingness to be constrained in any way. Thus, in the 1990s, the United States pushed for the expansion of NATO right into the territory of the former Soviet Union, posing a direct challenge to a weakened and demoralized Russia. It pursued laissez-faire capitalist free trade to the extreme of punishing poor countries that broke pharmaceutical patents in order to treat AIDS patients and driving small farmers in the developing world out of the market in favor of mass agribusinesses. In the ultimate act of foreign policy unilateralism, the United States mounted an invasion of its erstwhile ally, Iraq, without a mandate from either the United Nations or the NATO allies.

From the chastening vantage point of 2013, the idea of limitless American power and wealth seems both naïve and hubristic. The September 11 attacks revealed the fundamental vulnerability of the American homeland to attacks by terrorists and the damage that could be wrought by a handful of determined civilians. The idea that the United States could act at will anywhere on the globe was proven manifestly false by the invasions of Iraq and Afghanistan, which became open-ended military quagmires. And the financial meltdown of 2008 made clear that the American economy could not continue to expand without limit.

The realist perspective would argue that, once again, international relations has come down to the question of power and that, with its power diminished, the United States would need to engage the world on a much more even footing—a cornerstone of the political platform of the man the country elected president in 2008 and 2012. President Obama's aggressive use of unilateral action to kill Osama bin Laden and expanded employment of unmanned drone strikes makes clear that the United States will continue to act in its interests even with a chief executive seen as more dovish than many of his predecessors.

While the realist school can offer critical insights into U.S. foreign policy, so too can the competing perspective of *foreign policy idealism*, which emphasizes the projection of domestic values and ethics onto the world stage. Idealists argue that international relations need not be a zero-sum game and that, by patient negotiation and quiet consensus building, the world can take incremental steps toward peace and prosperity. Certainly, the greatest triumph of the insight of idealists has been the successful construction of the European Union, transforming a continent of antagonists into a community of partners among whom warfare has become unthinkable. Other institutions, notably the United Nations, may have fallen short of their promise, but they still provided important forums for international dialogue and the enunciation of worthwhile goals such as the Universal Declaration of Human Rights.

Some elements of U.S. foreign policy—from the Marshall Plan to help reconstruct Europe after World War II, to the Peace Corps to promote development in impoverished nations, to funding of medications for the AIDS epidemic in the developing world—have played a critical role in actualizing the vision of idealists and improving the lives of peoples around the world. Globally, the United States has championed human rights in repressive regimes, provided more foreign aid than any other nation, intervened militarily to prevent massacres and genocides, and assisted with disaster recovery, postwar reconstruction, and peacekeeping endeavors around the world. Despite the lure of unilateralism that has so often tempted the United States, many of the world's most important multilateral institutions, including NATO, the United Nations, the World Bank, the International Monetary Fund, and the World Trade Organization would not exist without its participation and, often, leadership. Even the U.S.-led invasion of Iraq was in some ways as much a manifestation of idealism as of realism, a manifestation of the hope that American-style democracy could be instilled in even the seemingly most inhospitable locales.

And while it is true that U.S. foreign policy during the Cold War could often be harsh, it is important to remember that the enemy was truly implacable and terribly dangerous. Communist regimes in the twentieth century were responsible for more terror, torture, famine, and human suffering than any others in history, including even the Nazis. Communism emphatically proved itself to be an economic system incapable of producing prosperity, a political system unable to survive without systematic repression, and a moral disaster of massive proportion. The United States could have compromised or withdrawn or appeased its Communist rivals, but instead it risked global nuclear war. When necessary, it also consorted with unsavory dictators and manipulated the politics of smaller states, in the name of the larger good of defeating what Ronald Reagan—in classic "idealist" language—termed "the Evil Empire" of the Soviet Union. It was thus truly a victory and a vindication that such an enemy could be defeated with so little bloodshed, collapsing because of its own weaknesses in the fall of 1989 to be replaced by more free, democratic, and capitalist societies.

Ultimately, the promotion of democracy and capitalism around the world may not be only an act of idealism but also a realist strategy for promoting peace and prosperity. Perhaps the single most compelling observation about the role of democracy in the making of foreign policy is the so-called democratic peace theory. Although in theory there is no reason why two well-established democracies could not wage war on one another, in practice this essentially never occurs. In Europe, the spread of stable democracy after World War II ended centuries of conflict and bloodshed, including the remarkable reconciliation of Germany with the neighbors it had repeatedly invaded. In Latin America, the collapse of the military regimes of the 1980s and the restoration of democracy ended most border tensions and threats of war, such as the perpetual tensions between Argentina and Chile over their southern border. By contrast, nondemocratic Russia continues to have tensions and even military clashes with former Soviet territories, such as the 2008 invasion of Georgia, and China's borders with nearly all of its neighbors remain tense and heavily militarized.

One difference, argues the democratic peace theory, is that the democratic process of negotiation and alternation in power promotes a culture of compromise that predisposes democratic countries to work out their differences rather than go to war with one another. In an era of global economic interdependence, countries generally stand to gain more from patient negotiation than they could achieve through armed conflict with one another. And domestic electorates prefer peace and prosperity over conflict whenever possible, an issue that is always a prime consideration for the reelection minded. Thus, democracies still go to war with nondemocracies, as seen in NATO actions against an aggressive Serbia in Kosovo and against the Taliban regime in Afghanistan. But the shared attribute of democracy itself seems enough to nearly guarantee peaceful relations with other states and also tends to dampen internal conflicts, civil wars, and even famines, which are often more a product of politics than the result of actual food shortages. In all, democratic peace theory presents a powerful rationale for the imperative to spread democracy across the globe.

Conclusion: Why It All Matters

One of the key attributes of any sovereign state is the ability to enter into relations with other states; one of the key responsibilities of any sovereign state is to defend its territories and protect its critical national interests. How any particular state carries out its foreign policy is the product of multiple different influences. Some relate to the country's institutional structures, such as whether the executive is able to act independently or must rely on support from the legislature or other political actors. Other influences on foreign policy involve the domestic political context, including the influence of a free press, the opinions held by voters, and the pressure brought to bear by organized interests. Still others relate to the capacity of the state, such as the scope of its military forces, the skill of its diplomats, the personal qualities of its leaders, and the power of its ideas.

Both of the two major schools of thought about foreign policy, realism and idealism, can offer important insights into how the United States conducts its foreign policy. With its emphasis on the balance of power in the world and on narrowly defined national interests, the realist view can help to explain a great deal about U.S. behavior during the Cold War and, in recent decades, on such issues as globalization, terrorism, and the environment. At the same time, no portrait of American foreign policy would be complete without considering the idealist perspective. Promoting democracy, advancing capitalism, promoting human rights, fostering international cooperation, and providing humanitarian aid are also all hallmarks of U.S. foreign policy.

Further Reading

Beasley, Ryan, et al., eds. *Foreign Policy in Comparative Perspective: Domestic and International Influences on State Behavior, 2nd Edition.* Washington, DC: Congressional Quarterly Press, 2012.

Breuning, Marijke. *Foreign Policy Analysis: A Comparative Introduction.* New York: Palgrave Macmillan, 2007.

Neack, Laura. *The New Foreign Policy: U.S. and Comparative Foreign Policy in the 21st Century, 2nd Edition.* Lanham, MD: Rowman & Littlefield, 2008.

Web-Based Exploration Exercise

The manner in which different countries conduct their foreign policy is determined by many factors, including their position in the global arena, their domestic political arrangements, and their vital national interests. Visit the website of the U.S. Department of State (www.state.gov/policy), and read about any three foreign policy issues. Then visit the websites for the foreign ministries of any other two countries, and review coverage of three foreign policy issues (ideally the same ones that you read about on the U.S. website). What major similarities and differences did you find in terms of how the issues were framed? How do you account for these similarities and differences? A comprehensive portal to the world's foreign ministries (many with at least some English sections) can be found at http://www.ediplomat.com/dc/foreign_ministries.htm.

Question for Debate and Discussion

The realist and the idealist perspectives place a different emphasis on how states actually act as well as how they should act in the conduct of their foreign policy. To what extent do you see U.S. foreign policy as being essentially a realist response to the balance of power in the world? In what ways is it an idealistic response designed to promote liberty, democracy, and capitalism? Should it be different? And, if so, how could it be changed?

Conclusion
The American Anomaly on Balance

As we have seen throughout this book, it is not very meaningful to speak of the United States as having the world's best or worst political system. Indeed, such judgments are meaningful only when placed into the context of a set of political values to be maximized and needs to be met. Which is to be preferred: stability over time? Flexibility amid changing circumstances? Responsive politicians? Accountable parties? What is the correct balance between competing values, and how can these best be reconciled? Different individuals will answer these questions differently according to their own political beliefs and personal experiences. Similarly, each country must make these decisions based on its particular circumstances, some of which are permanent and fixed and some of which are likely to change over time.

Although it may not be possible to generalize about the U.S. political system as being the best or worst in an objective sense, it certainly is possible to identify how different values are maximized or minimized by the particular forms taken by American political institutions and processes. It is also possible to consider how well these dimensions of American politics meet the needs of contemporary life in the United States. This brief conclusion offers some thoughts on how well U.S. politics and government maximize certain key values and what might be learned from the experience of other countries.

Stability

One of the most striking characteristics of U.S. politics and government has been its stability throughout the country's more than 230 years of history, during which time the country expanded from a cluster of settlements along the eastern seaboard to become a continental power and then a world superpower, mostly under the auspices of the same basic governmental framework. In a world in which tumultuous political change seems to be more the norm than the exception, the U.S. political system has provided an extraordinary degree of political predictability and order.

Consider these anomalous facts. The U.S. Constitution is the first and oldest continuously functioning national constitution in the world. The same two political parties, and only those two political parties, have alternated in power for the past century and a half. Presidential power has been, without interruption, smoothly transferred for more than 220 years. Elections have been held in the same stable two- and four-year cycles since the founding of the Republic. And once politicians are in office, their terms are fixed, so that governments cannot fall overnight, and, except to fill occasional House vacancies, federal elections are never called on short notice. Such executive and legislative stability is in stark contrast to what is found in parliamentary systems, enabling longer-range planning and fostering a sense that elected officials have a legitimate right to govern for the duration of their terms.

Similar long-term stability can be found in the realm of domestic policy. Other than the one great constitutional failure of the U.S. Civil War, the American political system has managed radical social change, economic depressions, and social upheavals without having to face another revolution, a military coup, or even a dramatic interruption of the regular operation of government. Neither tyranny nor anarchy has managed to fatally undermine American democracy.

Continuity in foreign policy has been even more striking, particularly since World War II. To a striking extent, successive presidents of both parties have found their actions shaped by America's unique role in the world and its enduring national interests, creating broad continuity over decades. Thus, Richard Nixon campaigned against the escalation of the Vietnam War, yet it continued throughout his nearly six years in office. Ronald Reagan is credited with "getting tough" with the Soviet Union after 1981, but it was his much-maligned predecessor, Jimmy Carter, who began a more confrontational approach after the 1979 Soviet invasion of Afghanistan. In the 1990s, Bill Clinton completed George H. W. Bush's push to expand the NATO military alliance into formerly Communist countries, while Barack Obama moved only slowly and cautiously to end the wars in Iraq and Afghanistan begun by George W. Bush. Usually for better, though sometimes perhaps for worse, the United States has provided stability and consistency for decades in its role as a global leader.

Flexibility

While stability is a major goal, however, it can come at the expense of flexibility. The decentralization and dispersal of power in the United States make it difficult for the political system to adapt to changing circumstances, particularly on the domestic front. In order for a new law to come into effect, political actors must come to agreement at nearly two dozen points, with the power to obstruct progress residing with the chairs and members of a variety of congressional subcommittees and committees, the leaders and members of both the Senate and the House of Representatives, and the president. Then, the participation of state governments, the federal bureaucracy, and the courts may also be needed for the law to be enacted and enforced; each of these political actors also has great latitude and even autonomy from Congress and the president. All of these political players have their own constituencies and agendas and are often divided along party lines as well, making it a minor miracle that any legislation ever gets passed at all (and explaining why about 90 percent of proposed bills are never enacted into law). Yet, though ordinary lawmaking is arduous, it is exponentially harder to change the Constitution itself, with just seventeen amendments having been added since 1791, leaving the U.S. political system with many suboptimal or even outright archaic features. Although the meaning of the Constitution also evolves through new interpretations, this process is often highly contested and usually offers change haltingly at best.

With a limited ability to adapt to changing circumstances, problems can fester for years or even decades under the U.S. political system. Ethnic and racial socioeconomic disparities remain glaring a half century after the civil rights movement. Millions of people have insufficient health insurance in the wealthiest country in the world, a problem that even the landmark health care legislation of 2010 will be unlikely to resolve completely. And the United States incarcerates a higher percentage of its population than any other country on the planet. None of these problems is insurmountable, but they persist largely through governmental inertia. By contrast, many parliamentary systems can effect sweeping change at any time. But, of course, those changes can also be undone in short order; if the opposition comes into power after an election, it is usually free to undo the actions of the previous government, contributing to political instability and uncertainty.

Representation

The same fragmentation, decentralization, and dispersal of power that can compromise the efficiency of American government can also promote a high degree of representation. Consider the opposite extreme of the institutional configuration found in the United States, namely a parliamentary government with no upper house in a unitary state with little or no judicial review (such as exists in Sweden, Israel, or New Zealand). Citizens in such countries really have only one major point of access into the political system: their member of parliament, for whom they might cast a ballot as infrequently as every five years. Further, in most parliamentary systems, rank- and-file backbenchers have relatively little ability to influence the work of government and are limited mostly to following the lead of their party leaders.

The situation could hardly be more different in the United States, where the average citizen is represented by at least three elected executives—a mayor, a governor, and a president—and at least six elected legislators—a city or town council member, one member in each of his or her state's upper and lower houses, a member of the House of Representatives, and two U.S.

senators. Our citizen may also be represented by numerous other elected local, county, and state officials such as state attorneys general, state comptrollers, county executives, county legislators, sheriffs, and district attorneys. Given the heavy cost of campaigning and the candidate-centered nature of elections in the United States, each of these elected officials is likely to actively pursue the interests of his or her constituents rather than the broader "public good."

Although individual elected officials offer a broad variety of opportunities for representation, the U.S. two-party system deprives voters of the chance to choose from the range of political parties that is characteristic of most democratic political systems. In a multiparty democracy, voters are more likely to find a political party with clearly defined positions that fairly closely resemble their own. In systems of four or five parties, the choices are likely to span the ideological spectrum from far right to far left. In systems with eight, ten, or more parties, voters may also be able to find a party that reflects their ethnic, religious, regional, or other interests, albeit at the risk of hyper-fragmentation. In the United States, by comparison, it is much harder for the two major parties to cultivate clear platforms and to take sharply differing positions. Because the Democrats and the Republicans need to capture a majority of the electorate to win, a particular emphasis must be placed on the so-called swing voters who might be persuaded to support either party. Thus, the parties' policy prescriptions, when viewed in comparison with those that prevail in other countries, tend to be strikingly similar except on a few key wedge issues, and the parties' views usually hew to the political center.

Those who feel unrepresented by both the Democrats and the Republicans are left with the unpalatable choice of casting a "wasted vote" for a minor-party candidate with virtually no opportunity of winning or voting for the lesser of two evils. Many such individuals may choose to abstain from voting entirely, leaving them and their views completely unrepresented. Thus, it is no coincidence that, given that voters must confront frequent, complex balloting offering few ideological choices, U.S. voting rates are among the lowest in the world. Further, there is a distinct skew as to who does and does not vote in the United States: poorer and less educated populations, ethnic and racial minorities, and other disproportionately vulnerable populations are the least likely to cast a ballot or to participate in other forms of conventional political activity. Part of this trend can be explained by the various costs of participation and can be found in other countries as well. But part is attributable to the sense that the two major parties and the system they control do not represent the interests of some people enough to motivate them to vote.

Accountability

While the U.S. system promotes a strong connection between citizens and their individual representatives, it also greatly dilutes the power of political parties. As we have seen, political parties in other countries play a considerably larger role in nominations for election and the career advancement of politicians, giving party leaders far greater leverage for enforcing discipline on their elected officials. Similarly, in parliaments, the failure of a party to keep its majority in line can result in the collapse of a government; in the United States, the consequences are no more dire than a single lost vote on a particular bill. Thus, at election time, voters in parliamentary systems can reasonably consider whether they agree with the priorities articulated by a party and whether those goals have been capably met. In the United States, it is much harder for voters to hold parties accountable in this way: the parties do not speak with one voice, and party leaders cannot reasonably be expected to ensure that a particular agenda is carried into action.

Separation of powers and federalism only magnify the problem of accountability. Particularly when the House, the Senate, and/or the presidency are under the control of different parties, it is all too easy for the Democrats to place blame on the Republicans and vice versa and for different branches or houses to blame one another. Sometimes, no constructive agenda emerges at all, and the government becomes gridlocked into an inertial pattern; other times, compromise and consensus can lead to the formulation of sensible, centrist public policy. But in neither case can a party claim to have carried out its full agenda. Even when one party wields power at both ends of Pennsylvania Avenue, the institutional separation of Congress and the presidency can prevent the party from fully delivering on its promises. Federalism adds yet another dimension, in which state and federal level officials can blame one another for shortcomings, particularly in the way that federal mandates are carried out at the state level. And, finally, politicians can sometimes shift blame to the courts, which regularly employ judicial review to limit the power of legislators and executives. When the time comes for voters to evaluate the performance of their elected officials, it is little surprise that they often are unable to determine who should be held to account.

Conclusion

While there is no perfect political system, some systems can safely be argued to maximize more values for more of their citizens than others. For more than two centuries, the United States has had an unusual combination of political institutions and processes that have rendered it something of an anomaly among the countries of the world. On balance, the American political system provides stability at the cost of flexibility and representation at the expense of accountability. It is a system that in some ways functions well and in others would benefit from significant reform, perhaps brought into the United States by way of examples from other countries. (This theme is the topic of the book *Importing Democracy*, which was written by the author of *The American Anomaly* and is in some ways a successor volume to it.)

Looking forward, sweeping or sudden changes to the American political system seem unlikely and would, in any case, probably be unduly disruptive. The deference and respect afforded to established political processes provides a significant value in itself, and drastic attempts to change them could be more destructive than constructive. At the same time, there can be little doubt that the United States could find ways to maximize a broader range of political values more effectively to more of its citizens than it currently does. Indeed, the challenge of self-government is such that small, slow, incremental, but meaningful ongoing reforms are always necessary. When considering how they can improve upon their political system, Americans would do well to examine their own values and review their own history. But they also should consider the rich insights that the experience of the rest of the world can offer.

For Further Study
A Brief Bibliographic Essay on "American Exceptionalism"

This book is informed by a long history of studies in American exceptionalism, although this literature is not addressed directly in the text. *The American Anomaly* was deliberately written outside the framework of the exceptionalism debate in order to provide a fresh perspective, as well as to make this volume useful as a possible complement to standard introductory American and comparative politics courses. Ideally, for many students, *The American Anomaly* will mark just the beginning of their study of U.S. politics and government in comparative perspective. For those interested in further pursing this theme, several landmark works in the exceptionalist genre, many of which strongly influenced the writing of *The American Anomaly*, are introduced in this essay.

American exceptionalism is generally interpreted to be a school of thought that views U.S. politics and society as a distinctive product of unique circumstances. The exceptionalist perspective argues that from geographic isolation to social mobility, from the national creed to the immigration experience, the United States has been an exception to usual patterns of historical, social, and institutional development. The idea of exceptionalism sometimes also carries a connotation of superiority, implying that the United States is an exceptionally outstanding example of democratic practices and thus worthy of emulation abroad. At times in American history, American exceptionalism, under one name or another, has been used to justify territorial expansion within North America, invasion of foreign lands, and assertion of the moral high ground in international relations. On the domestic front, exceptionalism has been expressed by such ideas as the American Dream of upward social mobility and the United States as the "land of opportunity" for immigrants.

The late eighteenth century produced the earliest and single most authoritative collection of political commentaries explaining exceptionalism with regard to the institutions of the federal government: the Federalist Papers. Published as newspaper articles to urge ratification of the Constitution brokered at the 1787 convention, the articles were originally written under the pseudonym "Publius" but have since been attributed to three of the founders: James Madison, Alexander Hamilton, and John Jay. Among the eighty-five articles, several are widely recognized as masterpieces of political science and have been crucial in the interpretation and development of constitutional thinking. Among those by Hamilton, these include Number 15, making the case for a stronger central government, and Number 78, explaining the role of the judiciary. Madison's articles are perhaps the most important of all, notably Number 10, warning against the "tyranny of the majority"; Number 39, elucidating the new principle of federalism; and Number 51, laying out the logic behind separation of powers with checks and balances, especially between the legislative and executive branches. More than any other source, the Federalist Papers authoritatively explicate the vision of the founding generation for the young nation and its unprecedented new institutions.

Among nineteenth-century writers on the theme of American exceptionalism, two stand out. The first is Alexis de Tocqueville, a French nobleman who visited the United States and in 1835 and in 1849 published his oft-cited two-volume work *Democracy in America*. Drawing on his travels throughout the young republic, Tocqueville described a United States that was sharply different from Europe, stressing democracy, liberty, and equality rather than the more traditional hierarchical values of the Old World. Americans, he found, focused heavily on material accumulation, strongly asserted their individual rights, and actively sought to make their own way in the world. Remarkably insightful, even prescient, Tocqueville remains widely quoted today whenever distinctive patterns of U.S. politics are discussed.

Another outstanding figure of the nineteenth century is the U.S. historian Frederick Jackson Turner. In 1893, Turner published *The Significance of the Frontier in American History,* which placed less emphasis on the country's revolutionary ideals or distinctive social arrangements than on the defining reality of the westward expansion. Turner argued that it was on the ever-shifting frontier—where civilization met and mixed with the untamed—that the American character was forged, becoming more egalitarian and self-reliant, as well as more violent and distrustful of authority. Spawning a massive literature that is both critical and supportive, Turner's work remains a major influence more than a century after it was written.

In 1955, the political scientist Louis Hartz published *The Liberal Tradition in America,* which advanced the highly influential argument that American exceptionalism is rooted mostly in a lack of class conflict. In Europe, the political and economic spheres had long been controlled by a wealthy feudal aristocracy, who completely dominated the impoverished masses. As feudalism declined, class conflict ensued, through which the working people cultivated an ideology of socialism and a desire for social welfare programs. In the process, they came to accept high tax rates and a large government administrative apparatus. With no feudal legacy in the United States and far greater opportunities for individual social mobility, class conflict was relatively muted and neither socialist ideology nor "big government" ever developed. Many of Hartz's arguments about the central role of ideas and culture were validated and expanded by the survey evidence presented in Gabriel Almond and Sidney Verba's *The Civic Culture: Political Attitudes and Democracy in Five Nations* (1965), which compared Italy, France, Great Britain, Germany, and Mexico.

One of the giants of the study of American exceptionalism was the sociologist Seymour Martin Lipset. *The First New Nation: American History and Politics in Comparative Perspective* (1979) examines the social conditions that lead to stable democracy, contrasting the United States with Great Britain, Germany, and France. Lipset's *Continental Divide: The Values and Institutions of the United States and Canada* (1990) explained differences between the United States and its similarly situated neighbor as rooted in the former's revolutionary and the latter's counterrevolutionary histories and ideologies. Lipset also authored *American Exceptionalism: A Double Edged Sword* (1997) and *It Didn't Happen Here: Why Socialism Failed in the United States* (2001, with Gary Marks).

Another giant of the field has been the political scientist Robert Dahl, who is most famous for developing the theory of polyarchy. Polyarchal democracy, Dahl argues, is best understood as a system in which multiple groups and actors interact to produce political outcomes, with no one institution or elite faction having permanent or decisive power. In *A Preface to Democratic Theory* (1956) and *Polyarchy: Participation and Opposition* (1972), he set out basic criteria for polyarchal democracy, such as competitive elections, freedom of expression, and a broad electoral franchise. Dahl's early work is generally positive about U.S. political institutions and processes, but he became more skeptical in later works. In *Democracy and Its Critics* (1989), Dahl argues that no country can fully achieve democracy. *How Democratic Is the U.S. Constitution?* (2001) analyzes weaknesses and idiosyncrasies of the U.S. constitutional order, while *On Democracy* (1998) explores the interactions among political institutions and electoral systems. The comparative role of institutions and electoral systems has also been prominently examined by the political scientist Arend Lijphart in such works as *Patterns of Democracy: Government Forms and Performance in Thirty-Six Countries* (1999).

A number of volumes have been published that analyze the concept of American exceptionalism itself. Charles Lockhart's *The Roots of American Exceptionalism: Institutions, Culture, and Policies* (2003) analyzes the causes and consequences of American differences in public policy, comparing the United States with Sweden on taxation, Canada on health-care financing, France on abortion, and Japan on immigration and citizenship. John Kingdon's *America the Unusual* (1999) develops a theory of path dependency to explain how the unique course of U.S. history first created and then reinforced distinctive political institutions and views. Graham K. Wilson takes a different view in *Only in America?: The Politics of the United States in Comparative Perspective* (1998), arguing that the United States is actually only slightly distinctive. Given their heavily historical and cultural emphasis, all three of these books could serve as useful complements to the institutional emphasis of *The American Anomaly*.

Finally, readers interested in learning more about possible venues for reform of U.S. politics and government may wish to consider reading *Importing Democracy: Ideas from around the World to Reform and Revitalize U.S. Politics and Government*, written by Raymond A. Smith, the author of *The American Anomaly*. *Importing Democracy* explores twenty-one features found in other democracies but not in the United States and evaluates the potential impact of importing into the United States such ideas as proportional representation, a multiparty system, runoff elections, national referenda, synchronized congressional and presidential terms of office, limitations on the use of the veto, legislative overrides of judicial rulings, and streamlined procedures for constitutional amendment.

Glossary Terms

Administration In presidential systems, this refers to the tenure of any specific president (e.g., the Reagan administration) and in this sense is similar to how the word "government" is used in parliamentary systems. "The administration" is construed to include all the major actors of the executive branch, not just the president personally.

Adversarial legal systems An aspect of the common-law tradition whereby the judge acts as a neutral referee while two different sides of the legal question compete to better convince the jury of the rightness of their claims.

American creed The underlying philosophical principles of individual liberty and freedom from tyranny that bind Americans together politically.

American dream The belief that in a free society everyone should have the opportunity to be socially mobile and raise his or her standard of living through hard work and thrift.

American exceptionalism The cultural, demographic, geographic, and historic causes that have led to a divergence in society, politics, and public policy between the United States and the rest of the Western world.

Amicus curiae A brief filed in a legal procedure by an individual or institution that is not a direct party to the case but who has an interest in its outcome.

Apartheid Forced racial separation that channels legal, social, and economic benefits to one racial group at the expense of another. South Africa was notorious for its apartheid regime until the 1990s.

Appropriations Funding that a legislature designates to be used in the administration and execution of the laws it has passed.

Authoritarianism A type of government regime in which leaders are not democratically elected or accountable and in which military, police, or other types of force are often used to suppress political opposition and maintain social control.

Backbencher Members of a legislature, particularly a parliament, who do not have leadership roles or do not head government ministries.

Bicameralism The practice of having a legislature with two chambers. Under symmetric bicameralism, both chambers have equal power. Under asymmetric bicameralism, the lower house is more powerful.

"Big government" A term used by proponents of individual freedom to describe governments that interfere in market processes in order to take responsibility for the well-being of citizens.

Bill of Rights A statement or listing of protections by and from government, often as part of a written constitution.

Branches of government Under separation of powers, the subdivision of the functions of government into separate legislative, executive, and judicial institutions.

Cabinet, parliamentary The collection of ministers (led by a prime minister) that exercise collective executive power in a parliamentary system and are subject to confirmation and removal by the parliament.

Cabinet, presidential Executive actors appointed by and subordinate to an executive president and who head major government departments or ministries.

Candidate-centered elections Campaign style in the United States in which individual candidates, rather than parties, are largely responsible for their own fund-raising and the characteristics of the candidate play a central role in the decision of the voters.

Caucus The grouping of members of the same party in a legislature for the purpose of establishing a working majority, electing leaders, and coordinating legislative strategies.

Checks and balances Powers given to one branch of government to prevent the abuse of power in another, such as the presidential veto or congressional impeachment powers.

Chief diplomat role The power of the president of the United States to conduct foreign relations with other nations.

Civil disobedience A form of nonviolent social protest that makes use of boycotts, strikes, pickets, sit-ins and other forms of nonviolent resistance in order to coerce and embarrass the authorities into repealing discriminatory and exclusionary laws.

Civil-law systems Predominant legal system on the continent of Europe, where the principal meaning of the law is written in the statute itself and the judiciary has little role in interpreting or influencing its meaning.

Civil liberties Individual protections from the power of government, such as the freedom of expression or religion and the right to due process of law.

Civil rights Group protections by government against discriminatory practices, such as segregation or exclusion from employment or higher education.

Coalition government A parliamentary government composed of two or more parties, sharing in executive authority.

Commander-in-chief role The power of the president of the United States to deploy and direct the armed forces.

Common-law systems Legal tradition in which the judiciary and past precedent play a large role in the interpretation of the law and disputes are settled in courtrooms through an adversarial approach.

Communism A political ideology-endorsing rule by a single party, centralized economic planning, and nationalization of industries, in practice usually through the use of political and military repression.

Congress The collective term for the bicameral U.S. national legislature, comprised of a House of Representatives and a Senate; the term is also used for the legislative branch in some other separation-of-powers systems.

Confederation A state with a central government with extremely limited powers and little or no control over the constituent provinces or states, which are largely autonomous.

Congressional committees A division of labor within the Congress whereby different issues are assigned to specialized groups of members of Congress who are then given considerable influence over the makeup and fate of the bills that fall under their jurisdiction.

Congressional districts The geographic boundary set up by each state that establishes the constituents of each member of the House of Representatives.

Consociational democracy A form of political arrangement in which certain major groupings (e.g., religious, ethnic, or linguistic) are guaranteed significant participation in the governing process and, sometimes, a veto on issues of crucial importance to them.

Constituency The population of the geographic district represented by an elected official or, more informally, groupings of a politician's supporters.

Constitution The authoritative set of rules that organize a state, most typically compiled in a single written document that is considered binding in democratic systems.

Constitutional Convention Referring to the formal meeting of U.S. delegates in the summer of 1787 who ultimately voted on the text of the U.S. Constitution, this term could be used to refer to similar meetings in the United States (as on the state level) or in other countries.

Constitutional court A high-level branch of the judiciary that is tasked with interpreting the meaning and application of a constitution and that typically does not hear other types of cases.

Conventional political participation Modes of working within or exerting pressure upon the political system that are within the boundaries of socially acceptable behavior and established legal norms.

Corporatism A term in the field of political economy that describes how many some countries grant semiofficial status to associations or federations that negotiate policy with the government on behalf of their members.

Direct democracy As opposed to representative democracy, an electoral procedure in which major decisions are made by citizens via a ballot or a large meeting. Referendums are a common if more limited mechanism for direct democracy used in many representative democracies.

Districts The geographic boundaries within which representatives to legislatures are elected; they are periodically subject to redistricting to achieve rough population parity over time.

Divided government Made possible by the separation-of-powers feature of the U.S. government, divided government occurs when one political party controls the presidency and another political party controls at least one house of Congress.

Dual executives A scheme of government found in many parliamentary systems in which the day-to-day process of governing is handled by the prime minister and the ceremonial and symbolic duties of the head of state are executed by either a monarch or a figurehead president.

Duverger's law The observation advanced by sociologist Maurice Duverger that the number of parties in a political system is largely a function of its electoral process, with the use of proportional representation tending to create multiparty systems and the use of the plurality rule leading to two-party systems.

Electoral College The unique and peculiar system in the United States in which presidents are formally chosen by electors from each state rather than directly as a result of the popular vote.

Electoral thresholds In a multiparty system, this is the lowest percentage of votes that a party must receive in order to holds seats in parliament.

Ethnicity A common heritage that helps create a group's communal identity; often including language, religion, and cultural customs.

Exceptionalism The concept that the United States, because of geographic isolation, social organization, and other factors, has followed a distinctive historical and institutional pattern. Often called "American exceptionalism."

Executive The portion of a government tasked with executing, enforcing, or implementing laws and regulations, usually through a large bureaucratic apparatus.

Faction A segment of society that acts through or upon government to further its specific geographic or economic interests, which may be at odds with the nation's common good or needs.

Federalism The division of sovereign functions between a strong central government and multiple states or provinces, with each level having distinctive as well as overlapping areas of power and responsibility.

Filibuster A parliamentary maneuver that one or a handful of senators in the U.S. Senate can use to stall pending legislation through endless debate unless three-fifths of the chamber votes for cloture, which ends debate and allows a vote to take place on the measure at hand.

Gerrymandering A pejorative term used for legislative redistricting into oddly shaped geographic boundaries in order to boost the prospects of particular parties or candidates.

Globalization The process of increased worldwide economic interdependence that is the result of increased communications and transportation technology.

Government In presidential systems, this term usually applies to the entirety of executive, legislative, and judicial branches. In parliamentary systems, the term applies only to the current majority in the lower house of Parliament that exercises executive power.

Governor general A ceremonial position whose occupant represents the British monarch in a small group of former colonies of the United Kingdom.

Green parties Leftist political parties that represent voters who place a premium on policies that promote environmental sustainability and that also highlight those issues before the general public.

Gridlock A term for political inaction and stasis that results when divergent factions and/or parties in the government are unable to reach political compromise. Gridlock occurs most frequently during periods of divided government when political parties are internally homogenous, which leaves little room for agreement between the opposing parties.

Head of government The head of the executive branch in the actual governance of a nation. In a parliamentary system, this is the prime minister; in a presidential system, this is the president.

Head of state The head of the executive branch in a symbolic or ceremonial capacity with little or no actual power. In a parliamentary system, this is generally a figurehead president or monarch; in a presidential system, this is the president.

Idealist school of foreign policy An approach to international relations that argues that politics need not be a zero-sum game and that, through careful negotiation and diplomacy, seemingly competitive nations can achieve mutual benefit.

Immigration The inflow of people into a country from foreign countries, whether through legal channels or by illegal means.

Impeachment The charging of a government official with an offense meriting removal from office, generally carried out by the legislative body.

Incumbency effect A term used to describe how a politician can use the resources and influence of political office to gain the support of critical constituencies and potential donors to perpetuate his or her stay in power.

Incumbent A politician in a particular elected office who is up for reelection.

Information costs The time and effort that voters must expend to be informed and actively engaged in the political process.

Inquisitorial legal systems A legal system in which, rather than serve as a neutral arbiter, the judge plays an active role on behalf of the government in finding out the true facts of the case.

Interest group An organized group of individuals or organizations that makes policy-related appeals to the government.

Judicial activism In common-law system, this term is used (often pejoratively) to describe a judiciary that is viewed as meddling too much in the affairs of the legislative or executive branches of government.

Judicial review The power of the courts to declare legislation or the acts of an executive unconstitutional.

Judiciary The branch of government, composed of law courts, with the power to resolve legal conflicts and, in many countries, constitutional questions.

Legislature A branch of government tasked with passing laws and, usually, appropriating public funds.

Liberty The right to direct one's own life in a way that is free from external interference. Some conceptions of liberty also include the right of the individual to count on the state to create policies that enhance his or her freedom to act.

Limited government A policy preference of many conservatives who want as little government interference in the economy as possible. This policy preference may also extend to socially liberal voters who wish for little interference from the state in their individual lives.

"Living Constitution" One side of the debate over the interpretation of the Constitution of the United States, this term emphasizes that it is a document that steadily evolves and adapts with the times.

Lobbying Efforts by individuals or organizations to sway government officials to their position and/or to obtain benefits from government.

Lower houses, legislative The political body in a congress or parliament that is the most democratically elected and therefore is directly responsive to the wishes of the people. In most countries, this is the most important chamber in the legislative process.

Manifest destiny The belief that all or much of the territory in North America should be under the domain of the United States. This belief spurred the American westward expansion in the nineteenth century and is related to the concept of American exceptionalism.

Mass-membership party Political party in which a constituents who are members of an organization (typically a labor union) are automatically enrolled.

Military regimes Governments that rule by physical coercion and in which democratic elections and the will of the people are often ignored.

Mixed-member electoral system A hybrid electoral process in which each voter casts two votes in a legislative election, one for a candidate in a plurality election and one for a party list.

Monarchy Rule by a king or queen, usually hereditary, and often in a purely figurehead capacity alongside an elected parliament. Constitutional monarchs are no longer able to exercise actual political power.

Monroe Doctrine Foreign policy first initiated by President James Monroe that declared that any interference by European powers in the Western Hemisphere would not be tolerated and would be seen as an act of aggression.

Multimember district Under rules of proportional representation, the election of multiple representatives to represent the same electoral district.

Multiparty system A party system with three, four, five, or more parties that all contend for power and win some legislative seats.

NAFTA The North American Free Trade Agreement of 1993, which was seen as a boon to commerce by some and criticized as benefiting larger conglomerations at the expense of farmers and laborers by others.

Nation The collective identity of a people who are bound by a common geography, culture, and history.

NATO (North Atlantic Treaty Organization) Military pact formed in the early years of the Cold War that was designed to unite capitalist democracies in their opposition to the Soviet Union's military intervention in Europe.

New Deal The political program of President Franklin Delano Roosevelt that was put in place to help overcome the Great Depression and that greatly expanded the role of the federal government and created a limited social welfare system in the United States.

"Notwithstanding" clause A provision placed in the Canadian constitution that allows the federal government or a provincial government to reassert any law "notwithstanding" that the courts had struck down it down through judicial review.

Opposition In a parliament, members of parties that are not part of the governing coalition. The largest such party is sometimes called the "Official Opposition," and its head is the "Leader of the Opposition."

Pardon power The only directly unchecked power of the president, through which immunity for a federal crime can be granted to anyone the president chooses.

Parliamentary supremacy Principle in some parliamentary systems in which acts of the legislature or executive cannot be overridden by courts of law.

Parliamentary threshold The practice of excluding parties from legislative representation unless they win a minimum percentage of the vote, commonly 5 percent.

Plurality system An electoral process that awards a legislative seat or other political office to the individual with the largest number of votes, which may or may not be a majority when there are more than two candidates.

Political party A formally organized body that articulates public policy goals, contests elections, and forms caucuses within legislatures.

President In a presidential system, the elected head of state and head of government. In parliamentary republics, usually a figurehead with a ceremonial role but little actual political power.

Presidential model The separation-of-powers system of government, in which a single elected official is both head of state and head of government.

Presidential veto Prerogative of the executive branch that allows a president to refuse to sign an act of Congress, thus preventing it from becoming law. In the United States, a vetoed bill may still become law if the Congress in turn overrides the veto by a two-thirds vote.

Primary elections Feature of the American political system in which the nominees of each political party for office are chosen in an election by voters, usually those registered with that party, rather than by party leaders.

Prime minister In parliamentary systems, the head of government and leader of the cabinet who is also generally the leader of the majority party or coalition in the Parliament.

Proportional representation The awarding of legislative seats in close proportion to the number of votes won in any given district, usually in a multimember district.

Realist school of foreign policy Assumption that all nations on the world state are concerned principally with their own aggrandizement, power, and national interest and that therefore policymakers should focus only on practical policies to protect the homeland from foreign threats to its own interests.

Reapportionment The periodic reallocation of seats in a legislature to reflect changes in population over time.

Redistricting The process of periodically changing the boundaries and composition of legislative districts, often following a census.

Regimes The specific qualities of the legal, political, and cultural institutions that make up a state's governing structures.

Representative democracy In contrast to direct democracy, a system of government in which political and policy decisions are made by elected officials.

Responsible government Trait of parliamentary systems that fuse executive and legislative power and thus makes it easier for voters to know which political actors to blame or reward in the next electoral cycle.

Secret ballot Trademark of free and fair elections that guarantees that the privacy of the voter will be protected to ensure that his or her voting choices are uncoerced.

Semipresidential system A hybrid system of government in which executive power is shared by a directly elected president and a prime minister with the support of the parliament, sometimes resulting in confused lines of power and responsibility.

Separation of powers The subdivision of government powers into distinct executive, legislative, and judicial functions, usually institutionally isolated from each other and elected or appointed through different processes.

Shadow cabinet In a parliament, the "cabinet in waiting" of the Opposition.

Single-member-plurality system An electoral system under which each election can have only one winner, the candidate who gains the most votes, which is usually an outright majority in a two-party system.

Single-party systems Characteristic of nondemocratic regimes that have either outlawed or crippled all opposition political parties, effectively leaving the state with one-party rule.

Snap election A quick vote called on short notice, such as several weeks, by a prime minister rather than an election occurring on a fixed, predictable schedule.

Socialism A political ideology emphasizing redistribution of wealth and an activist role for government.

Sovereignty The universal recognition of a nation's autonomy and right to govern its domestic realm free from direct foreign influence. Sovereign states have no higher legal authority above them, although they may choose to bind themselves through bilateral or multilateral treaties.

Stare decisis Feature of the common-law system meaning "let the decision stand," referring to the legal tradition of deferring to past precedent.

State (concept) An independent and sovereign entity within the international system, characterized by a distinct population and territory and the legal right to exert control within its borders.

State of emergency A governmental declaration that some normal rights or political processes will suspended in order to more effectively address a crisis.

Subsidiarity The idea that as many decisions as possible should be made by the legal entity that is closest to the people, such as a local government.

Substantive democracy A definition of democracy with regard primarily to the equalization of socioeconomic status and access to basic human needs.

Supreme court Generally, the highest judicial body in a particular country or other jurisdiction.

Totalitarian regimes A political structure that seeks to control all aspects of the individual's life and subordinates it to the needs of the state.

Two-party system A political configuration in which only two major parties, relatively well matched in terms of electoral support, can effectively win elections, with minor parties relegated to virtually no effective political role. In a *two-party-plus system*, minor parties play a somewhat more active role.

Unconventional participation Political pressure exerted on the establishment that exceeds the boundaries of socially and legally acceptable behavior.

Unicameralism A form of government with only one legislative chamber to make laws.

Unitary states Countries in which all governing decisions are made at the national level and merely implemented by provincial or local governments.

Upper houses, legislative Chambers of legislatures that are designed to refine and temper legislation passed by the lower house. The members of many houses are less democratically elected than those of lower houses. Some upper houses share full authority with lower houses.

Veto The ability of an executive to reject legislation, usually subject to a legislative override. More informally, the term refers to the ability to effectively stop a piece of legislation anywhere in the process, such as at the committee stage.

Vote of no confidence A motion to determine whether a prime minister or cabinet still has the support of a majority in Parliament, without which it must resign and call a new election.

Voting Rights Act of 1965 Law proposed and signed by President Lyndon Johnson that fulfilled the promise of the Fifteenth amendment and legally prohibited the disenfranchisement of any American on the basis of race.

War Powers Resolution of 1973 A controversial act of Congress that places a ninety-day limit on the president's ability to deploy the armed forces without congressional approval.

Westminster model The parliamentary configuration first developed in the United Kingdom and since adopted, with some modifications, around the world.

Westward migration The massive flow of Americans in the nineteenth century toward the heartland and the Pacific coast in search of open spaces, cheaper land, and opportunity while the frontier was still open. This experience is closely related to the concept of American exceptionalism.

Winner-take-all elections Electoral system that allocates political office to the winner of the most votes even if the candidate falls short of a majority. Also referred to as "first-past-the-post".

World Trade Organization Powerful free-trade advocacy group that provides a forum for international agreements in an effort to encourage market relationships.

Zapatistas Leftist protest organization in Mexico that has used violent means to challenge authoritarian practices of the government, as well as to fight for policies that are favorable to the poor and indigenous peoples.

This glossary was prepared with the assistance of Brandon L. H. Aultman and Peter Capp.

Index

Page numbers in *italics* indicate charts, figures, or tables.

Aboriginal peoples 177
accountability 55–6, 201–2
activism 95, 110–14
ACT UP (protest group) 112
adversarial legal systems 95, 209
Afghanistan 71, 182, 186, 189, 193, 195
African Americans 37, 109–10, 169, 176
Ahmadinejad, Mahmoud 123
AIDS 112, 194
Albania 183
Allende, Salvador 191
Allied Powers 34–5
Almond, Gabriel 206–7
ambassadors 187
amending process, constitutional 21–3, 24–5, 25, 83, 200; *see also specific amendments*
American Creed 8–9, 209
American exceptionalism xiv, 159, 205–8
American Exceptionalism (Lipset) 207
America the Unusual (Kingdon) 207
antidiscrimination laws 178; *see also* segregation
apartheid 176, 209
appropriations 83, 87, 186, 209
Arab Spring 11, 94, 173
Argentina 10, 71, 188, 194
Armenian Americans 190
Armenians 173

Articles of Confederation 31
Asia, Southeast 61–3
Asian Americans 178
association, freedom of 114
asymmetric bicameralism 78–9, 81–2
Aung San Suu Kyi 62–3
Australia *xviii–xix*, 9–10, 79, 82–3, 84, 177
Austria *xviii–xix*
authoritarian regimes 12

Baathist Party 141
backbenchers, parliamentary 47–8, 52
Barbados 176
Barbary pirates 187
Belgium *xviii–xix*, 31, 68, 146, 191
bicameralism 78–9, 81–5, 209
Biden, Joe 72
"big government" 159–60, 169–70, 209
Bill of Rights (U.S.) 99; *see also* specific amendments
Blair, Tony 47, 52, 189
Board of Estimate (New York City) 81
Bosnia and Hercegovina 32, 146
Brady Campaign to End Handgun Violence 114
Brandeis, Louis 36
Brazil 22, 176
Britain: about *xx–xxi*; civil liberties 173; constitution 19, 21; elections 135; executive power 70; foreign policy 188, 190–1; judicial branch 98; labor

unions 116; parliamentary system 41–3, 47, 52, 55; political parties 141, 143–4; religion 117; as unitary state 34
Brown, Gordon 52
Brown v. Board of Education 99, 100, 112
Brunei 62, 63
Bulgaria 25
Bundestag (Germany) 144–5
burakumin (Japanese caste) 176
bureaucracy 73–4
Bush, George H. W. 199
Bush, George W. 54, 98, 133, 134, 186, 199

cabinet (parliamentary) 45, 46, 47, 51, 73
cabinet (U.S.) 72–3
cadre parties 149
California 23, 84
campaign finance 115, 123, 124
campaigns 123–4
Canada: about *xviii–xix*; civil liberties 173; civil rights 177; constitution 98; domestic policy 171; federalism 31; judicial branch 98–9; legislative branch 78–9, 81, 82; nationhood, development of 9; parliamentary system 52; political parties 141, 143–4
candidate-centered elections 201, 209
Carter, Jimmy 54, 189, 199
caste system 176
Catalans (Spain) 38
Catholic Church 117, 174
chancellors *see* prime ministers
Charter of Fundamental Rights (European Union) 172
Chaudry, Iftikhar 93–4
checks and balances 40, 48–51, 82
Cheney, Dick 72
Chiapas 106–7, 111
chief diplomat role 61, 62, 68, 75, 186, 209
Chile 191, 194
China 111, 172, 173, 182–5, 190, 194
Chretien, Jean 52
Christian Democratic Party (Germany) 145

church and state, separation of 117, 158
churches, established 158
Church of England 117
citizenship 125–6
Citizens United case 115
Civic Culture, The (Almond and Verba) 206–7
civil disobedience 112, 209
civil-law systems 94, 95, *96–7*, 97, 210
civil liberties 167, 171–4, *175*
civil rights 167, 175–9
Civil Rights Act of 1964 99, 176
civil rights movement, U.S. 109–10, 111–12
civil service 73–4
Civil War, Russian 187
Civil War, U.S. 109, 181
civil wars 108–9
class conflict 112–13, 206–7
climate change 189
Clinton, Bill 53, 54, 69, 188, 199
coalition governments 45, 48, 52–3
cohabitation 68
Cold War 169, 182, 191–3, 194
Colombia 108
commander-in-chief role 61, 186, 210
committees, congressional 85, 87, 210
common-law systems 94–5, *96*, 97, 210
Communism 172, 182, 183–5, 193, 194–5
competitive elections 122–5
Comprehensive Nuclear Test Ban Treaty 188
compulsory voting 126
confederations 28–31, *38*
Congress (Mexico) 89
Congress (Peru) 89
Congress (U.S.): about 77; committee system 85, 87, 210; foreign policy 186–7; importance of 89–90; party leaders 47, 48, 85–6; power, dispersal of 85–8; *see also* House of Representatives (U.S.); Senate (U.S.)
congressional committees 85, 87, 210
congressional districts 124, 129–30, 210
consent of the governed (concept) 13, 17

Conservative Party (Britain) 55, 143
Conservative Party (Canada) 143
consociational democracy 146
Constitution (U.S.): about *xxvi*;
  amending process 22, 23, 25, 83,
  200; anachronistic elements 23,
  25–6; brevity and vagueness 17, 18,
  20–1; civil liberties 174; elections
  121, 130; foreign policy 181, 186,
  187; importance of 10–11; legislative
  branch 23, 84; separation of powers
  40; social and economic protections
  18, 25–6; *see also* constitutions (general); *specific amendments*
Constitutional Convention 22
Constitutional Council (France) 92
constitutional courts 99
constitutional monarchs 65, 69
constitutions (general): amending
  21–3, *24–5*; Brazil 22; Britain 19,
  21; Bulgaria 25; Canada 98; France
  21; India 20; Israel 19–20; New
  Zealand 19, 21; North Korea 19;
  Peru 89; social and economic protections 18–19, 25–6; South Africa
  18–19; *see also* Constitution (U.S.)
Continental Divide, The (Lipset) 207
contra rebels 191
conventional political participation 105,
  106, *106*, 210; *see also* elections;
  political parties; voting
Convention on the Elimination of All
  Forms of Discrimination against
  Women 189
corporatism 116, 210
Costa Rica *xviii–xix*
Council of State (France) 92
Court of Cassation (France) 92
court system *see* judicial branch
creationism 157
Cuba 190
Cuban Americans 177, 190
Cultural Revolution 183

Dahl, Robert 207
Dalai Lama 183
Declaration of Independence 171
defense, national 169–70
Defense Ministry (China) 184

democracies, major: constitutional
  amendments *24–5*; executive power
  66–7; federal *versus* unitary states *30*;
  incarceration rates *175*; judicial
  branch *96–7*; legislative branch *80*;
  military spending *192*; political parties *142–3*; regional breakdown *5*;
  unitary states *30*; voter turnout *127*;
  see also specific countries
Democracy and Its Critics (Dahl) 207
Democracy in America (Tocqueville)
  206
Democratic Party (U.S.) 64, 117,
  148, 149–50
democratic peace theory 195
democratic regimes 12–13
Denmark *xviii–xix*, 165–7
desegregation 99, 100, 109–10; *see also*
  segregation
Detroit 110
dictatorships 122–3
direct democracy (concept) 119
directors-general 73–4
disabilities, people with 179
districts, congressional 124,
  129–30, 210
divided government 54, *55*, 210
domestic policy 165–80; about *xxviii*,
  165; big government, skepticism of
  169–71; Canada 171; civil liberties
  167, 171–4, *175*; civil rights 167,
  175–9; Denmark 165–7; importance
  of 179; socioeconomic policy 167–9;
  stability in 199
Dominican Republic 189
dual executives 64–5, 67–8, 210
Duverger, Maurice 139
Duverger's Law 139, 140

economy (U.S.) 14–15, 167–9
education 36–7, 167
Egypt 94, 123
Election Day 126
elections: about *xxvii*, 119; Britain 135;
  campaigns 123–4; candidate-centered
  201, 209; competitive 122–5;
  Constitution (U.S.) 121, 130; Egypt
  123; fair 121–2; free 120–1; Iran
  123; Iraq 123; Israel 119–20, 126,

132; Mexico 121; minor parties 125, 133; parliamentary system 45–6, 123, 132, 135; political parties 124; primary 124–5, 212; separation of powers 53–4, 134; snap 45; two-party systems 124–5; two-stage 133; Ukraine 121–2; winner-take-all 129–30, 134–5, 214; *see also* voting
Electoral College (U.S.) 23, 84, 133–5, 144
electoral franchise *see* voting
electoral thresholds 144–5, 210
El Salvador 189
emergency, state of *xxiv*, 89, 213
employment security 168
"end of history" thesis 193
environmentalism 112
equal protection 178
equal representation in the Senate 23, 83, 84–5
Equal Rights Amendment (ERA) 178
Esther, Subcommandante 107–8
ethnicity (concept) 4, 210
European Union 28–31, 49, 172, 182, 194
evolution 157
exceptionalism, American xiv, 159, 205–8
Exceptionalism Index 160
executive power 61–76; about *xxvi*, 61; Afghanistan 71; Africa 71; Brunei 62, 63; comparative perspective 68–70; democracies, major *66–7*; dual executives 64–5, 67–8; France 68, 72; Indonesia 62; Latin America 70–1; Malaysia 62; Mexico 72; Myanmar 62–3; nondemocratic countries 63–4; Palestinian Authority 68; parliamentary *66–7*; presidential *66*, 68–71; semipresidential *66*, 68; separation of powers 70–1; Southeast Asia 61–3; Ukraine 68; Vietnam 63; *see also* prime ministers
expression, freedom of 172–4; *see also* First Amendment
EZLN *see* Zapatistas (Mexico)

factions 114, 138, 210
Falkland Islands 188

federalism: about *xxvi*; accountability 202; advantages 36; Belgium 31; Canada 31; countries using *30*, 35–6; democracies, major *30*; disadvantages 36–7; forms 37–8; Germany 34–5; parliamentary system 49; Spain 38; Switzerland 31
Federalist Papers, The 40, 114, 138, 205–6
federations 28, *38*
Fifteenth Amendment 99; *see also* voting
filibuster 86, 210
Finland *xx–xxi*
First Amendment 117, 158
First Nations 177
First New Nation, The (Lipset) 207
"first-past-the-post" *see* single-member plurality
flag, burning of 83, 172
Flanders 146
flexibility 199–200
Florida 122, 134
foreign policy 181–97; about *xxviii*, 181–2; Belgium 191; Britain 188, 190–1; China 182–5, 190, 194; Congress (U.S.) 186–7; Constitution (U.S.) 181, 186, 187; European Union 182; France 190–1; Germany 188–9, 191; importance of 195–6; Japan 191; legislative branch 189; Netherlands 191; policymaking 185–90; realist and idealist perspectives 190–5; Russia 191, 194; Senate (U.S.) 187, 188, 189; separation of powers 189; Serbia 191, 195; stability in 199
Fourteenth Amendment 99, 178; *see also* equal protection
Fourth Amendment 174
Fox, Vicente 107
Fox News 159
France: about *xx–xxi*; civil liberties 173; constitution 21; executive power 68, 72; foreign policy 190–1; interest groups 116; judicial branch 91–2, 94, 99; legislative branch 81; political parties 149; political violence 110; regimes 11; religiosity and

moral values 157; socioeconomic policy 168; as unitary state 34
freedom of association 114
freedom of expression 172–4; *see also* First Amendment
French Revolution 91–2
Fujimori, Alberto 89

Gandhi, Mohandas 111
gay rights 112
Gaza Strip 120
gender identity 179
geography (U.S.) 13, 14
Georgia, Republic of 194
Germany: about xx–xxi; civil liberties 173; federalism 34–5; foreign policy 188–9, 191; naturalization procedures 126; political parties 144–5; regimes 11–12; snap elections 45; World War II aftermath 32, 34–5
gerrymander 124
globalization 182, 210
Google 173
Gore, Al 72, 98, 133, 134
government: big 159–60, 169–70, 209; coalition 45, 48, 52–3; divided 54, 55, 210; limited 17, 211; local-level 28, 81; national-level 28; responsible 55, 213; state 34, 81; as term 6; *see also specific topics*
governors general 65, 106, 211
Great Britain *see* Britain
Great Powers 182, 191
Great Recession (2008-9) 113, 152, 193
Greece 47
green parties 128, 133, 147, 211
gridlock 55, 211
Guatemala 191
Gulf of Tonkin Resolution 185–6

Haiti 176
Hamdan case 98
Hamilton, Alexander 91, 205–6
hard power 15, 184
Harper, Stephen 82
Hartz, Louis 206–7
head of state role 64, 65, 67–8, 68–70
health care 37, 54–5, 160, 167–8, 200

Hmong Americans 177
Holocaust 173
Honduras 189
House of Commons (Canada) 78, 79, 82, 143
House of Commons (Great Britain) 42–3
House of Lords (Great Britain) 42, 43, 117
House of Representatives (Australia) 79, 82–3
House of Representatives (New Zealand) 78, 79
House of Representatives (U.S.): elections 124, 130, 134; party leaders 86; power 82, 83; *see also* Congress (U.S.)
How Democratic is the U.S. Constitution? (Dahl) 207
human rights 18, 107, 148, 186, 194
Hurricane Katrina 37, 113
Hussein, Saddam 123, 192–3

Iceland xx–xxi
idealist school of foreign policy 194–5, 211
IMF (International Monetary Fund) 194
immigration 83, 148, 156, 170, 171, 177
impartiality of courts 93, 94
impeachment 53, 69
Importing Democracy (Smith) 202, 208
incarceration 174, *175,* 200
incumbency effect 124, 211
independence of courts 93–4
India xx–xxi, 20, 111, 176
Indonesia 36, 62
information costs 128, 211
Inglehart, Ronald 153
Inglehart Values Map 153–5, *154,* 156
inquisitorial legal systems 95, 97, 211
instant runoff voting 133
integration 99, 100, 109–10; *see also* segregation
intelligent design theory 157
interest groups 114–17, 189–90
International Monetary Fund (IMF) 194

international relations 190–5, *192*
Internet 173
Internet activism 113–14
Iran 111, 123, 152–3, 191–3
Iraq: elections 123; invasion of 182, 186, 188–9, 193, 194; parliamentary system 41; political parties 146
Ireland *xxii–xxiii*
iron triangles 116
Islam 117, 174, 182
Israel: about *xxii–xxiii*; constitution 19–20; foreign policy (U.S.) 189–90; political parties 145, 148; voting and elections 119–20, 126, 132
Italy *xxii–xxiii*, 53, 82, 145, 148–9
It Didn't Happen Here (Lipset and Marks) 207

Jamaica 176
Japan: about *xxii–xxiii*; civil rights 176–7; foreign policy 191; interest groups 116; public opinion and political values 152; snap elections 45; as unitary state 32–3
Japanese Americans 177, 186
Jay, John 205–6
Jefferson, Thomas 171, 181
Jewish Americans 189–90
Johnson, Lyndon B. 185–6
journalistic objectivity 173–4
Juan Carlos I, King 65, 67
judges, lifetime appointment of 94
judicial activism 95, 211
judicial branch 91–102; about *xxvii*, 91; Britain 98; Canada 98–9; democracies, major *96–7*; Egypt 94; France 91–2, 94, 99; impartiality of courts 93, 94; importance of 101; independence of courts 93–4; judicial review 97–100; Pakistan 93–4; parliamentary system 49; as separate and coequal branch 94–5, 97
judicial review 97–100
Jura (Switzerland) 84

Kadima Party (Israel) 120, 145
Karzai, Hamid 71

Katrina, Hurricane 37, 113
Kennedy, John F. 122
King, Martin Luther, Jr. 110
Kingdon, John 207
Knesset (Israel) 119–20, 132, 145
Koizumi, Junichiro 45
Korea, North 19
Koreans (in Japan) 126
Korean War 187
Korematsu v. U.S. 186
Kosovo 195
Kuomintang 183
Kyoto Protocol 189

labor unions 112–13, 116–17, 148, 149
Labour Party (Britain) 52, 55, 116, 143
länder governments (Germany) 35
Latin America 70–1, 89, 150; *see also specific countries*
Latinos 178
Law Lords 42
Leader of the Opposition 48
leaders, political party 47–8, 85–6, 88
League of Nations 188
Lebanon 146
legal defense
legislative branch 77–90; about *xxvii*; Australia 79, 82–3, 84; bicameralism, asymmetric 78–9, 81–2; bicameralism, symmetric 79, 82–5; Canada 78–9, 81, 82; comparative perspective 88–9; Constitution (U.S.) 23, 84; democracies, major *80*; foreign policy 189; France 81; Italy 82; Latin America 89; Mexico 89; New Zealand 78, 79; parliamentary system 55, *80*; Peru 89; separation of powers 88–9; Switzerland 84; unicameralism 78, 79, 81
Legislative Council (New Zealand) 78
Lewinsky, Monica 54
Liberal Party (Britain) 143
Liberal Party (Canada) 143
Liberal Tradition in America, The (Hartz) 206–7

Libertarian Party (U.S.) 125
liberty (concept) 8–9, 165, 170, 171–2, 211
Lijphardt, Arend 207
Likud Party (Israel) 120, 145
limited government (concept) 17, 211
Lipset, Seymour Martin 3, 207
Little Rock 109
"Living Constitution" (concept) 21, 95, 211
local-level government 28, 81
Lockhart, Charles 207
Lopez case 97–8
Los Angeles 190
Los Angeles riots 110
Louisiana 37
lower houses, legislative 43–4, 48–9, 211
Luxembourg *xxii–xxiii*

Madison, James 40, 114, 138, 205–6
Magna Carta 42
Malaysia 62
manifest destiny (concept) 8, 212
Mao, Zedong 183
Marbury v. Madison 97
Marcos, Subcommandante 107
Marks, Gary 207
Marshall Plan 194
Martin, Paul 52
mass-membership parties 149, 212
McVeigh, Timothy 108
Medicare and Medicaid 167
Mexico 9, 72, 89, 106–8, 111, 121
Mexico City 107–8, 111
military (U.S.) 186–7
military regimes 63, 212
military spending 191, *192*
Ministry of Justice (France) 92
minority rights 99–100
minor parties 125, 133, 144
Mitterand, François 157
Mohammed, Prophet 167
monarchs, constitutional 65, 69
Monroe, James 181
Monroe Doctrine 181, 212
Montana 149

moral values 156–9
Morsi, Mohammed 94, 123
Mossadegh, Mohammad 191–2
Mubarak, Hosni 123
multimember districting *see* proportional representation
multiparty systems *142–3*, 144–6
Musharraf, Pervez 93–4
Muslims *see* Islam
Myanmar 62–3

NAACP (National Organization for the Advancement of Colored People) 112
Nader, Ralph 133, 148
NAFTA (North American Free Trade Agreement) 107, 212
Napoleon Bonaparte 92
Napoleonic Code 92
nation (concept) 4, 6, 7–10, 212
national-level government 28
National Organization for the Advancement of Colored People (NAACP) 112
National Organization for Women (NOW) 114
national pride 159–60
National Rifle Association (NRA) 114
National Right-to-Life Committee 114
nation-state, as term 4
Native Americans 178
NATO (North Atlantic Treaty Organization) 181, 193, 194, 212
naturalization 126
Nazi regime 11, 182, 194
Nebraska 81
negative liberty 165, 171
neo-Nazis 172
Netherlands *xxii–xxiii*, 191
Netroots 113–14
Newark (New Jersey) 110
New Deal 169, 171
New Democratic Party (Canada) 143
New Orleans 37
news media 172, 173
New South Wales (Australia) 84
New York City 37, 81, 128

New York Times 189
New Zealand *xxii–xxiii*, 9–10, 19, 21, 78, 79
Nicaragua 191
Nixon, Richard 64, 70, 98, 122, 199
no confidence, vote of 52–3
nonviolent activism 110–14
Nordic countries, political parties in 145–6
North American Free Trade Agreement (NAFTA) 107, 212
North Atlantic Treaty Organization (NATO) 181, 193, 194, 212
North Dakota 36
North Korea 19
Norway *xxiv–xxv*
Notwithstanding Clause 98–9, 212
NOW (National Organization for Women) 114
NRA (National Rifle Association) 114
nuclear disarmament 112
nuclear weapons 182, 188

Obama, Barack: elections 113–14, 129, 136, 149; foreign policy 184, 187, 193, 199; health care 160; legislative branch and 85–6; separation of powers 54
Obamacare 98, 171
objectivity, journalistic 173–4
Occupy Wall Street movement 113
Ohio 122
Oklahoma City bombing 108, 110
On Democracy (Dahl) 207
one person–one vote standard of democracy 84
Only in America? (Wilson) 207
opinion, public *see* public opinion
opposition, parliamentary 48, 51
Orange Revolution (Ukraine) 122
O'Reilly, Bill 159
original intent 95
Orthodox Christianity 117
"Other Campaign, The" (Mexico) 108

Pakistan 93–4, 183
Palestinian Authority 68, 120
pardon power (U.S. presidential) 64, 212

Paris 110
parliamentary executive power 66–7
parliamentary supremacy 98–9, 212
parliamentary system: about 41; accountability 202; backbenchers 47–8, 52; bicameralism, symmetric 82–3; Britain 41–3; cabinet 45, 46, 47, 51, 73; Canada 52; checks and balances 48–51; coalition governments 45, 48, 52–3; coordination between legislative and executive powers 55; elections 45–6, 123, 132, 135; federalism 49; Iraq 41; judicial branch 49; legislative branch *80*; lower house of parliament 43–4, 48–9; opposition 48, 51; party leaders 47–8, 88; power, fusion of 43–6; prime minister 43–5; prime ministerial accountability to parliament 51–6; prime ministerial power 47–51; separation of powers *versus* 44, 46, 55; supranational entities 49; terms of office 46; upper house of parliament 48–9; vote of no confidence 52–3; Westminster model 41–3, *44*, 49, 50, 62; *see also* separation of powers
parties *see* political parties
Patient Protection and Affordable Care Act 98, 171
patriotism 159–60
Patterns of Democracy (Lijphardt) 207
Paul, Ron 125
Peace Corps 194
peace movements 112
Pearl Harbor 186
Pentagon Papers 189
Peron, Juan 71
Perot, H. Ross 144, 147
Peru 89
Pew Global Attitudes Project 156
Philippines 111
Planned Parenthood 114
Pledge of Allegiance 11
Poland 6–7
political participation: about *xxvii*, 105–6, *106*; activism, nonviolent 110–14; conventional 105, 106, *106*, 210; interest groups 114–17; Mexico

106–8, 111; unconventional 105, 106, *106,* 213; violence, political 108–10; *see also* elections; political parties; voting
political parties: about *xxviii,* 138; accountability 201–2; Belgium 146; Bosnia 146; Britain 141, 143–4; Canada 141, 143–4; case study, hypothetical 139–41, *140;* democracies, major *142–3;* elections 124; electoral systems 139–41; France 149; Germany 144–5; Iraq 146; Israel 145, 148; Italy 145, 148–9; Latin America 150; leaders 47–8, 85–6, 88; Lebanon 146; multiparty systems *142–3,* 144–6; Nordic countries 145–6; single-party systems 141, 213; Switzerland 146; two-party-plus systems 141, *142,* 143–4; two-party systems 124–5, 138, *142,* 146–50; *see also specific political parties*
political values *xxviii,* 152–6, *154,* 159–61
political violence 108–10
polyarchy 207
Polyarchy (Dahl) 207
popular sovereignty (concept) 13, 33
population (U.S.) 14
positive liberty 165, 171
poverty 169
Powell, Colin 177
power: dispersal of 85–8; fusion of 43–6; hard 15, 184; pardon 64, 212; soft 15, 184; *see also* executive power
precedent 92, 94–5
Preface to Democratic Theory, A (Dahl) 207
premiers *see* prime ministers
presidencies (African) 71
presidencies (ceremonial) 65
presidencies (Latin America) 70–1
presidency (France) 68, 72
presidency (U.S.) 51–2, 53–4, 64, 68–70
presidential executive power *66,* 68–71
presidential system *see* separation of powers
presidential veto 40, 77, 88, 90, 212

pride, national 159–60
primary elections 124–5, 212
prime ministers: about 43–5; accountability to parliament 51–6; power 47–51; removal 51–3; *see also* parliamentary system
Prime Minister's Question Time 51, 69
Prodi, Romano 53
proportional representation 120, 130, *131,* 132–3
public opinion 152–62; about *xxviii,* 152–3; "big government" 159–60; importance of 161; pride, national 159–60; religiosity and moral values 156–9; U.S. public opinion in comparative perspective 155–6; World Values Survey 153–5, *154*
Putin, Vladimir 188

Quebec 10, 98–9
Question Time, Prime Minister's 51, 69

race 176–8
racism 109–10, 176, 177–8
Reagan, Ronald 69, 171, 193, 194, 199
realist school of foreign policy 190–4, 212–13
realpolitik 184
reelection rates 124
Reform Party 147
regimes: about 6; authoritarian 12; defined 213; democratic 12–13; France 11; Germany, Federal Republic of 11–12; military 63, 212; Nazi 11, 182, 194; Poland 6–7; totalitarian 11–12, 213; traditional 11; United States 10–11
religion 117, 156–9, 174
representation 200–1
representative democracy (concept) 119
Republican Party (U.S.) 64, 148, 149–50
Republikaner Party (Germany) 144–5
reserve powers 65
responsible government (concept) 55, 213
review, judicial 97–100

Revolution, U.S. 170, 171
Revolutionary Institutional Party (Mexico) 89, 106–7
Rice, Susan 187
Roman Catholicism 117, 174
Romney, Mitt 113, 149
Roosevelt, Franklin Delano 172, 186
Roots of American Exceptionalism, The (Lockhart) 207
Royal Canadian Mounted Police 171
Rumsfeld, Donald 193
runoff elections 133
Russia 182, 188, 191, 193, 194; *see also* Soviet Union

Saddam Hussein 123, 192–3
Sarkozy, Nicholas 157
Schroeder, Gerhard 45, 188–9
SCLC (Southern Christian Leadership Conference) 114
Second Amendment 174
secretary of state 187
secret ballots 120–1, 213
segregation 99, 100, 109–10, 176–7; *see also* integration
self-reliance 169–70
semipresidential system *66*, 68
Senate (Australia) 79, 82–3
Senate (Canada) 78–9, 81, 82
Senate (U.S.): authority 82; equal representation in 23, 83, 84–5; foreign policy 187, 188, 189; party leadership 86; *see also* Congress (U.S.)
separation of church and state 117, 158
separation of powers: about *xxvi*, 40–1; accountability 55–6, 202; bicameralism, symmetric 83; checks and balances 50–1; Constitution (U.S.) 40; elections 53–4, 134; executive power 70–1; foreign policy 189; impeachment 53; inefficiencies 54–6; legislative branch 88–9; parliamentary system *versus 44, 46, 55;* party leaders 47, 48; *see also* parliamentary system
separatism 109
September 11 attacks 37, 152, 182, 193

Serbia 191, 195
settler-frontier-immigration thesis 170–1
sexual orientation 178; *see also* gay rights
shah of Iran 111, 192
Shining Path 89
Significance of the Frontier in American History, The (Turner) 206
single-member plurality system 129–30, *131*
single-party systems 141, 213
single transferable vote 133
slavery (U.S.) 169, 176
Smith, Raymond A. 202, 208
snap elections 45
Social Democratic Party (Germany) 145
social movements 110–14
Social Security (U.S.) 167
social welfare programs 158, 165, 166, 167, 169–70
socioeconomic policy 167–9
soft power 15, 184
South Africa 18–19, 176
Southeast Asia 61–3
Southern Christian Leadership Conference (SCLC) 114
sovereignty (concept) 6, 183, 213
Soviet Union 182, 191, 194–5
Spain 38
stability, political 198–9
stare decisis 94–5, 213
state (concept) 4, *5*, 6, 10–11, 213
state governments (U.S.) 34, 81
state of emergency *xxiv*, 89, 213
State of the Union Address 69
"Stolen Generations" (Australia) 177
Stonewall riots 112
student activism 113
subsidiarity (concept) 36, 213
Supreme Court (Canada) 98–9
Supreme Court (U.S.) 94–5, 97–8, 99, 100
Supreme Court (Ukraine) 122
Supreme courts (U.S. states) 125
Sweden *xxiv–xxv*, 116

Switzerland *xxiv–xxv*, 31, 84, 146
symmetric bicameralism 79, 82–5

Taiwan 183, 184
Taliban 195
Tea Party movement 113
term limits 124
terra nullius (concept) 177
terrorism 173, 182
Thatcher, Margaret 52
third parties 125, 133, 144
Thirteenth Amendment 176
throne speech 69
Tibet 183
Tocqueville, Alexis de 114, 206
totalitarian regimes 11–12, 213
Trade Union Congress (Britain) 116
traditional regimes 11
treaties 187–8, 189
Treaty of Versailles 188
Turkey 173, 190
Turner, Frederick Jackson 206
Twitter 173
two-party-plus systems 141, *142*, 143–4
two-party systems 124–5, 138, *142*, 146–50, 201
two-stage elections 133
tyranny (concept) 40

Ukraine 68, 121–2
unconventional political participation 105, 106, *106*, 213
unemployment insurance 167, 168
unicameralism 78, 79, 81, 213
Uniform Code of Military Justice 186
unions, labor 112–13, 116–17, 148, 149
unitary states 28, *30*, 32–4, *38*, 213
United Kingdom *see* Britain
United Nations 189, 191, 194
Universal Declaration of Human Rights 194
upper houses, legislative 48–9, 81–2, 83–4, 213

values: moral 156–9; political *xxviii*, 152–6, *154*, 159–61

Verba, Sidney 206–7
Versailles, Treaty of 188
veto, presidential (U.S.) 40, 77, 88, 90, 212
vice presidents 71–2
Vietnam 63
Vietnam War 113, 169–70, 185–6, 187, 189, 199
violence, political 108–10
vote of no confidence 52–3
voter eligibility 125–6
voter fraud 122
voter registration 126
voter turnout *127*, 128–9, 201
voting 119–20, 126, 128, 133; *see also* elections
Voting Rights Act of 1965 99, 176, 214

Wallace, George 148
Wallonia 146
war, declaration of 186–7, 189
War of 1812 181
war on drugs 174
War on Poverty 169–70
War on Terror 186
War Powers Resolution of 1973 187, 214
Washington, George 64, 138, 181
Watergate 98
Weathermen 109, 110
welfare *see* social welfare programs
West Bank (Palestine) 120
Westminster model 41–3, *44*, 49, 50, 62; *see also* parliamentary system
westward migration 170, 181, 206, 214
Wikipedia 173
Wilson, Graham K. 207
Wilson, Woodrow 182
Winfrey, Oprah 177
winner-take-all elections 129–30, 134–5, 214; *see also* single-member plurality system
women 178
World Bank 194

World Trade Organization 49, 194, 214
World Values Survey 153–5, *154*
World War I 181–2, 188
World War II 32, 34–5, 169, 182, 186, 191
Wyoming 23, 84

youth empowerment movement 113
Yuschenko, Victor 122

Zahir Shah, Mohammed 67
Zapata, Emiliano 107
Zapatistas (Mexico) 107–8, 111, 113, 214
Zurich 84